The Advertising Budget

The Advertising Budget

The Advertiser's Guide to Budget Determination

SIMON BROADBENT

Vice Chairman
Leo Burnett Ltd

NTC Publications Limited
Institute of Practitioners in Advertising
1989

The Advertising Budget
The Advertiser's Guide to Budget Determination

Published for the Institute of Practitioners in Advertising by NTC Publications Ltd, 22–24 Bell Street, Henley-on-Thames, Oxon RG9 2BG, United Kingdom. Telephone: 0491-574671.

British Library Cataloguing in Publication Data
Broadbent, Simon
    The advertising budget: the advertiser's guide to budget determination.
    1. Great Britain. Advertising. Expenditure
    338.4'3

    ISBN 1-870562-35-6

Printed and bound in Great Britain by The Print Business Ltd, London.

Contents

DETAIL 177

For Leanne

Acknowledgements

I have worked with advertisers on both sides of the Atlantic for many years, both on their advertising budget decisions and on how to measure the effects of advertising. I am grateful for this shared experience, which has taught me much more than any published papers or books.

At the time I started work on this book, I was Director of Brand Economics in Leo Burnett, Chicago. I have also written an American version, published in 1988 by Lexington Books, with the title, *The Advertiser's Handbook for Budget Determination*. The two books are similar, but more has been changed than the spelling and terminology. American data, research experience and marketing practice all differ in important ways from those found in Britain. The books, therefore, also differ in detail, and especially in references to media data, scanner data, electronic test markets and budget allocation over regions. I have used British examples where relevant, but have kept some American examples because their experience can usefully be added to ours.

The Institute of Practitioners in Advertising asked me to write the British version of this book. It was only then that I started to assemble this record of what I have so often seen. I was very pleased to get this invitation from David Wheeler, the IPA's Director-General. Janet Mayhew, the Research Officer, reviewed for me the many Marketing Appraisals the IPA has anonymously written over the years and which I have quoted with permission. She also ensured that I received help from others at the IPA, including Charles Channon, Director of Education and Training, and Bridget Hynard, secretary to the Recruitment and Business-to-Business Committees. Several IPA members contributed ideas and material, particularly two successive Chairmen of the Publications Working Group, Alan Wolfe and Dan O'Donoghue, and the Chairman of the Business-to-Business Committee, David Lowe. Gerald Eva worked on the original plan for this book. The section on the Ideal Campaign Evaluation in Chapter 6 is based on the editorial I wrote for *Advertising Works 2*, with the permission of the IPA.

David Lamb and Peter Pickersgill, of Rowntree Mackintosh Confectionery, gave me the data used in Example 8.5. The Director of Research of the Advertising Association, Mike Waterson, and the Managing Director of Media Expenditure Analysis Limited, John Stockley, provided both valuable data and advice.

Jeff Fergus, Managing Director of Leo Burnett, London, generously allowed me the time and resources I have used here. Among those who have helped at Leo Burnett are Brian Jacobs, Media Director, and Lynne Farrar, Information Manager. Special thanks to two secretaries who stayed cheerful through many revisions and a few word-processing catastrophies: Imma Trillo in Chicago and Gill Beattie in London.

Simon Broadbent

Preface

In 1987, the IPA's Marketing Appraisals and Publications Working Group was attempting to revise one of the IPA's most successful books, *Setting Advertising Budgets*, published in 1978 and now out of print. The Group felt that there was a real need to update this book.

After weeks of literature searches and discussion, and much ground work, the Group realized that a simple revision and updating of the original book would not be adequate.

The IPA was fortunate that Simon Broadbent, working at the time with Leo Burnett in Chicago, accepted the invitation to write this book. Whilst early discussions were going on with Simon before his return to London at Christmas, 1987, he took the opportunity to write an American version which was published by Lexington Books in Massachusetts in October 1988. This has already been well received and is most successful.

The basic theme and form of the two books are similar, but the UK edition, commissioned by the IPA, is in its detail very different, using examples culled from a wide range of published material in the UK and from a number of willing helpers.

With his usual efficiency Simon's manuscript was completed in September, to praise from its IPA 'readers', all of whom are in the front line of advertising. The unanimous reaction was that this is a most valuable, practical and useful book, and it is written with such clarity that it cannot fail to be of use to all those who are involved in determining advertising budgets. The substantial investments by companies in advertising have to be justified both in terms of rational media expenditure and advertising effectiveness. To this end, this book is an invaluable aid.

For those advertisers whose money is at risk, it can help to reduce uncertainty and provide guidance towards a disciplined procedure for setting advertising budgets. They are the prime target market of this book. It will at the same time be invaluable to those in advertising agencies who have the responsibility to advise on the setting of advertising budgets.

I am grateful to Simon Broadbent for the way in which he has applied his experience and his skills to providing both an interesting and a practical book. It is a vital work for all advertisers and agencies involved in the business of advertising budget-setting. The examples and case histories used provide illuminating and practical information on real-life solutions. The references and notes at the end of the book suggest extensive and up-to-date further reading for those who wish to read more widely.

One cannot help but be impressed by the scope and scale of the book; in particular, the stress put on setting the budget as a process, the considerable attention given to the long-term effects of advertising and the clarity with which some misleading assumptions are exposed.

I am sure that this book will provide an important and essential contribution to the planning of more effective advertising. It is an important work and will prove to be a very influential one.

David Wheeler (Director-General, Institute of Practitioners in Advertising)

Background

1   How to Use This Book

This book was written to help advertisers to determine their working media budgets. The basic question that every advertiser has to face is: how much should be spent to get advertising to the people it is aimed at? The book should make that question easier to answer. The fundamental question raises many others. Some of them are listed in the next section, as are the places in the book where they are discussed.

Few people will read this book straight through. By using this chapter as a guide, the reader can select the sections which will be most helpful for particular problems.

The book is mostly about mass consumer advertising: selling fast-moving packaged goods, durables, and services. The sections in Chapter 6, about direct marketing and corporate or business-to-business advertising, are exceptions. These important applications are not discussed in detail, but some of the ways they differ from traditional advertising are examined.

I describe who the book is written for: different people in the company and outside it are concerned with these questions. All the people working on the brand should appreciate that the advertising budget is a business investment. It is not determined separately from other company decisions or in isolation from the budgets for other marketing activities.

The amount to spend on advertising is determined by a process, not by a formula. This practical guide examines the whole of this process, from understanding the brand's budget to evaluating, after the advertising campaign, what has been achieved. Action points at the end of each chapter summarize the work to be done.

This chapter includes short sections on timing, the need for mathematics (very little), and comments on the vast amount previously written on this subject. Setting the budget is not an academic exercise. We can learn from theory, and some is included in this text, but only as much as makes sense in the Boardroom.

The Big Questions — and Where They Are Answered

Is There a Formula I Can Use to Set the Budget?

The answer is definitely no, but there are many *methods* that suggest an amount to spend. Fifteen are described in Chapter 5, and there are variations within them. These come quite late in this book because there are steps you should take *before* any of these methods are used. There are also decisions to make *afterwards*. The results will be specific to your brand at this time: generalizations are not really helpful to you.

If Not By a Formula, How Should the Budget Be Set?

Determining the budget is a *process*. At the end of Chapter 4, the steps to take are set out as a flow chart. By following the action points and this flow chart, you will see the process which is recommended.

Will This Book Make It Easy to Set the Budget?

It is never possible to be certain that you have set the 'right' budget, if you are a normal packaged-goods, durables or services manufacturer. In special cases, the advertiser can get closer to the best amount to spend. Direct marketing is the best known of these, and the approach used there has a lesson for other marketers (see Chapter 6).

Taking the steps to determine a budget requires business judgement. One aspect of the decision must be weighed against another. The major choices are outlined in Chapter 4. There is nothing unusual about this: most business decisions are made with incomplete information. Investments are made every day and determining the advertising budget is an investment decision.

I cannot make it easy to determine the budget; but I can make it easier, by helping you to think about the alternatives systematically and responsibly.

Why Is the Decision Hard?

The comparison is sometimes made between the investment in advertising and the purchase of raw materials and machinery. Surely, it is said, the marketing director can justify the recommendation in much the same way as the production director carries out quality control on materials or runs tests on machines. However, the two are not comparable, since the purchase of advertising involves judgements of a different sort.

The difficulty is that you do not know enough about the effects of your advertising. Until you know all the benefits, and how they vary if more or less is spent, you cannot be sure that you have invested the right amount.

The fact that it is hard to measure all advertising's effects does not mean that advertising is ineffective or that the investment is imprudent. It means only what it says, that the investment in advertising cannot be evaluated precisely.

You have to decide, in your own case, which effects advertising is likely to have. The first half of Chapter 2 gives a description of what advertising effects may be produced. The second half discusses ways they may be observed, and ideally measured. It is unlikely that you will get a complete understanding, even about the past, but to make the problem really hard you have to forecast the future.

Reviewing what effects are likely, and trying to measure them, means that your ultimate decision is made with better information. These preliminary tasks are not easy; they might in some cases involve such specializations as modelling and experimental design and analysis.

The advertising budget decision is linked directly to what the brand itself is intended to achieve (see Chapters 3 and 4). Since there are often several objectives, there is no single criterion by which to set the budget. Nor can you expect there to be one way to do it, any more than one military strategy will win every battle.

Do I Need to Know the Effect of Advertising on Sales Volume in the Current Year?

This information would indeed be very helpful. In Chapter 7 there is a discussion of the detail in which you would like to have the answer. But even if you had this, you need more. Advertising may do more for your brand than have merely a short-term effect on consumer sales. There are at least three further considerations:

1. The benefits of being an advertised brand may endure beyond the current year. Suppose you did not advertise at all one year: you

might start the second year at a disadvantage.
2. In addition to your consumer targets, you should also consider the channels of distribution between factory and consumers. Advertising may affect the trade, that is, wholesalers, retailer buyers, and even your own salespeople.
3. In the minds of consumers, good advertising adds a value to the brand, and the added value helps make other marketing activities more effective. For example, the price you are able to charge may depend on how valuable the brand is seen to be.

Thus advertising may be working in the long term, on the trade as well as on the consumer, and by interaction with the rest of the marketing mix. Again, a description is given in Chapter 2.

Do I Have to Know All These Things Before I Can Set a Budget?

You would be exceptional if you ever knew all these things. The decision will not be made with perfect knowledge but by balancing likely alternatives. This is the central part of Chapter 4. You should review the evidence you have, to help you estimate what advertising may do for you, and then weigh the different elements according to your needs.

Do I Need These Estimates Just For My Brand?

You should consider more than just your brand, unless it is truly unique and without competition. First you need some information about the category and competitors. Budgets cannot be set in isolation: they have to perform in a competitive marketplace. Chapter 4 describes the way marketplace data should enter, and Chapter 5 reviews competitive comparisons, as well as brand history.

More than one brand in your company may be advertised; portfolio management is discussed in Chapter 6.

Should I Be Concerned With Only the Working Media Budget?

This book concentrates on how to determine the working media budget, or media spend: the amount paid to the media actually to do the work. I also call it adspend: the amount spent on the advertising that people see. The working media budget, or adspend, is only part of the total advertising budget. The remainder of this larger budget is discussed in Chapter 3.

Deciding how much to spend on advertising has an impact on the whole budget for the brand in two special ways:

1. The total advertising budget is an expense and must be affordable.
2. Because the media spend should affect sales, the brand budget should be drawn up with this effect in mind.

Both these points are discussed in Chapter 4 and the detail is in Chapter 3.

Several key ratios in the brand's budget can help you decide how much should be spent on advertising (see Chapter 3). The brand's objectives are key in determining what the advertising has to do, used in the Task method (see Chapter 5).

How Does the Content of the Advertising Affect the Amount to Be Spent on It?

Your view of the advertising investment depends on how effective you think your copy actually is. Your analysis of the history of the brand and of the category will assist this judgement. Because this book is about the budget, creative strategy, copy, creative execution and the media department are not highlighted. Nevertheless, getting the budget right must not distract you from getting the advertising right. Media planning and buying matter too.

Nor is this book about the administration of the budget after it has been set. Most company procedures are more than adequate for this, and in any case differ in detail.

Should I Be Concerned With the Amount Spent, or With the Number of Exposures of the Advertisement to the Target?

Pounds spent impact the budget, and data about competitors' advertising are often expressed as a sterling estimate. But exposure of the advertising does the work, so the answer to the question is that you need both. You have to translate pounds to the number of opportunities to see the advertisements.

For simplicity, TV language is used in most of this book, but of course equivalents exist for other media. Sometimes, the media mix has not been determined when the budget is set and a guess must then be made at the main medium and at the appropriate language. If another medium is chosen or part of the budget goes to other media, you may repeat the process.

I do not detail how you decide who the target is or what 'see' means. Consult your advertising agency or a textbook (1: note that references are numbered at the end of the book and that the References and Notes section contains detailed comments, to avoid cluttering up the main text). I give TVRs (Television Rating Points) the simple definition that one rating point bought means that one per cent of the target has an opportunity to see (OTS) your advertisement. When you have bought one hundred rating points, all the target (on average) sees your advertisement once. Of course, some miss it, and others see it twice or more often. I do not go much into the details of cover (see it once or more), or frequency (how often), though these terms are important in media planning and in definitions of the response to advertising (used in some of the methods). This book is concerned with the average (2).

Advertising Accountability

Advertising is not a game, though it can be fun. Money spent on advertising is a serious business investment, and decisions on how much to spend must be justified as thoroughly as possible. The central problem is that making advertising accountable is far from easy and there is a wide range of attitudes to this difficulty, from overconfidence to despair. To understand this diversity of views, we need to know where these different beliefs come from.

Paying close attention to the advertising budget is not new. It is traditional, but incorrect, to attribute this scrutiny to current high media costs and to the rise of alternative marketing activities (consumer promotions, trade promotions, price deals). Actually, there never has been a time when a pound was thoughtlessly spent on advertising.

What has changed in recent decades is the attitude to advertising's effects. In the very early days, these seemed obvious. There was no question that a store ad in the local paper, or a poster for a soap, beneficially accelerated changes in retailing or in mass-production manufacture.

Claude Hopkins tells the story of his employment by a Chicago meat-packer. Results were expected — and quickly. He was told: 'Father is very nervous about this money spent in advertising. He considers it an utter waste. The results so far are not very encouraging. You have been here nearly six weeks, but our sales of Cotosuet have hardly increased at all.' Sales effects became the subject of regular measurement when direct-response advertising was normal and Hopkins' *Scientific Advertising* was a popular book title in the 1920s (3).

This period was followed by scepticism, after the advent of television, the rise of the retailer and the decline of direct response. Advertising did not always produce immediate results, for reasons which were obscure, and its practitioners retreated. The low point was in 1961 with the publication of DAGMAR: *Defining Advertising Goals for Measured Advertising Results* (4).

Rather than encouraging agreement to defining goals as a first step, and measuring appropriate results as a second, DAGMAR led people to find out first what could be measured easily and then to set it as a goal. Communication became advertising's objective. DAGMAR was an apparent success (translated into nine languages, and in its ninth printing in 1986) because it let advertising off the hook. The intermediate goal was no longer directly related to financial contribution. Unfortunately, this shift of focus also made advertising appear less valuable to accountants. Furthermore, it was often just assumed that the intermediate effect *was* positively related to sales, which is not always the case (see Chapter 5).

But even in the 1960s good marketing executives realized (as they still do) that such simple communication objectives could not encompass all that advertising had done for great brands. At the same time, they thought that the measurement of sales effects was generally impossible. These people, however, did not fall into the trap of making advertising accountable on only one of these dimensions — or in some other simple way. Instead, they listed their overall marketing objectives and then made the advertising help to accomplish all of them. They did not use one numerical measure alone to determine the advertising budget, any more than they evaluated copy by a single score.

What is a successful brand? The answer is found in the bottom line and in the long term. A great brand is one which continues, taking one year with another, to make profits for its manufacturer. This usually means good consumer sales volume, at a high price to retailers and with low price discounting, supported by an economic amount of advertising and promotional spend. The brand can continue to meet these criteria as long as it operates in a healthy category and fights off its competitors.

This is a simple description of objectives and is expanded in the next two chapters. But it allows us to see the scope for advertising effects.

They are not limited to short-term changes in consumer sales volume, important though these are. The base level of sales, about which these variations take place, has also to be maintained. Adding value to the brand is what allows the high price and low discounting. Reducing the advertising-to-sales ratio is a sensible management objective, but can be done by raising sterling sales as well as by cutting advertising. Making the promotional budget work harder, again by raising the perceived value of the brand, is also one of advertising's tasks. Since the category should be kept alive, part of the objective is to support it (even though this may help competitors to survive also).

One-dimensional assessment of advertising is still with us. Ironically, the recent success of measuring part of advertising's sales effects (5) has been to reduce its total value. Advertising may be seen only as the producer of immediate consumer sales volume changes, since this is what is being most often calibrated. A limited aspect of its role is then compared directly with other ways of producing immediate sales, such as promotions.

The following kinds of comments (6) are now commonplace:

'Clients are taking money over to places that can be measured. And they are spending less on things they can't measure so precisely.'

'Words like performance and value . . . are probably more important today than they were yesterday.'

'Clients are looking at this thing and saying we've got to make sure the return on this investment is adequate.'

The fact that advertising may have effects other than short term on volume is too often overlooked, because such effects are complex and hard to quantify. Today, anything without a number attached is invisible. This book tries to return the reader to a wider view. When advertising is evaluated, it is important that the job is done properly.

Whether the chief executive is a believer, an agnostic, or a sceptic in this debate often determines the trend of the advertising budget. He may have an instinct for branding, and see the clues which justify its long-term financial benefit. If so, the case for the budget is made more easily. He may insist on numbers, or his priorities may be only short term. If so, the budget will be continually under attack.

Gut feeling plays a large part in business. Not being able to prove a case does not mean that it is lost. Advertising is not guilty of ineffectiveness when it cannot be clearly associated with dividends. We are comparing probabilities in the marketplace, not carrying out calibrations in a laboratory.

Is This Book For You?

More than one person in the company is involved in determining the advertisement budget. Below, and in Chapter 4, I discuss the viewpoints of the chairman or managing director, the finance director or accountant, the marketing director and the brand manager. The sales director figures occasionally, sometimes as an opponent who champions the promotional budget at the expense of advertising. There also may be a budget committee or other management group to whom budgets have to be presented for approval. These names may differ in your own organization, but you will recognize the responsibilities.

The marketing director is the key player, who is responsible for the brand manager and reports to the managing director. Brand managers who read this book may be helped by seeing the bigger picture; top management may be able to view the advertising budget as more than a financial decision.

The person who does most of the work is rarely the main decision-maker: the brand manager makes a case that is judged by a higher level of management. He has to have a narrower view and more limited objectives. To help higher management make up its mind, the brand manager has to forecast the effects of a number of different plans. He or she has to put up with a series of budget revisions, but in compensation should be given a clear directive on priorities. The reconciliation of brand managers' plans with company objectives is a major responsibility of company management.

In setting the budget, priorities are often assumed to be contribution, volume and the brand's goodwill, in that order. But often advertising's effects are in exactly the reverse order. The largest and clearest effect is on the standing of the brand, or its value (the words used here all mean much the same and are explained in Chapter 2). Volume sales and contribution are, however, affected by many other factors, so it is less easy to see what advertising achieves here; its effects are often smaller than the results of other marketing activities.

The marketing director and brand manager specify what advertising has to do. Usually this is stated as a set of direct and short-term objectives: the results expected during the period over which the budget is set, often a year. Who is the advertising target? How is its marketplace behaviour expected to change as a result? The answers to such questions are the basis of the company's brief to the advertising agency.

The far-seeing marketing director and managing director do not limit their horizon to the current year, nor do they consider only the effects on volume. They also take into account the other effects suggested above and described in more detail in Chapter 2.

Usually the company's chief profit-earner is a brand, which has the added values to which advertising contributes. The brand is more important than the current formulation and packaging of the underlying product. Chapter 4 discusses the balance that has to be struck between the maintenance of value and short-term financial pressures. This is often the main decision in agreeing on an advertising budget and requires information about branding and its worth (occasional 'brand audits' are suggested in Chapter 2). It means also that policy has to be set at the highest level in the company. 'It's becoming apparent that brand management is moving to the office of the chief executive . . . The most important asset any company owns is going to be brand names' (7).

This lesson is also being learned by the establishment. At the time of foreign bids for Rowntree and while Cadbury-Schweppes seemed a likely target, a *Times* leader criticized the financial viewpoint (8):

> 'They have strong brand names, in some cases of world stature, built up over decades of skilful marketing . . . Nestlé is prepared to pay £1.5 billion for Rowntree's brand names, quite apart from its more tangible business assets . . . Too many British companies have neglected the value of brand names . . . World brands attract little awe on the stock market, where the loyalty that makes them almost priceless is viewed as sentiment rather than virtue.'

Money is always in short supply and is needed for many urgent purposes: dividends have to be paid, as do workers; research and development cost money; a new factory may have to be built; and so on. Other brands within the company compete for cash. In any case, is the brand worth long-term investment, or is it a cash cow to be milked?

With these different perspectives and priorities, it is not surprising that agreeing a budget is a matter of negotiation. The information used has to be shared and a framework for this is needed. In addition, the real criteria for the advertising are complex. The budget is not only affected by internal priorities; it also responds to external changes — movement in the category, competitors' activities, and media costs. In times of need, the advertising budget may be cautiously starved; in times of investment, it may be generously fed. For all these reasons, the temptation to make the decision over-simple should be resisted. If we do make it simply, we are almost certainly making it incorrectly. The book emphasizes the improvement which will be likely if we are methodical but wide-ranging.

Although there is the full cast of characters just introduced, I use the word 'marketer' to stand for all of them. Not always, because at times it is necessary to distinguish among the players. Indeed, in some companies, we cannot assume helpful cooperation in this important decision. Big budgets are a source of power in the company structure, and the internal competition for resources may be so fierce that selling the brand's advertising budget to management may require almost as much work as selling the product to consumers. Advice is available (9) on explaining advertising's effects, developing the necessary case histories, and generally pre-selling to the budget committee.

For the most part I write of a single marketer who makes rational and honest decisions. The complications of company politics and of company marketing strategy are outside the scope of this book, but they may play a vital role when the advertising budget is being set.

'Managers do not make decisions as isolated entrepreneurs, but in an organizational environment . . . all the attention given to techniques of budgeting — models, experimentation, or "rules-of-thumb" — is meaningless unless placed into the appropriate organizational setting' (10). Most commentators have missed these points; Nigel Piercy, of the Cardiff Business School and whom I have just quoted, is almost alone. It is particularly necessary for academics to appreciate this, otherwise they send out into business young people who can be alarmed at first by what they imagine is unusual and bitter conflict. Those who concentrate on a part of the whole problem may put forward what they see as conclusive solutions, when all they are doing is sub-optimizing at best, over-simplifying to an absurd extent at worst. There will be more on this in Chapter 7.

Even those who see the whole of a problem often do not allow sufficiently for the difficulty of changing other people's minds. A brilliant code-breaker and mathematician is only one example: 'Having set down a highly intelligent plan, Alan [Turing] tended to assume that the political wheels would turn as if by magic to put it into effect. He never allowed for the interaction required to achieve anything in the real world' (11). This interaction was a problem even between people on the same side in wartime; in the jungle of the corporate structure, tooth and claw are, not surprisingly, redder.

Small Budgets and Large

Compare the positions of two companies in different categories. Their turnovers are the same, but one has a high proportion of marketing effort going to sales representatives, trade promotion and so on. Its attitude to the advertising budget is inevitably different from the other's, whose advertising budget takes the majority of its marketing spend. Both want the advertising budget to earn its keep and wonder whether it has a measurable effect on sales and whether more should be spent or less.

The importance of these questions and the chances of answering them are not the same in the two companies. The company that spends a small proportion of its marketing budget on advertising may view it like fire insurance. The company cannot drop it completely but wants to spend as little as is reasonable and to make its decision quickly. The heavy advertiser knows that advertising is important to his business and is willing to spend in order to find out.

There are obvious differences between the marketing director of a multi-million-pound consumer goods company, with an advertising budget in the millions of pounds, and the new franchisee of a fast-food chain who is preparing for a meeting with the local newspaper sales rep. The same principles apply to both, and this book is intended to help both. The differences lie only in the scale of operations, the data available, and the time worth spending on the decision. If I have concentrated on the large advertiser, it is because it is there that most of the methods have developed and the examples have been published.

The Advertising Agency

Outside the manufacturing company, the people most interested in the budget decision are at the advertising agency. This book is also for agency people who want to understand better the realities and techniques involved in budget-setting. In general, it is the client service director or account handler at the advertising agency who should be asked for advice about setting the budget. He or she is responsible for the business side of the advertising.

Others in the agency will have a view. The media planner is essential for the calculation of the media exposure which can be bought for a given working media spend. The account planner is not usually a business planner (12), but may advise on whether the task set, or the expectations of the team, are compatible with this amount of advertisement exposure. The planner will certainly work on the objectives of the advertising, and hence on the effects expected, and on campaign evaluation. There may also be modelling expertise in the agency, perhaps in a specialist group.

The *Advertising Works* papers are largely written by planners, and here the effectiveness of advertising is described not only as causing changes in the real world, but as profitable for the advertiser. The papers in these books represent the cream, and show that this job can be done. Short-term cost-effectiveness is, however, demonstrated in the real world only rarely.

I have witnessed the adversarial system, where the agency executive is thought too self-interested to be helpful. But even if the agency is paid by commission rather than by fee, the agency knows that it will flourish only if its advice is sound. Its bias is perhaps admitted and allowed for, and this does not disqualify it from helping. There is, in fact, often more experience of budget-setting at the agency than at the manufacturer. Conversely, the marketing director or managing director may be thought by the agency to be too concerned with the bottom line and the short term. The correct response is discussed in this book.

There may also be involvement by consultants of various kinds. Media owners may help with data, descriptions of category norms and so on.

Timing: Plans

Although the company usually has a long-term outline plan, there is a tradition that the advertising budget is decided annually. Usually there is a run up to the start of the fiscal year. During this preparation, the major budget decisions are made. In some companies, this is a quarterly event. If the overall budget has been over-optimistic, the adjustments often happen in the last quarter of the year. If these require price-cutting to retailers to make volume targets, with a corresponding cut in advertising spending to meet the contribution targets, then the last quarter is often a frenzied time of budget re-writing and media re-planning. This is generally a wasteful and dangerous way of working, to be avoided if possible. The solution is more realistic initial budgeting. Of course, changes cannot all be avoided and some are healthy: in marketing, you should react to opportunities and to attacks. But there is no need for self-inflicted wounds.

A few companies believe that revenue must be made before it is invested. They spend the first part of the year waiting for a positive cash balance before they approve advertising budgets. This approach can also be inefficient and comes from a false view of the flow of cause and effect (see Chapter 3).

In other cases, there is a continual, or perhaps monthly, monitoring, and adjustments are made to all parts of the budget as required. This is the recommended method, provided that the considerations set out below are kept in mind and changes are made deliberately and not too often. This is better than a shock at year end or when starting next year's plan.

For simplicity of presentation, this book assumes the traditional annual plan. Bear in mind, however, that at the other times you may have to re-plan.

The decision on how much to spend may be seen as merely adjustment. No one argues whether we *should* be advertising; we wonder only whether we are spending too much or not enough. We discuss shaving off a fraction or marginally upweighting. But sometimes the very existence of the ad budget is in doubt, and deciding how much to spend may include deciding that this should be zero.

Most of this book is about the first case, considering variations of, say, plus or minus a quarter of the size of the budget. The second case is a crisis. Stopping the advertising or supporting a previously unadvertised product, are major decisions. Chapter 2 considers the different ways in which advertising may play a part, to help show the implications of such choices.

Timing: Evaluation

There is a quite different point to be made about timing. I am no longer discussing when decisions are made, but the time frame in which they are evaluated. Advertising may be thought of as an expenditure which must justify itself within months. However, like eating all the seed corn in the winter, the result can be starvation next autumn.

There are three pressures which favour short-term over long-term evaluations. The bottom line is inspected frequently — perhaps too frequently — by analysts and shareholders. The future is uncertain, and many feel that if they look after the pence now, the pounds tomorrow will look after themselves. Finally, brand managers move fast between assignments and between companies, and even chief executives feel they have to make their mark within months. 'No doubt most managers would do more [advertising] experimenting if they believed they were to be responsible and remunerated on the basis of a brand's cumulative profits over the next ten years rather than the next ten months. As it stands, the manager who experiments incurs the short-run costs but receives no credit for long-run profits' (13).

Investment may be required now: but the pay-off may not be gained this year. This dilemma is recognized for new products, but less so for established brands. The cash benefit from reducing advertising is immediate but the damage may be years away (and then someone else's problem).

The solution to this dilemma lies in the character or style of the company, set by the chief executive. The advertising decision is like those made on product quality, or on research and development. The bottom line can always be improved — temporarily — by cutting these investments. The good manager balances the short and long term. The contribution the brand makes this year is important, but so is the property handed over next year: the sales share and the standing of the brand with consumers and trade.

Mathematics

In most of the book, I have avoided technical terms and the only number skills needed are the use of a hand calculator; it is also useful to plot one variable against another. A spreadsheet PC program is more than adequate.

The explanation of models in Chapter 7 is necessarily mathematical. You do not, however, have to follow every step, and many readers should skip the whole chapter. Using a model depends, nonetheless, on the assumption that the equations used represent reality, and managers tempted into this area should know enough to be cautious about the assumptions. Models can provide suggested answers to parts of the problem, but these should provide only one input. Models should not set the budget.

One of the worries that advertisers often have is that they should be more 'scientific'. Should so much depend on judgement, even on style? There are indeed regularities in the marketplace, but you can be sure that they are not permanent. You cannot say when or how the rules will change, but you know the time will come. There should be no surprise here, because changes in the environment affect all areas of business: finance, distribution, retailing, the product, and media opportunities. Does this mean that formal methods should not be used, and modelling never be attempted? The answer is that if regularities in the marketplace are discovered, they should be used, but cautiously. This caution, or the balance between logic and flair, is nothing but style.

References

Anyone with a good library service and persistence in following up bibliographies will soon accumulate a long list of books and papers on this subject. As long ago as 1978, there were over 2000 such references. Some of them explain useful methods, contain good common sense, and reassure the fainthearted. More of them, however, over-simplify and can even mislead.

Two previous publications require comment. In 1978 the IPA published a review called *Setting Advertising Appropriations* (14). In 1970, *Spending Advertising Money* (1) first appeared, and its fourth edition was issued in 1984: one of its chapters is called 'How much to spend'. That chapter is in some ways a summary of the thinking in this book, although it discussed the setting of the budget from the point of view of the media planner. The three questions suggested there still look sensible, and indeed find their place here:

1. What can the product afford? is expanded here as the checks and balances process of Chapter 4.
2. What is the advertising task? is an indispensable question, covered here in Chapter 2 and as part of the methods of Chapter 5.
3. What are competitors spending? asks for information about the category, and leads into the examination of history, ratios and so on.

This book is much fuller than either of the two publications mentioned. There are three other differences:

1. This book is written for advertisers, while the others concentrate more on the advertising agency input. The agency plays a very important role, but it cannot have a complete understanding of the priorities, pressures, and process which actually make the decision.
2. Previous publications concentrated on methods, which here take second place to the process.
3. Because it is now seen to be possible to learn more about advertising's effects in the marketplace, this receives more attention here.

I have tried to distil into the text what the best published work has to teach us. In the References and Notes section I list and comment on them. If you need more detail, these are the recommended sources.

Chapter 1: Action Points

The organization of this book is as follows.

Chapter 2 reviews how advertising might affect your brand and how to look for these effects. Chapter 3 reviews the brand's overall budget and how to determine the financial results of advertising expenditure decisions. Chapter 5 gives a checklist of methods that suggest the amount to spend on advertising your brand.

The heart of the book, Chapter 4, recommends a process to determine the budget that uses the reviews described in Chapters 2 and 3 and some of the methods from Chapter 5.

The fastest way to see how this book may help you is to read the Action Points summaries at the end of these chapters and to follow up the points that apply to your brand.

The rest of the book is to be used selectively, by picking out the special cases, techniques, and case histories that seem relevant.

Here is a summary of the ideas in the book.

1. There is no easy *formula* for setting an advertising budget. This book suggests a *procedure*.
2. Various *methods* are available to suggest possible budgets. The results are no more than suggestions: it is the procedure which determines the budget.
3. The *objectives* for the brand and the advertising must be agreed before a budget is determined.
4. The advertising budget *should not be set in isolation*. Information about other parts of the marketing mix is needed in order to make a good decision.
5. Advertising can do *more* than *directly* influence *consumers'* behaviour: it can have *trade effects* and it can improve the efficiency of *other marketing activities*.
6. Advertising can have effects *over longer than the financial year*, but these returns have to be paid for now. The brand may already benefit from previous advertising that was paid for earlier.
7. Short-term effects of advertising, felt over a few weeks or months, are additional to long-term effects. *Both* long- and short-term effects should be considered.
8. The budget itself is decided as a cash amount, but what it will buy, in terms of our target purchasers and consumers seeing *advertisements*, should also be known.

9. Numerical *modelling* of the effects of advertising can sometimes help, but such techniques are only an aid and should not be trusted completely, nor used in isolation.

2 Advertising Effects on Your Brand

Every advertising question should be answered by the salesman's standards.

Let us emphasize that point. The only purpose of advertising is to make sales. It is profitable or unprofitable according to its actual sales.

Treat it as a salesman. Force it to justify itself.

Claude Hopkins (1923)

You cannot plan an activity without anticipating the effects that it will produce. You should think through what your advertisements will do for your brand.

For our present purpose, it is not so important to decide *how* your advertising will work. I do not discuss what actually happens when advertisements are exposed to people, or the value of recall, or what makes an advertisement persuasive. Of course, these subjects are vital to the people making the advertising. Here we are concerned only with the results, not the mechanisms.

You should not expect *general* agreement on the results expected from advertising. This is because advertising can perform different tasks, and it is unlikely to do them all equally well in every campaign. It is a different question, and a vital one, to consider what your own *particular* campaign is expected to do. You then take into account the situation faced by your own company and your own brand.

In this chapter, I describe what an advertising campaign *may* achieve. Check, for your own situation, how much of this is relevant to you.

Advertising has to fit into the general plan for the brand. It is the effectiveness of the whole that matters, and you need to understand the part that advertising plays in this whole, not how it might work on its own.

Most traditional methods of setting the advertising budget are over-simple, not only addressing advertising in isolation but as if there were only this year's advertising and this year's sales. The true situation is more complex in two ways. Advertising may have long-term effects and also may interact with other marketing activities. Hence, after describing possible direct advertising effects, I turn to the effects of price and promotion as well.

After these descriptions of effects, I outline the ways they may be researched and ideally quantified.

Ways in Which Your Advertising May Work

First, advertising should have direct effects on consumer behaviour, both long term (over years) and short term (over weeks and months).

Long Term

A 'brand' is 'that unique combination of product characteristics and added values (non-functional as well as functional) that have become attached to a product by means of its name, packaging, advertising, pricing, etc. — which differentiate it from competitive brands in the consumer's view and which suit it to providing the greatest satisfaction to some consumers' (1).

More briefly (2), 'a brand is a product that provides functional benefits plus added values that some consumers value enough to buy', the added values coming from:

'— experience of the brand,
— the sorts of people who use the brand,
— a belief that the brand is effective,
— the appearance of the brand which is the prime role of packaging.'

Branding is part of the reason consumers buy one product rather than another. It helps to create and defend sales, and is itself partly created and defended by advertising.

Advertising is usually the major contributor to branding. It differentiates between similar products. Its effect can be seen most clearly in the elements of the brand that can have come only from advertising, or when changes in the brand image are associated with changes that we have made in the content of advertising. Other activities also contribute to branding, and we usually cannot isolate completely or put a financial value on the advertising effect alone.

It is recommended that this long-term contribution of advertising is recognized formally. An occasional 'brand audit' should be done, that lists, and if possible quantifies, the ways in which our brand differs from other branded, or unbranded, products. There will be more discussion on this later.

The sales of a brand are like the height at which an airplane flies. Advertising spend is like its engines: while the engines are running, everything is fine but, when the engines stop, the descent starts. The effectiveness of branding is like the aerodynamic design of the plane. Great creative, or better design, means that by spending the same money, or by using the same engines, we take the brand or the plane higher. If we cut spending on advertising, or stop the engines, the better brand or plane will stay up longer. But both will come down! Note that, in this analogy, advertising both creates increases in sales (gets the plane up) and is needed to maintain sales (to stay at the same height is an achievement).

Be warned that some people are not convinced by such arguments. They see the product's existing sales, except perhaps for the blips mentioned below, as 'independent of advertising'. They do not take these sales into account as part of the benefits of advertising. It is argued below that advertising does contribute to them and should get some credit. The debate on this topic continues; it flared up particularly in the 1970s, as the references given show (3).

The misguided view has support from two directions. First, brand images move slowly, perhaps over years. Even stopping all advertising may result in no detectable change in sales for some time. The contribution of advertising, some argue, ceased when the brand image was created. No harm, or very little, can be done when advertising is cut. Second, consumers rarely report such advertising effects on their routine purchases. Their memories of the advertising may be woolly. How can behaviour, it is argued, be affected by something so vague and distant?

The brand image is a mass of great momentum which is slow to alter direction, and often we are dealing with unquantified effects. This does not mean that they are unreal. True marketers have the instinctive and correct feeling that the brand is their most valuable property, that it will evaporate slowly unless supported, and that long-term effects are the main justification for the advertising investment.

Short Term

Short-term sales effects of advertising may be seen only when the following conditions apply. The advertising content must *be* sales-effective (this cannot be assumed). There must be sufficient variation in advertising levels over time; in other words, there must be some peaks, followed by low spending. Other influences on sales (and there are many) must be reasonably steady, or must occur at times different from the advertising peaks, or must somehow be allowed for in the analysis.

When all these conditions hold, we should see blips in the plot of sales over time that correspond to peaks in the advertising. Even if blips are not seen because our advertising has been fairly continuous, we may presume that there are such short-term effects. They have been often enough observed and measured econometrically to be considered normal. The mechanism must be mainly a reminder to purchasers. It is not that some new information startles the viewer into unusual action, but that the brand moves a little higher in the purchase repertoire. In an ideal world, if we invested an extra pound in advertising, we would be able to identify, say, three pounds of extra sales caused by this advertising. This is the sort of evaluation expected from an area test or from any other way of measuring short-term sales effects.

Note that when we estimate the size of such a sales blip (or of any other sales effect of advertising), it is not necessarily in relation to sales in the period before, or even in relation to sales last year. Short-term advertising effects should be judged against the trend in the brand's sales. In this way we attempt to see what would have happened if the advertising peak had not occurred. This principle applies to evaluating all marketing activities. Thus it is only if sales are steady that a comparison with the period before is really appropriate. A comparison with the same period last year has the advantage that it may remove seasonality, but only if annual sales are steady.

Example 1
Sales are falling steadily at 6% a year. Compared with the previous bi-month, sales are 1% up. The best estimate of the real increase is +2% (+1% against the expected change of −1% in a bi-month).

In addition to these direct effects of advertising, there should be indirect ones.

The Trade

'We know of many cases where frantic pressure for immediate sales has distorted the appropriation to the point where far greater sums are being spent to jolly the dealer along than to build a reputation for the product which the dealer cannot be expected to appreciate at the moment but which in the last analysis will prove his greatest strength' (Leo Burnett, 1936).

The previous two sections have assumed that the brand is distributed via retailers, is available to its purchasers on the shelf, is reasonably displayed, has retailer support, and so on. All this does not happen by chance. A lot of it is paid for directly (the sales force, trade deals, and so on). Trade press advertising plays its part. The question we consider now is: does *consumer* advertising also play a part?

At one time, when the balance of power first swung from manufacturers to retailers, the answer to this question would have been considered obvious. Media advertising was how the marketer went over the head of the retailer to create consumer demand for his brand. It pulled sales through the pipeline.

This argument is heard less often today. Brand proliferation is the reason: if the marketer does not play by the retailer's rules, another manufacturer may be found who will. The retailer's power has escalated. But the argument still has force. The real defence that the manufacturer has against retailer power is the brand's franchise with purchasers and consumers. The trade — by which I mean the channels of distribution from the production line to the shelf — is still indirectly influenced by a manufacturer's advertising.

The effects are also direct: from the manufacturer's own employees to the checkout clerks, a well-advertised brand is seen as special in some way. Branding applies to this target as well as to purchasers and consumers. Advertising is seen as the marketer's act of faith in the product, as a guarantee of quality, of perseverance, of the brand's consumer franchise.

It has been argued (4) that the trade effects of advertising can be allowed for explicitly, and that they justify larger advertising budgets than consumer effects alone:

'In calculating the sales effect of their firm's advertising, these Canadian managers included advertising's impact on distributors (whether they stocked and promoted the brand) as well as on consumers. Indeed, when asked whether the chief "strategic emphasis" of their advertising was distributor or consumer oriented, 35 per cent of the marketing executives at convenience-goods firms and 58 per cent at shopping-goods firms responded that the principal emphasis was on influencing distributors.

'Retailers . . . exercise varying degrees of market power as buyers in the first-stage manufacturer/retailer market and downstream as resellers in the second-stage retailer/consumer market. The degree of competition in these two markets, as well as the relative bargaining power of the manufacturer and its retailers, is a function of the strength of a brand's consumer franchise. In turn, the latter tends to be closely and positively related to the size of its advertising budget.'

A case history (Death of a Brand) in Chapter 8 demonstrates the importance of this trade effect. After advertising stopped, it was not a consumer change that explained the sales fall but loss of trade support. In launches also, trade influence is critical.

Example 2
Café de Rio was launched in Australia by a banned commercial, never publicly shown, starring Ronnie Biggs. The resulting PR, and its effect on retail buyers, was enough to make the brand known.

The Timing of Effects

'On most lines, making a sale without making a convert does not count for much. Sales made by conviction — by advertising — are likely to bring permanent customers' (Claude Hopkins, 1923).

A word used to explain branding effects on consumers is goodwill, which encourages positive attitudes to the brand. Spending on advertising adds to goodwill. Thus spending is an investment on which we expect to get a return over years. Goodwill also depreciates over time, however, and needs topping up. The connection between goodwill and sales varies by campaign; it is hard to specify exactly, but is expected to be positive.

The concept has been formalized (5): the units for goodwill are financial. A similar concept is adstock, which spreads the purchased advertising exposures over subsequent weeks; it is during these weeks that we expect to see their short-term effects; the units are the rating points bought (6). Both ideas emphasize that returns are not immediate and that even short-term sales depend on past but recent advertising as well as on the current level.

The rates of decay of the two effects are not the same. After a whole year, it is likely that three-quarters or more of our goodwill still remains; in contrast, three-quarters of the short-term influences represented by adstock will be over in three or four months.

These ideas have led to the suggestion that advertising costs be capitalized and amortized over later periods, and not all shown in the accounts in the period they were spent (7). This is not a generally accepted accounting procedure; the evidence, like most direct links between advertising and sales, is too weak for such a major change, but there is little doubt in my mind that this is how some advertising effects are felt.

Two developments at the end of 1988 deserve comment. First, in the USA, there is a threat to disallow advertising expenditure as a fully deductible expense for tax in the year in which it was incurred. The logical ground for this move is precisely that advertising has long-term, brand-building effects, though the necessity to raise tax revenue is in practice a stronger motive. Second, there is debate in the UK about adding an amount for brands in the company's capital statement. General goodwill (here a financial term) has often been included previously, though usually as a small amount; what is new is putting a specific value on brand names. This increases borrowing powers and is a defence against takeovers which may be aimed as much at brands as at tangible assets, shown dramatically by the Nestlé purchase of Rowntree, mentioned in Chapter 1. For example, Reckitt & Colman and Grand Metropolitan have both put acquired brands as assets on the balance sheet. Ranks Hovis McDougall, in November 1988, declared the development of Mr. Kipling, Hovis, Mother's Pride, and so on, as worth £678 million.

In both countries, 'brand equity' is the key to the argument. This American phrase means the value added to the name by every kind of manufacturing and marketing investment: a better product, and one seen as superior to competitors both by purchasers and the trade, has a large brand equity. Through a bigger sales share, or a higher price, or better trade terms, this pays off both in volume and in profit. Advertising, often a major marketing activity, is one contributor to equity. Manufacturing costs are already partly capitalized (the factory, for example), so some of these costs are spread over years. Advertising, so some Americans say, should be treated similarly. Once brand equity has been created, some British companies agree, it is an asset and should be recognized as such. However, they go on to say that maintaining it by further advertising and other means is a current cost. Advertising has short-term effects but long-term benefits.

The full implications of these financial debates are not yet apparent. It has not been properly recognized that some advertising is largely, or entirely, for the short term (recruitment, for example); that sales promotion, and research and development, and staff training might all be treated similarly; that, while some brands grow, others fail — how will accountants treat brand equity then?

Category and Competitor Effects

Beyond direct effects on the brand, two other effects are possible. First, the size of the category may be affected; in general, and over the long term, we expect some association between category size and media spend. The positive influence of advertising is particularly likely if the category is growing. Advertising often explains how brands are used, and this education of the users about the benefits of all the products in the category can accelerate the penetration of the category. In any case, there is always some confusion between brands in consumers' minds, so advertising Brand A may influence sales of Brand B. Thus all advertising is expected to have some effect on the total category. In reverse, when a category is declining, there is often a reduction in advertising. It is very rare that a category advertises itself out of trouble, though a well-managed brand may do so. Even in these cases, how much do the sales changes cause advertising spend changes, and how much is it the other way round? The first is usually more important.

Do not expect growth effects in mature categories, since Brand A's gain is often simply Brand B's loss. There are categories in which the advertising industry argues vehemently that it does *not* influence category size: tobacco and alcohol, for example. In a review of 18 mature food categories, between 1975 and 1983, Harry Henry concluded (8) that while 'advertising clearly affects brand shares within markets, [it] appears to have little or no effect on total market sales.'

Second, our advertising may affect competitor brands by encouraging them to retaliate. Alternatively, the level of advertising in the category may be such that potential competitors decide the cost of entry is too high, which has the long-term effect of maintaining our brand share.

These ideas do not usually play much of a part in setting a brand budget, though they do enter into discussions by economists.

Creative and Media

So far, the copy that will be run has hardly been mentioned. This is not a book about advertisements, but advertising budgets are rarely decided in isolation from creative work. Normally we know we are going to spend the money on existing copy, or we have a good idea what the campaign will be like. We also know that the sales effects depend critically on how effective this advertising is. This does not mean that it is impossible to measure or to estimate the effect of financial changes, but only that the results are specific to that particular situation and to those particular advertisements.

The effects of the chosen media on the advertising carried are often discussed. It is rare that advertising is thought to influence the medium. However, by setting the agenda, a campaign can make editorial matter more favourable to the product. An example is the Greater London Council's anti-abolition campaign in 1984, which, it has been claimed, even had an influence on legislation (9).

The Expected Size of Effects

It is sometimes necessary to estimate the short-term sales effect that will be produced by changing advertising weight. Here weight means the number of advertisement exposures to individuals, assuming that advertisement length or size remains the same. It is not the same as adspend because weight is also affected by changes in cost. Media inflation from year to year, or special arrangements for an area test, may require more adspend just to get the same exposures.

For example, we would dearly like to know the likely result of 25% fewer TVRs (Television Rating Points) next year; or what may happen if we run an upweight test with 50% more TVRs.

The difficulties of making these estimates are enormous. Even if we are guessing, however, we may be forced to give at least an order of magnitude. This section attempts to make the guess a realistic one.

Obviously, the answer turns on how sales-effective, in the short term, our campaign actually is. Anything we already know about its sales effects should of course be used in making this judgement. It is very hard to admit that the advertising, which the team has worked so hard to create, is anything less than brilliant. The sad truth is that most advertising is average and a lot is below average in effectiveness.

We should increase our optimism about the effect of weight changes if

— our share of voice is high but actual adspend is not very large,
— penetration of our brand is low,
— our trade relations are good, and our brand is at least at cost parity in the store,
— our advertising communicates a relevant benefit (physical or psychic).

It is hardest to cause big short-term effects when a large, mature brand without uniqueness sells in a competitive market with a lot of advertising against it. Movements are then generally long term and advertising is mainly defensive.

In Chapter 7, the difficulties are explained and the foundations are laid for the estimates now given. They depend on classifying the sales effectiveness of the campaign as:
— outstanding
— very good
— good
— average
— poor.

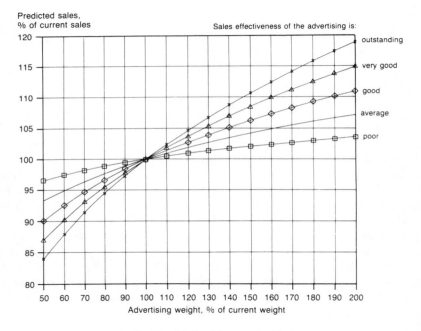

Figure 1   Predicted Sales Changes, for Various Advertising Weight Changes.

After this decision, and with the relevant percentage change in advertising weight, use Figure 1 to give you an estimate. Usually we compete within a category, and it is then necessary also to include in our estimate of future sales any category volume changes we expect.

Example 3
Our advertising effectiveness is rated average. Category sales are expected to grow next year by 5%. The planned increase in TVRs is 50%. What volume change can we expect? The chart indicates a sales index of 104, at average effectiveness, and TVRs at 150% of current. Thus the combined index from the category change and our advertising is $1.05 \times 104 = 109$. So + 9% is predicted.

Changes predicted in this way are sometimes disappointing. People expect payout too rapidly from adspend increases. They also forget that maintenance of the current position of the brand (continuing the long-term effects of previous advertising) requires expenditure.

Note that the figure shows diminishing returns: the lines are convex curves. For the 'outstanding' line, for example, the increase from 100 to 110% of TVRs grows sales from 100 to 102.4. But the increase from 190 to 200% of TVRs grows sales from 117.4 to 118.9, an increase of 1.5, which is less than 2.4. These apply also to decreasing TVRs. The lines fall faster the more we reduce advertising.

Do these effects pay off? This question requires information about the brand's budget and is answered in the next chapter.

Price and Promotions

So far, my description of the ways advertising may work has ignored other parts of the marketing mix. Many people think this way: they look for advertising effects only directly on brand volume, and often only in the short term. The rest of the mix is supposed to work independently, unaffected by advertising. The effects of price, promotion and so on are thought to be constant: advertising effects should be visible against a steady background.

These assumptions, once stated, are obviously unrealistic. They limit the role of advertising unnecessarily. They gloss over the complications introduced into observing advertising's effects, even on sales volume in the short term. It is therefore necessary to make a digression at this point, and to investigate the ways in which price and promotions may work. When we return to advertising's effects and how to quantify them, it will be with more realistic expectations. When the brand's budget is discussed in the next chapter, price and promotions will again be included.

I start with the truism that purchasers do not just select a brand; they have to pay for it. A successful brand is one which is thought to be good value for money. That is, it offers the right combination of quality and price. The physical performance of the brand is fixed, at least temporarily, so it is up to the marketer to find the right mix of marketing activities which affect both value and price.

At his disposal is media advertising, the subject of this book, as well as trade and consumer promotions in all their variety, and list price, or the nominal cost of the brand to the retailer. I say nominal because discounts and trade deals often reduce the list price in practice.

Clearly one of advertising's tasks is to maintain and add value. The brand has to be seen as worth its cost. The performance of the product is rarely enough on its own: when I make a choice I often have to be told what to look for, and to feel that the brand is 'for me'. Equally clearly, list price works mostly at the money end, but not entirely: a high price actually implies value to many purchasers, and a low price can imply that the product is shoddy.

In between come the various sorts of promotions, and their functions can be mixed. Even when a consumer promotion is apparently reducing the price only temporarily, it may change perceptions of the brand and have long-term effects (there will be more on this in Chapter 8).

Although most advertising people would agree with this distinction between money and value, be aware that the words are not always used in this way. The Institute of Sales Promotion has offered this very different definition (quoted in Mintel: 10):

'Sales promotion is a facet of marketing which is *adding value* [my italics], usually of a temporary nature, to a product or service in order to persuade the end user to purchase that particular brand.'

However, there is as yet incomplete agreement on what activities count as sales promotion (11). Nearly everyone would include cash refunds and coupons, special promotional packs or tags and collars, in- and on-pack premiums, and tailor-made promotions. Many would add special merchandising, sampling and door-to-door distribution, money off, banded packs and twofers (two for the price of one), extra quantity free, collection items and trading stamps. The total number of activities included in the Institute of Sales Promotion's 1987 Survey was 65.

There is debate within the sales promotion business itself on the balance between, on the one hand, getting measurable results quickly or moving boxes, and, on the other hand, making the brand message stand out from the mechanics used or creativity (12). It is likely that most brands' promotion objectives give priority to the first of these.

Some of the sales during a promotion would of course have been made anyway, either at the time, or soon after (in the latter case, sales are advanced). Some of the cost of a promotion may of course be the price of getting extra distribution or new buyers.

The long-term effects of price promoting can be detrimental. Most advertised products face competition from cheaper and often lower-quality goods. Some promotions, such as straight price reductions, do not reinforce the belief that a brand is worth paying more for; they often do not mention the brand's values at all. They do, however, draw attention to price as a choice criterion. In the long run they can destroy confidence in value.

It is recommended that every promotion being considered for your brand be evaluated for its likely effect in changing value as well as for its part in lowering price.

'Sales promotions *may*, if we are very lucky, also enhance the quality, but they are usually directed towards lowering the perceived price' (13).

A coupon may be simply money-off, trading on the existing brand standing, and may provoke the response: 'It can't be much good if they have to make it that cheap'. But a relevant self-liquidating offer ('Get this deck chair') or additional product ('20% added free') may be seen as the brand sharing with its purchasers, as a friend would. It may be planned to make use of the values from theme advertising without harming them, or even to reinforce the advertising effects.

Paradoxically, it is often the strong branding created by advertising that may make promotions at first appear to be so effective in comparison with advertising. 'A valuable brand *and* at a bargain price!' It is the overuse of this tool which can, in the long run, reduce the brand's franchise.

Similarly, a successful consumer competition may be announced in a tactical print campaign or on-pack, quite separate from the mainstream advertising budget. If these announcements recall the main advertising theme, can you doubt that the mainstream campaign contributed to their success?

Some direct marketing activities (see Chapter 6) overlap or are similar to promotions. The same distinction should be attempted for these activities. When you use direct mail, door-to-door drops, or telephone methods, is your approach consistent with the value-adding objectives of advertising? Or are you cashing in these values, not reminding the recipient of mainstream advertising themes, or even being unfriendly and threatening (as some telephone selling has been described)?

For your own brand, you should review all the marketing activities: not only advertising, but promotions, direct marketing, and any other way you make an impact on purchasers. You must make up your own mind how much each activity increases or sustains value, and how much it trades on it.

Example 4
One manufacturer has seen clearly that the long-term and indirect effects of advertising are what matter. Pedigree Petfoods (14) is a major advertiser, and advertising is their third largest expense (after raw materials and cans). It is therefore 'critically examined as is any other major investment or forward purchase such as capital equipment, purchase of a raw material, forward purchase of a commodity or foreign exchange.'

If the purpose of advertising were merely to boost sales volume, it would be far too expensive. 'Even on a medium size brand of around £20 million per annum turnover, a simple calculation would show that you would need a large sustained uplift in sales and a big margin to justify, say, a £1 million network TV burst of a few months. There are in fact far more effective ways of boosting volume in the short term such as: price promotions, in-store feature/display, retail outlet-led promotions.'

The investment is made for the long term: to create brand images, to reinforce and re-emphasize the messages which communicate these images. 'The value of the advertising can be measured by the success of the brands.'

However, it is necessary to allow for the other links in the whole chain also working well (the two other main links are the quality of the product and production capacity), before 'the effectiveness of advertising could be measured by the capability to continue the investment in all aspects of the brand including advertising in order to continue its growth'.

Example 5
In a review of the management of mature products, Nielsen (15) gave an example in a canned food category. Here private label growth was a real concern, and marketing expenditure was shifted from advertising to promotions to counter this attack. Over a period of eight years, media expenditure for one particular brand moved from about three-quarters of the total budget towards half. In addition, the total marketing spend fell 10%.

Special analyses showed that, in the retail chains supporting each promotion, there was a definite share lift for the promoted items during the promotion, then sales fell back to their previous level. This improvement did not achieve the objective of reducing the private label share, which continued to grow in these chains. Nor was total brand share improved: there must have been switching between packings (different sizes of units, or flavours) within the brand's total sales. Category sales were similar in the stores supporting the promotion and in those that did not.

These disappointing results compared with a relationship found between category sales, over 12 years, and total advertising expenditure for the category. In the years when advertising was high, so were these sales. In later years, with reducing media spend, the category was in decline.

It is best to look within your own category and brand for associations between advertising spend, perceived values and consumer price (or return to the manufacturer). This is far more relevant than general relationships, although these have been investigated (16). The effects of all these activities on the budget are considered in the next chapter. Here their effects on sales take priority.

Trade deals are mostly price reductions. These may or, more often, may not be passed on to the consumer. They are part of the negotiations between the retail buyer and the manufacturer, part of the price of doing business. The buyer is not motivated as much to lower the absolute price (this makes his own profit harder to find) as to be price-competitive with other retailers. Buyer and seller are playing a complicated game here.

At the end of the day, when the brand has a high value, it can command a high price. As its value decreases, so does the price which purchasers are willing to pay. As Andrew Ehrenberg has pointed out (17), 'brand-differentiation ("strong branding") will pay off not so much in terms of market segmentation or in targeting on a suitable advertising platform (the past evidence of success for these purposes is not strong), but in providing the basis for more profitable pricing policies. Strong brand differentiation serves to allow more aggressive pricing.'

Everything the marketer does to maintain value, including advertising, has an effect on the saleability of the brand. A brand audit, which is where we look for long-term advertising effects, therefore includes price as one of the important dimensions. The audit considers the frequency and depth of price-cutting promotions. The higher the relative price, the more effective and the less frequent the promotions, then the higher are the added values, to which advertising has contributed.

We also look for long-term branding effects. How does the trade view the brand? How well does it do with consumers, compared with other products which are not so different, in unbranded or blind tests? What uses of the advertising are explicitly made elsewhere? Or implicitly?

We should not look for advertising's effects in volume sales alone: we look at the brand's financial return too and at the efficiency of all its marketing activities. It may be found that, in the past, advertising has made a major contribution to the brand and so to the company. Future advertising is likely to do the same. But 'what has posterity ever done for us?' is a hard question to answer.

Advertising oils the wheels for other marketing activities. Unfortunately, it is often part of the background, and this role may be taken for granted. For example, trade relations and the effectiveness of the sales representatives have both been built up while the brand has been advertised. We do not have any other sort of experience. Such effects cannot be experimented with, without putting at risk the brand itself. The situation calls for a management with sympathy for the value of branding, which understands the long time it can take to add this value — and the short time it may take to lose it.

Because this is a book about advertising, price and promotional effects are considered partly as possible beneficiaries of advertising and partly as complications in observing what advertising does. They should also, of course, be studied in their own right and evaluated just as stringently as advertising.

How to See Advertising's Effects

'There is no more difficult, complex, or controversial problem in marketing than measuring the influence of advertising on sales' (18).

This book is not about researching the effects of advertising, so this section will be short. Your research department and suppliers, and your advertising agency, should be the best guides through this jungle. The two greatest dangers are:

1. The desire for an easily-applied and standard system, which does not allow for the different jobs which advertising can do.
2. An incomplete view of what effects advertising can have, and of how it achieves them.

There are reviews of this vast subject (19), but they should be used with caution. If you have the time and interest, it is best to read case histories and so build up a repertoire of approaches, services and suppliers appropriate to your particular situation. Each case history teaches us about the effects of a single campaign. Do not expect uniformity: a lot depends on the way the advertising actually worked in the circumstances which the brand faced. In Chapter 5 there is more on the collection and use of historical sales data, and on experiments. These, and consumer research, are the main tools for assessing advertising's effects.

Activities Other Than Advertising

I have already mentioned the major difficulty in quantifying advertising's effects; other factors influence the results.

The first factors to consider are the *product* itself and its *name*. Clearly, product performance is key: advertising can sell a poor product once only. *Packaging* is important: it should reflect the brand image we are aiming for and so should mirror the advertising (and vice versa). It is amazing how many names and packages fail to capitalize on, or are even inconsistent with, advertising. These factors seldom change.

Price, however, changes all the time. It is price comparison which shoppers make, and the price of competitors is not in our control. Price relative to competition is a major influence on sales in at least three ways. First, our general price level may be at the category average — or very different. It is not unknown for an advertised brand, supported by excellent product performance, to cost twice as much as its competitors. Second, variations occur in this average price through special low pricing by the store, or by the manufacturer: price-off packs, for example. The third influence comes from couponing and other promotional activity. Note that temporary low prices of the second, and especially the third, kind are often associated with activities other than the price itself. The coupon which causes the price to be lower, for example, was itself distributed in some way, perhaps in a newspaper ad, which draws attention to the brand. Thus low price may have more than just a price effect.

Promotions have already been mentioned and have major and often very visible short-term sales effects. These effects are sometimes themselves inefficiently evaluated; not all coupons redeemed represent additional sales, for example. Remember that we should compare what *did* happen with what *would* have happened if the activity had not occurred. Promotions also have long-term effects: on consumers, who are being trained to buy on price; on retailer buyers, who have come to expect manufacturers to support their own store's marketing; and on brand managers, who learn to use them as a tool to generate short-term volume.

The list of other factors that can affect sales is a long one. In addition to our marketing activities and our competitors', we should include everything that retailers do as well as price manipulation, from stocking to displaying, from the position in store to the shelf-footage allocated. The general consumer environment is a factor: sales of certain food products alter with health beliefs, even in the short term; the spending power of purchasers alters with employment levels, interest rates, and so on. Even the weather may play a part in sales.

In round terms, measured factors (price, couponing, etc.) may account for 50 to 90% of observed sales variation. Unmeasured and often unexplained factors cause the rest.

Advertising's direct effects are often a smaller source of this variation than, say, price. It follows that advertising effects are usually hard to disentangle and, not surprisingly, there is a traditional belief that its sales effects cannot be measured. It does not, however, follow that advertising is uneconomic because its effects, at least in the short term, are small.

Investment in advertising is usually also a small part of the brand's turnover. Increases in this expenditure can still bring a sound return through only a small sales increase (more on this in Chapter 7).

Research Methods

The first major distinction here is whether we are to look at advertising's effects on *sales*, or on behaviour, compared with *other*, indirect dimensions (for example, attitudes to the brand). To the purist, only sales measurements can show advertising's economic effects. However, in an imperfect world it is admissible to make judgements. These may be based on qualitative data, or on measured dimensions other than sales (for example, awareness of advertising claims about the brand is sometimes relevant).

This is a difficult position, but I know of none better. If we restricted budget-setting input only to measurements of advertising's sales effects, then few budgets would be set. It is an ideal to *try* to find quantified sales effects. Even when we fail, we shall get useful information. But we cannot ignore the indirect ways of estimating what our advertising is doing, even those that are imperfect in strict logic.

The second distinction is seen among *a snapshot observation* (for example, a survey on brand image at one point in time), *repeated observations* (for example, the same survey repeated, or sales shares from a continuous store audit) and *experiments* (for example, we have deliberately changed the level of adspend before the second survey). The one-off observation cannot, of course, show changes but may help in a brand audit.

Within these two broad classifications of the research to use are many choices. There is more detail, as well as an outline of an ideal campaign evaluation, in Chapter 6.

The main sorts of effects to look for are discussed below, with some suggestions as to the appropriate research technique for each. This is not an exhaustive list, nor are the descriptions detailed. For your own case, you have to select what to look for and the appropriate way in which to find it.

Long-term Consumer Effects

Most advertising is written for the long term; most evaluation techniques are suitable for the short term. Thus, where advertising may perform best, it is least measurable. Advertising is usually aimed more at brand maintenance, at the refreshment and updating of the values it adds. The economics of advertisement production, the need for repetition, the shortage of totally different things to say about a brand — all these drive advertising into presenting and re-presenting the basic values in the brand.

Of course, there are short-term tactical opportunities, Olympics and local advertising, re-launches, and announcements of improvements, but all these are usually schemes to take temporary advantages. The main theme campaigns are intended to be long running.

A well-managed brand is a combination of excellent product quality, strong branding maintained largely by advertising but supported by other activities, and a certain amount of local excitement. The latter includes short-running, tactical advertising but is mainly promotions.

The values added to the brand by advertising help in the short term, but to judge theme advertising only by its short-term, direct cost-effectiveness undervalues its real contribution. Some ways to look for long-term effects follow, beginning with one that is the most convincing but hardly ever available.

It is rare that an experiment is run long enough to estimate long-term effects. If we see a trend in the results of, say, upweighting, this may help us to guess what the long term will show. Normally we are restricted to a snapshot of how things are now. There are a few examples of stopping advertising (see Chapter 8) but this is not a generally recommended technique!

The brand audit already mentioned is a review of how the brand stands with consumers. It summarizes, for example, the results of a Usage and Attitude or Image survey, comparing these with how competitive brands stand. When we can identify that certain dimensions come from the advertising, this is helpful. Often what we see is the result of advertising years ago: attitudes and images change slowly.

Where tracking data are available on consumer attitudes we look at them first in an overall way. Are we maintaining our position or is there a consistent trend? Later we examine their short-term movements.

The audit may combine this qualitative information with an analysis of consumers' repertoires and switching patterns. Panel data show not only who buys our brand but who our real competitors are in the repertoire. Often buying behaviour looks more random than expected: loyalty is an over-rated concept.

Branded and blind product tests may establish differences in preference levels which are not explained by product performance.

The brand's history is used in several ways. In Chapter 4 we inspect where we are in order to evaluate the task that advertising is expected to do. In Chapter 5 we look at history for parallels to the budgets we might set. We also introduce — and expand in Chapter 7 — the idea of mathematical modelling.

We can look for advertising's effects on the way all other marketing activities affect the brand. Do our promotions benefit from the main theme advertising, for example?

It has been suggested that branding causes the difference between a public company's capitalization value and the worth of its physical assets.

Price: a Major Long-term Advertising Effect

Of all marketing activities that benefit from branding, price is the most important. The purpose of advertising is often to make the brand more saleable; the purpose of the pricing policy, and of promotions, is often to cash in on this saleability. How do you see pricing as an advertising effect? There are two main methods: static and dynamic.

For a static analysis, look at the average prices of different brands in your category. Plot the position of each brand on a map that shows their sales shares and their relative prices. An example of such a map is given in Chapter 5. Record the brands' average media spend. This map often shows the relation between price and share to be one that the economists do not expect.

The cheaper brands do not necessarily sell more. The plot does not look like the one for a single brand for different periods. Instead, the more heavily-advertised brands may sell more at the same price as competitors, or have higher prices and sell the same.

'Advertised brands cost more' is a familiar consumerist complaint, but frequently this is not comparing like products with like. The advertised brand may be of better quality, or, if a durable, have better guarantees or service arrangements, and so on. Advertising often makes people aware of a product's benefits and has produced a brand that is simply more valuable to people than those of its competitors. Of course, sometimes advertised brands cost less because advertising has helped them to reach sales volumes at which economies of scale are possible.

Advertising is not the only factor involved in branding. Product performance is paramount, but do not forget the part advertising plays in setting the agenda, that is, drawing attention to those aspects of performance where our brand does best. Thus it makes the use of the product more satisfactory and increases the bonding between the brand and its users. This may show in other ways as well as price, of course, just as other factors play a part in branding. Only the insights of qualitative research can help your judgement about the importance of advertising here.

The price of a brand also affects its sales in the short term. If you plot the brand's share at different periods against its price relative to other brands, you often see a downward-sloping association. The higher the price, the less the demand or the lower the sales. The relation is called the demand curve (see Example 5).

Advertising may make the brand suffer less when we charge more or when competitors cut prices: it reduces the brand's price elasticity. Elasticity is discussed more fully in Chapter 7; it is the percentage by which sales volume falls when price goes up 1%. It is related to the slope of the demand curve: the flatter this relation the smaller the elasticity. This has often been observed: 'heavily advertised products exhibit lower price elasticities than little advertised products' (20).

When several brands are compared over the same periods, they usually have different demand curves. Sometimes it is instructive to consider the association of these curves with the amounts the brands spend on advertising.

There are plenty of examples of more advertising, or better advertising (21), moving the demand curve. The new relation will be above and to the right when there is an improvement. This does not necessarily mean that sales, or share, have on average changed. You may have raised price as well as getting better results via advertising. The joint effect may be to leave share unaltered; but contribution may have improved through the higher price.

Example 6

A panel of households recorded their purchases in a three-brand category. For each purchase we know: the brand bought, the price paid (in pence per unit weight) and the week. For each brand, its share by weight for each week was calculated, and also its average price that week (compared with the category = 100). The weeks for which each brand was at each relative price were grouped: for example 85 to 95, 95 to 105 . . . Then the average brand share for those weeks was calculated.

In Figure 2, the A at 100,70 means that when Brand A's relative price was 100 its share was 70%. The three brands' share relationships to price clearly lie on different lines. We are seeing here three different demand curves. For example,

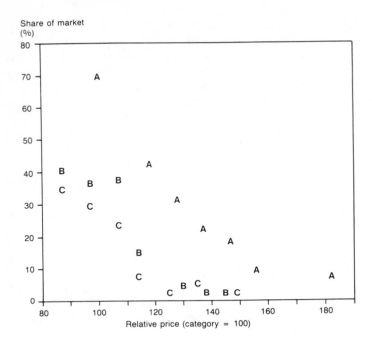

Share of market
(%)

**Figure 2   Shares of Market for Three Brands Against
Their Prices Relative to the Category.**

when Brand A is at a relative price of 110 we would expect a sales share of about 55%. But at a relative price of 110, Brand B would sell only about 15%, and Brand C only 10%.

The relative weights of TV advertising at the time were:
— Brand A: 100
— Brand B: 20
— Brand C: 0

The coincidence between the advertising weights and the positions of the demand curves is too great to be by chance only; and qualitative research confirms that advertising claims are making a contribution in purchase decisions.

In this example, it is tempting to put a value on the higher price that Brand A can charge. Brand A is at the same share as Brand B when Brand B is about 25% less expensive. If Brand A were able to command only the same price as Brand B, this would be 25% less than now. Thus, on average, the brand name is worth 25% of the selling price.

Example 7

This case history is about a Lever Brothers brand in a cleaning product category (22). It demonstrates a change for the better in price elasticity: that is, the elasticity was made smaller. This was claimed to be the result of restaged advertising. It also shows how this price elasticity is made up among different groups of people: those more loyal to the brand are those with the lower price elasticity. Hence the mechanism by which the price elasticity was improved: by increasing brand loyalty, advertising put more consumers in the groups with lower price elasticity. It also raised brand share.

Frequently, loyal users, however defined, are the most important segment of our target. Keeping them, or, better still, adding to them as here, is a major objective. The 20/80 rule suggests that we often find that 20% of the 'ever use' account for 80% or so of total usage. This example shows that their loyalty can be demonstrated by their disinclination to switch away from our brand as a result of competitive marketing activity.

Before the advertising was changed in this case, a survey divided purchasers into five groups, based upon their answers to questions about the brand normally purchased and the action they would take if it were not available. This excludes the 1% who said that they would never buy the brand. A price elasticity for each group was found by a regression analysis on separate data.

Group	Definition	Percentage of sales of our brand	Price elasticity
1	Normally buy our brand and would not substitute another.	25	−0.8
2	Normally buy our brand but would substitute another.	15	−1.2
3	Normally buy our brand but would buy a specific substitute.	30	−2.2
4	Have no regular brand.	12	−2.8
5	Normally buy another brand but would substitute our brand.	17	−3.0
	Weighted average		−1.9

The brand's advertising was then restaged, and this was deemed 'quite successful': sales share increased by a quarter without a substantial increase in adspend, or a major change in relative price.

This was due mainly to an increase in the number in Group 1 and a decrease in Groups 4 and 5. As a result of this, the overall price elasticity of the brand was reduced from −1.9 to −1.7. This makes clear what it means to add value to the brand.

It may be that moving the demand curve to the right, as a benefit of advertising, is demonstrating the same phenomenon. Suppose the way that the benefit is taken is not to increase the price but to sell more at the same price. Suppose also (as often seems to be the case) that the slope of the new line is the same as that of the old. Since the price elasticity is

(slope) × (average price) ÷ (average sales)

the elasticity will be lower after the new advertising.

These are just some examples of the relationship possible between price, advertising and sales. And the case history, Death of a Brand, in Chapter 8 could be described as a long-term relationship between distribution, advertising and sales.

Finally, at an even longer-term and higher level, other important effects may be considered (23). For example, heavy advertising may be deliberately intended to deter competitive entry. Analysis of the category history may indicate such effects.

Short-term Consumer Effects

It is usually necessary to have some comparison in order to see a short-term effect of advertising. A single moment in time is not enough to distinguish a difference from trend. It is *changes* we are inspecting: how a difference in advertising weight associates with differences in what we measure. Thus we look at data over time or at an experiment.

The same sources as in the section above are relevant, including brand images, purchase repertoire, relative price and other promotional tools. Tracking studies, or repeated measures over time, are helpful. The usual warning is necessary about image changes: they may not be related to the sales results we really want. (Examples are given in Reference 24; see also Examples 15 and 16 in Chapter 5).

Thus the ideal evaluation of a weight change is to have measures for both:

— overall sales (and of other factors affecting sales)
— consumer and purchaser behaviour and beliefs (which give us clues about how sales were changed, for example via copy point recall when this is relevant).

The two classical situations where we make these measurements are as the data actually fell, and in an experiment. The latter is normally an area test (more details of which are given in Chapter 5).

Long- and Short-term Trade Effects

Compared with the relations that manufacturers enjoy with consumers, little has been published about the way they relate to retailers. Most companies rely on their own data on deliveries, list price and trade deals. Their competitive position in this area may also be partly quantified by trade research, rare though this is. There is store environment research (distribution, stocking, shelf-footage, display, and so on).

Qualitative measures on the brand's standing with retailers are very rarely available. We normally rely more on the opinion of the sales force about the advertising support they are given. Few will say they can do without trade advertising. However, all advertising is seen by salespeople as an alternative to spending directly on themselves or the tools they use (trade promotions), so they are not disinterested in this evaluation. The level of management to which both media advertising and sales force report is the lowest at which an evaluation is trustworthy.

For price effects and some others, the same tools apply as with consumers. We can map where the brand is positioned, in list price, discounting and advertising support. Just as with consumers, we may see a high price or lower discounts justified by advertising. As far as the retailer is concerned, this is usually because the brand sells faster, or is a loss leader, or in some other way its standing with consumers shows through. Often this is because the brand maintains a healthy market share at a higher list price, discounting less, or no more, than average.

It is again through changes that we see short-term effects of advertising on the trade. How do wholesalers and retailers react when we approach them with a new formulation, package, or deal? Does the advertising behind the change gain it higher acceptance, so the changes work through to consumers faster and more completely? Does the sales force report that advertising helps in the inevitable bargaining of small-scale negotiation?

The Shape of the Relationship

I have argued that advertising may affect sales in the short term. The more we spend, the more sales we get within the financial year. Figure 3 shows the relationship between annual sales and annual adspend, as it is often assumed to be. Note that I do not commit the error of extending the curve to the zero adspend point and calling all sales below this level 'independent of advertising'. Within the financial year the direct effects may be so, but these are not all the effects, nor is this year the end of the story.

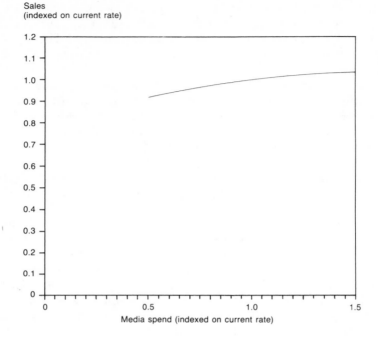

Sales
(indexed on current rate)

Media spend (indexed on current rate)

**Figure 3   Annual Sales of a Brand Against the Media
Spend in That Year.**

From the shape of this curve we see it implies that more is better (for volume sales), but also that there are diminishing returns. This means that at high media spends we do not get as much more for an extra pound as we did at low media spends. The shape is not a straight line.

Diminishing returns are often poorly defined. Further, it is not enough that the curve falls away from a straight line to show that extra spend is not worth while. Diminishing does not mean negative. In fact negative returns have very rarely been shown to exist even at high spends.

The curve may be used to decide how much needs to be spent to reach a volume target. This is legitimate, provided that we have estimated well enough where the curve lies. It comes under the Task method in Chapter 5. It may also be used to set an optimum contribution level. This means that we find, at various points on the curve, how much extra sales we get for a pound more adspend. These sales add to revenue but also add to production costs. At some point, the extra marginal revenue equals the cost of advertising. This has been put forward seriously as determining the best adspend: where marginal revenue equals costs (this argument is expanded, and criticized, in Chapter 7).

Another way in which this curve can be used is to deduce a second curve: how contribution changes as we change adspend. The highest point on this relationship again determines the optimum. More important is that the second curve is rather flat around this point: that is, changes in adspend make little difference to contribution. In other words, provided we make a reasonable guess at how much to spend, contribution is not very sensitive to the exact value we guess.

In the example given in Chapter 7, a brand can withstand changes between £800 000 and £1 200 000 on adspend while the contribution differences are around only £40 000. Perhaps this is one reason why very different budgeting practices can co-exist: their financial effects are not especially critical.

For TV commercials which are not themselves media events (discussed above), it is likely that the overall return in increased sales does not pay off until the ads receive a decent amount of exposure. It normally does not make sense to spend tens or hundreds of thousands of pounds on production, plus the trouble of writing and agreeing a script, unless much more is spent showing the film. Thus, if you plot the overall return from different amounts in the total advertising budget, not in adspend, the curve will probably be below zero return at the left end.

Such thinking may be behind the famous S-shaped response curve. According to this belief, we do not get much response (or financial return) at small amounts spent on advertising, but response picks up beyond some threshold. This is not to say that consumer sales would not move at low adspends. Some hold (and I am one of them) that the effect on consumers at low adspends is not negligible.

The shape of the curve is convex: it is actually growing faster when it starts (there will be more discussion of response in Chapters 5 and 7). Note also that the trade might deride small media expenditures, and indirect trade effects may show through as consumer sales effects.

Finally, I repeat that the plot above does not tell the whole story. One way of stating the problem of setting an advertising budget is that the contribution is immediately affected, sales are affected later, and the slowest effects are on the brand's standing. The last item does not appear in the plot.

It is always possible to maximize profit — for a time — by losing share and destroying the brand. But this strategy is for corporate raiders, not for brand managers. Marketing management's job is to defend or maximize the long-term contribution of the brand. To do so they should hand over to their successors a brand in as good shape as they found it — or better.

Chapter 2: Action Points

Review the possible effects of advertising in the chart below, for those that may apply to your brand.

	Purchasers and consumers	*Wholesalers and retailers*
Long term	Maintains the brand's value. Keeps the brand in the repertoire. Maintains sales levels or helps trends.	Maintains company and brand standing. Keeps distribution, facings.
	Justifies price and position: the brand is more saleable and promotions in general are more attractive.	Reduces reliance on trade deals: the brand is more saleable so price to the retailer is firmer.
Short term	Reminder: brings the brand forward in the repertoire, hence blips in sales, and in tracking study scores.	Helps sell-ins and trade promotions.
	Makes changes in price or short-term promotions saleable.	Helps introduce new packs and product formulations.

Moreover, there are category and competitor effects.

Whether or not you have supporting data, decide how important each of these effects is and how dependent it may be on the number of advertisement exposures (and so on the working media budget).

Review the data and techniques that might help you to see and ideally to quantify these effects; how they react to changes in adspend and how they might decay in the absence of advertising. The most likely sources are:
— brand personality or image research
— usage and attitude research
— blind vs branded tests
— tracking studies

— trade surveys
— area experiments
— analyses of delivery and retail sales data, especially:
  mapping the average positions of your brand and competitors: share of units, share of sterling, share of voice, actual opportunities to see, relative price, use of promotions and so on;
  plotting relations in detail (by period, or by region) for share of market against share of voice, relative price and so on.

3 The Brand's Budget

'One placard at a time would strike the eye,' said Mr Vavasor, counting up the expense to himself. 'There's no doubt of it,' said Mr Scruby in reply. 'One placard will do that, if it's big enough, but it takes four-and-twenty to touch the imagination.'

Anthony Trollope (1864)

Definitions

The advertising budget decision should be seen in the context of the brand's total budget and in competition with other marketing activities. Suppose there is just one other marketing investment which is called here 'promotion' and which might be directed towards consumers or to retailers. Suppose also that the average price of the brand to retailers (list price) is known. This is before special price deals to retailers are allowed for. The price to consumers can be controlled much less, but suppose that variation in the price at which the manufacturer sells to retailers corresponds to variation in consumer price. That is, if you increase the average price to retailers by 5%, then the price to consumers also goes up by 5%. The two decisions we now consider are: how much to spend on advertising, and the list price of our brand.

There are two places in the brand budget where the effects of each of these decisions will be seen most importantly: the volume you expect to sell, expressed in the budget as so many cases or tonnes, and your bottom line.

Changes in units are also approximately changes in category share, when you are working within a defined category and the brand has a share less than, say, 25%. This reminds us that there are nearly always competitive brands. We normally disregard effects on category volume and (too often) how competitors will respond to our activities.

For the moment, imagine that you are working in a category of fixed volume and that competitors will not react. These are sometimes more realistic assumptions than might be expected. For example, smaller brands treat the competition as a uniformly hostile but unchanging environment.

You can now draw up a list:
— planned, annual, unit, volume sales
— planned average price to retailers
— hence, revenue (volume × price)
— planned advertising budget
    — of which, part is for advertisement production, part perhaps for research, trade press, and various overheads (see below),
    — leaving the adspend or working media spend: this is the amount that buys time and space for the advertisements actually to reach your target and to defend or advance sales.

Some fixed costs are nearly always necessary. This does not mean they cannot be altered during the budgeting process; you may, for example, make more or fewer TV commercials. It means that once they are settled, variation in the total budget for advertising is not directly proportional to the effect on consumers.

Suppose that production and other costs take 0.2 of the total advertising budget and media take 0.8. If you add a half again to the total advertising budget, but treat production and other costs as fixed, then the media spend, and so the expected impact, goes up by more than half (0.8 increases to 0.8 + 0.5: the increase is more than 60%).

The number of items that may be included in the advertising budget is large. Lists (1) have been published that show over half of a sample of 'consumer advertisers' agreeing that they include 11 items as well as space and time and over half of a sample of 'industrial advertisers' agreeing that they include 26 such items.

The most frequent are some relatively small items such as consultants, association dues, subscriptions, *Yellow Pages*, and other directory listings. Then we also see audience research, corporate advertising, pre-testing services, overheads and salaries. Finally, there are potentially major items like direct mail, cooperative programmes, point of sale material, and catalogues.

This book is not concerned with the 10, 20, or more items in the advertising budget which do not directly influence purchaser and consumer. These other expenditures should be subject to normal cost-control disciplines. I am concerned with media advertising, or adspend, which is normally the major part of the budget.

If fixed costs for advertising and promotion are included in other fixed costs, the brand budget list may be rewritten as follows:
— volume, price, revenue
— fixed costs
— adspend and promotion spend.

Next, we need to consider what connection there is between these items and contribution, which is the profit made by the brand and in effect paid by the brand to the manufacturer. The money needed to make and distribute the product has first to be subtracted from revenue. Then, other costs are subtracted, for example, the advertising budget.

Companies differ in their accounting conventions and in the headings used to describe parts of the budget. For example, factory overheads may be allocated by brand and subtracted before contribution is defined, or the factory overheads may be taken from the contribution.

It is important to distinguish in 'the money needed to make and distribute the product' those items that are fixed and those that vary according to the volume sold. For example, raw material costs are usually directly proportional to volume. There may in some cases be production restrictions that lead to steps up or down in costs as certain volume barriers are crossed. For example, starting up an additional production line may add a major sum to overall costs. What matters is that we determine the variable costs that alter when we change the volume sold (within known limits). These include the raw materials already mentioned. They also include packaging and may include warehousing, transport, and so on. To ascertain this part of the budget accurately, your cost-accounting practices may have to be examined in some detail. For the moment, assume that a genuinely variable manufacturing and delivery cost per unit is known: 'variable cost'.

We already know the average revenue per unit: it is simply total revenue divided by total volume. The difference between revenue and variable cost per unit is gross margin. It is gross because we have not yet subtracted all the other costs in the budget, only manufacturing and delivery.

We can finally write out our brand budget list in the format required to help our decision-making process:
— volume, price, revenue
— variable cost, hence gross margin
— adspend and promotion spend
— fixed costs, contribution

Example 1
Suppose that, for an imaginary brand, adspend, the part of the advertising budget allocated to working media, is £1 million. Promotion spend is the same, at £1 million. The brand sells 5 million cases at an average price to retailers of £4 per case, so generating £20 million revenue. The variable cost is £2.40 per case, so the gross margin is £1.60 per case (£4 minus £2.40). After the deduction of all costs, including £2 million fixed costs, the brand makes a contribution of £4 million.
    The budget may be written:

		£ *million*
Variable cost (5 million × £2.40)		12
Gross margin:		8
fixed cost	2	
adspend	1	
promotion	1	
contribution	4	
Revenue (5 million × £4)		20

Important Ratios

Various ratios in this budget turn out to be important, compared either with the ratios of other brands or other companies, or to what management feels comfortable with: good practice:

1. *Contribution/revenue* (here 4/20 or 20%) is first, because it shows how much the brand finally returns to the company, after all costs, as a proportion of turnover.
2. *Gross margin/revenue* (here 8/20 or 40%) tells us how much is left after meeting the variable costs of the product. The higher this is, the larger the marketing activity that can be afforded. Sometimes its complement, variable cost/revenue (here 60%), is talked about and the converse applies.
3. *Adspend/revenue* (here 1/20 or 5%) is the well-known advertising-to-sales or A/S ratio, considered as a budget-setting method in Chapter 5 and discussed again in Chapter 8.
4. *(Adspend + promotion)/margin* (here 2/8 or 25%) shows how important these marketing activities are. The lower the variable cost, the higher the gross margin; and the lower the variable cost the more likely it is that increasing marketing activity will pay off. Equally, the lower this marketing spend, the cheaper it is to make a big proportional change in it. Thus, if this ratio, (A+P)/margin, is low, the easier it will be to make a case to increase this marketing spend. The same is true of the ratio adspend/margin. More discussion of this will be found in Chapter 6.
5. *Adspend/(adspend + promotion)* (here 1/2) indicates roughly the proportion of marketing spend going to consumers and to value-building, or brand-building, as opposed to trade discounts and

price-cutting. It is a frequent recommendation that this ratio should be one-half or above.

A Common Over-simplification

The following practice is often followed but is not recommended. Instead of splitting up the brand budget in the way set out above, it may be presented in the following form:

Revenue (5 million cases at £4)　　　　　: £20 million
Production and fixed costs　　　　　　　: £14 million
Contribution, adspend, promotion spend　: £ 6 million

This is produced by setting volume and retail price forecasts, hence the £20 million revenue. The cost of producing and distributing this volume, plus other costs, is then calculated at £14 million. What is left has to be divided between contribution, adspend, and promotion and is now £4 million to contribution and £1 million each to advertising and promotion.

It may be pointed out that these are the same figures as before. What is the objection? The problem with this presentation and way of thinking is that it is production-led. The sales forecast may be set before the marketing activities are agreed. This is fine as a first step, provided we go back and consider the influence of these activities on sales. But it is common to take the sales forecast as fixed. Hence the second line is also fixed. Thus contribution, adspend and promotion spend are parts of a fixed total. Spending more on marketing means less to contribution. Contribution usually has priority. So it is easy to say, 'Advertising should drop to £800 000 and contribution will go up to £4.2 million.'

This view of the budget may be represented as follows:

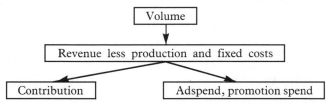

Another view represented by this chart is that cash-flow restrictions prevent any spend on advertising until sales have reached a certain level. Money can be spent only when it is in. The fallacy, except in cases of extreme cash shortage, is that this presentation suggests that marketing activities do not influence sales volume.

You should be aware that, even when the procedure outlined just above is not followed exactly, something very like it exists in the minds of many managements and accountants. Sales are real, so is revenue. There is at the end only a limited sum to divide. Contribution may be sacred: it is certainly a priority. Marketing spend may be the last decision, not the first. To raise contribution, it seems obvious that advertising may be cut. Often, of course, it can, in the short term. The long-term effect may be a different story.

The Advertising Budget as a Reserve

This book assumes that the budget being set is a realistic one. All the forecasts made are in good faith and the whole of the budget will be spent. In some companies, part of least of the advertising budget is not set in this way. This part is treated as a reserve that may be raided in a crisis. Even if this is not formally stated to the managing director and accountants, it is in the mind of the marketer. Part of the budget is kept in the back pocket. If all goes well, the whole may be spent, but more often than not the money is more urgently needed elsewhere. The fight between contribution and the advertising budget is an uneven one, as drops in advertising in the last quarter of the financial year frequently demonstrate.

This flexibility is understandable, because media money can be cut more easily than some other expenditures. The practice leads to inefficiency in media buying and encourages a cynical attitude about advertising's effects.

To reduce the chances that the advertising budget is seen as an alternative to contribution, we can reverse the order of the previous chart.

A More Realistic Way

The following dynamic viewpoint of the budget is recommended. This starts with the decisions about the three factors we might change and ends with contribution:

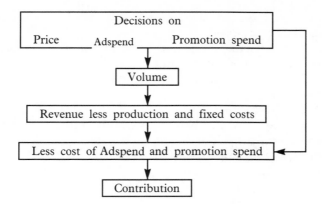

Where to Start

In practice, both the flow charts above are hard to follow. We should not start with fixed volume *and* contribution; nor can we start with a decision about adspend in the abstract.

To break into this system, we need a starting plan that is later refined by cycling round the decisions. Only adspend is shown below, but all marketing activities should be decided in this way.

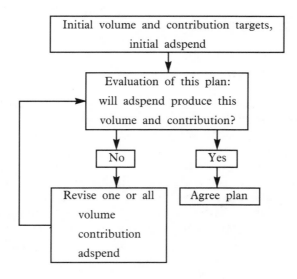

Thus decisions on adspend are made, while at the same time considering these questions:
— How do I expect adspend to affect volume in the short term?
— How does adspend affect price?
— How does adspend affect promotions
    — as a support?
    — as an alternative?
— What are the priorities in agreeing both volume and contribution?
— What are company long-term objectives in
    — the saleability of the brand?
    — volume and contribution?

Another way of showing how difficult it is to break into the cycle is to discuss this sequence.

Profits → media spend → sales → profits

The first step points out that the money spent on advertising comes from actual or anticipated profits. When a brand is in trouble at the bottom line, spend on advertising is often reduced. There is a clear connection between profits made and the amount spent, as is explained below, as can be seen in aggregate industry figures and as is also often experienced at brand level. Next, the very reason we spend on advertising at all is because we intend our sales income to be higher because of the values which advertising adds to the brand. So more spend should mean more sales. Of course, it is from these sales that our profit comes, and so the circle is closed.

The purpose of this section is to introduce these ideas: they are discussed in depth in Chapter 4.

Will Changes Pay Off?

This question is discussed in several places in this book, mainly in Chapter 7. It is impossible to answer in general and very difficult to answer even in particular cases. This section turns the estimated volume changes you expect from changes in advertising weight (example, ratings) into financial results.

Remember that the changes we are talking about are short term only. The results are those we expect within the financial year. Long-term effects are additional. Adding to adspend will assist the brand beyond this year. Cutting adspend reduces the branding on which we shall depend in years to come.

The key figures we need are among those defined above:

— volume sales predicted before the change in advertising weight, and the gross margin per unit
— or, gross revenue predicted (volume × gross margin)
— the sterling change in adspend resulting from the advertising weight change.

The calculation required is one which credits the brand with the increased revenue, but subtracts the increased cost.

Example 2

Suppose that you expect 4% volume improvement from +50% advertising weight. Does this pay off? It is normal to disregard possible additional sales due to category movements; these are not credited to the advertising change.

We expected to sell 5 million cases at a gross margin of £1.60, so gross margin was £8 million. The additional gross margin from +4% volume is 0.04 × £8 million or £320 000. Adspend was planned previously at £1 million and the 50% upweight is expected to cost £500 000.

This calculation tells us that we should recover £320 000 or over 60% of the extra media investment. The remainder, £180 000, must come from long-term benefits. It is unlikely we can value the latter financially.

The situation in this example is common: the marketer has to balance, on the one hand, a contribution fall, against, on the other hand, two benefits. The fall in contribution is not the total cost of extra advertising, £500 000, but only £180 000. The benefits are the forecast immediate volume gain (4% of 5 million cases is 200 000 cases), and the long-term maintenance or improvement in branding. We have an example here of the priorities problem raised in the last section.

It would be surprising if the reverse situation were normal, that is, that the marketer could easily improve both contribution and volume by spending more on advertising. This would imply that his advertising budget was previously clearly too low; there is every reason to raise it. Life is not often as easy as this: we expect to have to compromise.

Promotional Budget

This section will not be long, for this is not a book about the promotional budget. In many ways, such a book would be very like this one. The recommended procedure would require the same steps. You have to understand the brand's situation, objectives and budget. You should review what the brand's history, and those of competitors, can teach you about promotional effects.

Visible Short-term Effects

There is no doubt why brand managers write consumer promotions into their plans, especially when volume is in trouble: they 'work'. Say, for example, a coupon is used. Perhaps a small fraction only of those coupons distributed is redeemed; say that many of these redemptions are for sales that would have been made anyway but are brought forward, or are by heavy coupon users who switch merrily from brand to brand and will never be loyal; the long-term effects may not be good, but there is still an immediate lift in sales volume.

Visible and rapid effects may drive out the less tangible, long-term added-value benefits of advertising: this is why a proper balancing of the two sorts of activity is so hard.

Even if the short-term effects are uneconomic, the brand manager may judge it to be worth his while to buy the extra volume. Success and failure are not necessarily economic terms. In one review of promotions (2), 'a successful promotion was almost as likely to be a financial failure as a financial success . . . Of 45 promotions deemed by managers to be successful in overall terms, only 30 were actually financially successful. Moreover, of 46 promotions judged to be failures, 19 were actually successful. This finding seems to suggest that marketing executives do not place profitability as a primary objective of promotions; indeed, moving volume was the primary stated objective.'

Comparing Advertising with Price-cutting

Price can be altered in two ways: by setting the average or nominal level, and by discounting from it with trade or consumer promotions. When we think about the average price decision, at the same time as we decide whether to spend more or less on advertising, we see there are four main directions in which we can change both. The comments which follow assume that the present position of the brand is satisfactory:

1. *Price up and adspend up.* This is the brand leader route. The two decisions complement each other. The additional income from the price rise provides the revenue which can be spent on advertising. The added values justify the higher price.
2. *Price down and adspend down.* The reverse of the policy above and the primrose path to commodity marketing. This may indeed be a

valid decision, but remember that, when we reduce the reasons for purchase, except that the product is cheap, we cannot expect it to retain all the advantages it now has from earlier advertising.

3. *Price up and adspend down.* Milking the brand may again be a valid strategy but is an even more short-term policy than the one above. A higher price can in some categories imply value and may generate enough revenue to give the purchaser reasons to buy other than media advertising (improvements in the product, for example). These may well have a better effect than advertising in sustaining sales, and this is the decision to examine.

4. *Price down and adspend up.* This can be appropriate when volume is the priority. We are buying our sales, fighting off competition and investing in the future. The effect on the bottom line must be appreciated before this route is followed.

The mix of advertising, consumer promotions and trade promotions was described in Chapter 2. For many brands, the budget shows expenditure on each of these in proportions near 5:2:3. Now we consider this allocation more deeply.

It has been said that successful brands spend not less than half this total in 'consumer franchise-building activities': see the case history in Chapter 8. This distinction is like the value against price balance set up in Chapter 2. Without disputing this view, the case is now put forward that comparing the two sorts of expenditure is unrealistic. The first, advertising, buys actual communication with retailers and consumers; the second is a book-keeping transaction.

Consider in the budget example above the £1 million on media advertising and the £1 million on promotion. Suppose the first is spent on TV, the second on trade deals (consumer promotion comes between these two and is reviewed later). The TV spend buys exposures of the advertiser's message to purchasers, users and the trade. These cause a change or reinforcement of images and beliefs. The intention is to shift or maintain behaviour. A trade deal is also meant to shift or maintain behaviour; in this case retailer orders, display, and so on. But the £1 million does not change hands in the same way as media money. Rather, it is allowed as a discount off orders. In other words, the trade discount money is not spent at all: it was never in the manufacturer's hands. The budget above could be written:

Production and fixed costs	:	£14 million
Adspend	:	£ 1 million
Contribution	:	£ 4 million

Revenue (5 million cases at £3.80)	:	£19 million

Is there an important distinction here? It depends on your point of view. To the brand manager, given a list price and a total advertising and promotion budget, all the promotional spend is real. Most of it is also real to the sales representative, given his trade discount allowance to allocate. But to the managing director, or accountant, most promotional spend is a price cut. Volume targets may have been met, but at a cost in revenue and, worse, the long-term result is that retailers come to expect the discounts, so the price decrease becomes permanent. The same is true, though less so, for consumer promotions.

Sometimes price allowances are made to a retailer specifically in order to support the retailer's own advertising, in which the brand is featured. This practice may be seen as a low-cost way of getting the brand at least some advertising, and to be associated with a major retailer in this way may be considered an advantage. It is, however, a mistake to count advertising allowances automatically as part of the brand's advertising budget. It has been reported (3) that some of these allowances are not actually spent, but finish up in the retailer's pocket as part of a price discount. Even when they are spent, they may benefit the retailer far more than the manufacturer; in fact, they can be a major contributor to the retailer's total adspend. In addition, when the only point made in the copy is a price cut, which is often the case, the dangers present in any price-cutting promotion are intensified. Ideally, such advertising should be tailored to a particular occasion and the copy should be provided by the manufacturer, who ensures that it maintains brand values.

Example 3
A survey by Andrew Roberts (4) of 26 grocery and toiletry brands' marketing expenditure gave their average advertising and promotion budget at 20% of turnover (when turnover was before price discounts). About half of this was spent on consumer advertising. An analysis of the remainder showed the majority (8% of turnover) was in fact price discounting. Only 2% of turnover was spent on promotions which could possibly have had an effect beyond price, such as paying for in-store displays, merchandising, competitions, self-liquidating premiums, public relations and so on.

The analysis for these brands was continued by using information on how their sales had been seen to react to changes, both in their selling price and in their spend on media advertising, using techniques similar to those explained in Chapter 7. This step was taken because 'The real problem with the traditional method is that it hides an important marketing decision — what price should be charged for the product? This should be separated from the question of the size of the advertising budget or expenditure on other forms of promotion . . . the real issue is not the allowance between above and below the line expenditure, but the price and advertising decision.'

The result of the analysis was that most brands were deemed to be spending about the right amount on advertising, when short-term profit was the criterion. In contrast, 'half the brands are seriously underpriced' by the same criterion. Thus 'the profit implications are equally serious, because pricing has a crucial effect on profitability.'

It is no wonder that manufacturers, at least marketers in senior positions, say they would like to prune back the growing promotional entanglement (5). Stores which offer 'every day low prices' are saying much the same to some receptive consumers. At the time of writing, however, I see few signs of the dilemma being generally resolved.

To be fair, advertising is also seen as an expense which manufacturers would cut if they could: 'I would not hesitate to get rid of advertising tomorrow if I could find a better way of doing what advertising does,' said the Chairman of Unilever in 1964.

The practical conclusion, in your own company, is unlikely to be that promotional spend is stopped. Rather, the conclusion is that it should be critically examined for its overall effects. If value is falling and price dominating, ask yourself whether the trend is healthy. Allocate your resources in order to move the balance towards where you want it to be. Here are two suggestions about the consumer promotional budget. First, try to spend it in ways which improve the brand's value to some degree, not simply as a price reduction. Second, try to set specific objectives: to bring in current non-users, to reach target consumers who get below-average media coverage and so on. As far as trade promotions go, most is spent on price-cutting, and this may be a game you have to play. Try not to treat the list price as fixed and discounts from it as real costs. If you do, they inevitably compete with the spend on activities which add value.

You have a whole armoury of marketing tools to use. It is wasteful to use each only one at a time, especially as some work best in combination with others. The budget includes decisions about list price, about that sort of promotional spend which is really price-cutting and that promotional spend which is not price-cutting, in addition to the advertising decision. All of these interact with each other. Example 3 demonstrated one sort of interaction. The following example indicates a positive step which can be taken to improve the budget.

Example 4

For the budget which started this chapter, the list price was £4 per case, and advertising and promotion each took £1 million. It has now been decided to increase the trade promotions budget by 50%. One possible route is to spend £500 000 on advertising and £1.5 million on promotion. Another is to raise list price to £4.10 per case, leave the advertising spend at £1 million, and raise the promotion budget to £1.5 million.

Stating the strategy as badly as this, our representatives might not convince retail buyers. But such a strategy can be sold. Value is maintained, our consumer franchise is unharmed and the trade promotions budget is increased.

Budget Decision Totals

Another way to approach the advertising budget is in the aggregate. What are the results, in a category or nationally, of all the individual brand decisions? If we understand the major forces influencing these results, we gain insight into the factors likely to affect our brand. We also learn in this way about our competitors' decisions. This is close to the individual brand analysis discussed in Chapter 4.

Advertising Totals

In the United Kingdom, we have exceptionally good data on media advertising expenditure. Individual advertisement insertions are monitored by two companies, Media Expenditure Analysis Limited (MEAL) and the Media Register. Differences between these two services are important to their users but are currently changing and are not discussed in detail here.

Because there is also good research on media exposure, it is possible to calculate, sufficiently well for our purpose, the audience to these insertions. For detail on this data, ask your advertising agency or consult a textbook (6). However, you cannot know exactly what your competitors paid for their advertisement insertions. TV ratecards are complex and include a pre-emption system, so that the same spot may cost different advertisers dramatically different amounts. The price paid for a spot reflects the demand for it, a point we return to below. The top ratecard figure used in a BARB report (from the Broadcasters' Audience Research Board) is an indication only of the true cost. In other media, ratecards may be flexible, that is, subject to negotiation and discounts. The result is the same: different advertisers may be paying different amounts.

The revenue of individual media owners is, however, sometimes known in total, across all insertions. If not known, it may be estimated. From the ratecard income, and the actual income, an average discount can be found. If you are unhappy about using this average, because of some special circumstances, an estimate of the real discount can be used. Your agency will advise on these special cases. For example, a large advertiser who has flexibility over time, and is known to plan well in advance, generally pays less than average. An advertiser who buys late and irregularly may have to pay more.

Thus, for any advertiser, and in most media, there is a list of insertions and of the audiences to these insertions, plus an estimate of what he actually paid. In this chapter we are concerned with the money, but note that we do also have a figure for his actual advertisement exposure. This actually predicts the results of his advertising better than his expenditure, and is used later.

The media expenditure data just described are also reported in summary and convenient form by the Advertising Statistics Committee of the Advertising Association. This source concentrates on spends in total and for individual media groups, but also gives broad product group data, derived from MEAL data. It does not publish figures for individual advertisers or brands. MEAL and the Media Register do, however, give this detail, and can use the discount estimates described above, so they can provide estimated actual spends for your category and for your competitors. From the sources mentioned, and from Industry Forecasts Limited, there is a wide range of reports, special analyses, reviews, pocket books, and forecasts, in addition to the *Advertising Statistics Yearbook*, 'the industry's statistical bible'. There are also frequent and regular articles on advertising expenditure in *Admap* and other trade publications.

These data are put to many different uses. First, I answer the question, how much does a typical or a large advertiser actually spend? Then I discuss some of the influences on the expenditure totals. The numbers are also used as input in many of the methods described in Chapter 5. See particularly the section on advertising-to-sales and other ratios in Chapter 8.

What Do Advertisers Spend?

To answer such a question you need up-to-date numbers, and particularly for your own category. An indication, however, is given here. This is based on the MEAL Top Spenders report, which amalgamates expenditure over the variants of each brand. It gives the

1000 'brands' spending most on display advertising (TV, newspapers, magazines and radio in key regions). A similar 500 brand analysis is reported by the Media Register. Note that a 'brand' here includes some advertisers not normally thought of as a brand in marketing terms, for example share flotations, which can be quite untypical.

For this book, MEAL carried out a special analysis on 1987 data, in which ratecard expenditure for TV was adjusted for estimated discounts of 22%. Similarly, newspaper and magazine discounts were estimated at 23%. Radio was included at the cost on the ratecard, but was for ten contractors only.

The total spend by all advertisers on the four media just listed was £2950 million. The top 1000 brands spent £1850 million, or 63% of the total. It is not the purpose of this book to discuss media choice, but in passing I record that about three-quarters of the TV contractors' revenue came from the top 1000: TV depends heavily on the large advertiser. Of the total spend by these brands, 64% went on television, 34% went on print. Radio got 2.5%. Of course, few individual brands matched these proportions; most concentrate on either TV or print.

The average brand in the top 100 spent over £6 million. For the next 100, the average was much smaller, under £3 million. In the tenth 100 the average spend was £700 000. For the 700 between these, the averages were between £2 million and £750 000. Thus, to spend half a million pounds or less does not qualify you as a large advertiser in this sense, though spending this amount may make you a big fish in a small pond in some categories. A typical large brand spends one or two million pounds.

Total spend on display advertising is considerably influenced by total spending by consumers: the more money manufacturers are competing for, the more it is worth their while to invest. Thus one of the explanatory terms which forecasters often use is consumers' expenditure. Inflation is reflected conveniently (for the analyst) in this figure. We must not expect the ratio of total advertising to consumers' expenditure to be constant, nor each category or manufacturer to have the same proportion of turnover spent on advertising.

A second factor which helps to explain how much is spent on advertising in total is the amount of manufacturers' profits. No one would draw a causal arrow simply from advertising to profit. Nor is it entirely in the other direction. But when the economic climate is favourable, companies tend to invest in all kinds of marketing activity, and, on the whole, they make profits. Conversely, when times are hard, and profits fall, there are cuts in every sort of expenditure that can be pruned, including advertising. These may also be explanations for the changes in advertising expenditure for the individual brand, but some firms will always be exceptions, perhaps all the more powerfully just because they are exceptions. The belief that next year's market will be tougher may be a reason for less advertising overall, but not for your own advertising to be reduced, though you may not be able to match the confidence shown by W.K. Kellogg (7):

'When the 1929 crash stunned the business world, Mr Kellogg displayed the same sort of courage he had shown in the previous panics of 1907 and 1921.

'In the summer of 1929, he and Lewis Brown had agreed upon a large appropriation for the 1930 campaigns, and had approved the advertising copy.

'In the fall, Mr Kellogg left to spend the winter in California, stopping off in Hot Springs en route. He was in Hot Springs when Mr Brown telephoned late in October and strongly recommended that all advertising be cancelled because of the stock market crash.

' "We started this company during a panic", Mr Kellogg told him, "we've weathered several periods when times weren't too good, and so I don't think we'll cancel our advertising now. In fact, we might even increase it".

'This courageous decision proved correct. Earnings for 1929, 1930, and 1931 set new records.'

A third possible influence on advertising spend is the cost of time and space. This is a combination of audience size and of the amount paid for an insertion. Cost per thousand increases when the audience falls or when you pay more for an insertion. What has unsympathetically been called whingeing by advertisers on the rise of media costs has provoked much discussion. One viewpoint already described is that costs, in TV at least, are only a response to demand and all that advertisers see is the operation of the free market. In the press, however, rates do not rise similarly in response to demand. This is because the supply of space can to some extent match demand. TV is effectively a monopoly, advertisers argue, since TV-am, Channel 4, satellite and cable, at the time of writing, still supply only a small proportion of total viewing. Hence TV advertisers cannot react sensibly, by using another supplier, when ITV ratings decline or ratecards rise.

This is a comment on total expenditure. How individual advertisers should behave is discussed in Chapter 5, because media cost changes are often temporarily responsible for individual advertising budget changes. In the Task method, for example, a requirement for ratings is translated to a budget via the cost of a rating point. But with a broader perspective, the reverse is true. Unit costs respond long term to advertiser demand. Media can take only what advertisers are willing to spend. After that, the supply of space and time, the number of readers and the time spent viewing and listening, help to determine the costs. The advertising agency media department will provide the data relevant to a particular brand. See also the Advertising Association forecasts.

Promotional Tools

As mentioned in Chapter 2, promotional spending statistics have suffered from problems of definition. It was argued above that some of the money reported was never even spent (if it was a trade price reduction). Therefore you cannot expect the same precision with data about promotional expenditure, or about the A + P total, as for advertising on its own.

In November 1987, the Institute of Sales Promotion's *News* estimated that the 400 companies represented in the Institute spent annually somewhere between £800 million and £3000 million. My own view tends towards the lower figure. Mintel (8) reported in 1987 its conjectures (the word is used advisedly) on sales promotion expenditure since 1980. This includes manufacturers' own expenditure which does not all go through specialists. In the year (1986) when total advertising expenditure was estimated at £5600 million, the figure for consumer promotions was £2200 million and for trade promotions £3300 million. Thus, in round figures, the estimate is that advertising took half the total A + P budget (I believe it really took more). Consumer promotions got 20% and trade promotions 30%. Incidentally, the amount spent on direct marketing (including direct mail, which is counted in the figures above) has been estimated as £1000 million (9). The Mintel report indicates the range of techniques used in promotions, simply by the headings used in the data tables: tailor-made special offers, reduced price offers, coupons, cash refunds, self-liquidators, free mail-ins, pack inserts and give-aways, banded packs and multi-packs, and competitions. When the trade side is added, we have also to list exhibitions, public relations, merchandising, and so on. The overlap with normal trade selling, with direct marketing and with such media as direct mail is very obvious.

These UK estimates may be compared with US data, which are also rather uncertain. Donnelley Marketing publish each year estimates made by marketing executives who manage sales promotions. These estimates include the proportions of the total advertising and promotion budget allocated to the three main activities. In the *Ninth Annual Survey*, published in 1987, the following shares were given for 1986. They are compared here with the shares for 1976.

	1976 %	1986 %
Media advertising	42	34
Consumer promotion	19	29
Trade promotion	39	37

In other words, during these 11 years, the media advertising share fell (steeply from 1982) while consumer promotion rose. Increased emphasis on short-term returns, and management need for demonstrable pay-offs, have encouraged this trend (10). Further, many more respondents expected consumer promotions to increase rather than to decrease. Overall, trade promotion took a steady share.

The survey is valuable in describing the dollar importance, to the respondent companies, of various types of promotion. In 1986, the leading consumer promotion was direct consumer couponing: 73% said it was 'most important'. It was followed by money-off promotions: only 12% said 'most important'. The coupon vehicle most used was the free-standing insert: 82% said 'most important', while direct mail couponing followed with 6%.

Nielsen's Manufacturers Coupon Redemption Center, quoted by *Marketing and Media Decisions* in June 1987, agrees in allotting most consumer coupons delivered by media to inserts (68%). This is followed by run-of-paper (15%). A July 1987 figure, attributed to Dancer, Fitzgerald, Sample, allocates 76% of consumer promotions to coupons. This is followed by 9% to on-pack offers.

Much of the UK growth in recent years has been the adoption of promotional techniques by categories which had not previously used them. Fast-moving consumer goods categories, which have been heavy users, may not be the main explanation for growth. It could follow that the extremes of couponing and support of retail displays found in the US need not necessarily happen in the UK. Moreover, straight price reductions are taking a smaller proportion of consumer promotions than they used to.

Chapter 3: Action Points

1. For your brand, set out the current annual budget in the following format:

(a) revenue = units sold × average list price per unit
(b) variable cost per unit = raw material + packaging + distribution cost
(c) total variable cost = units sold × variable cost per unit
(d) fixed cost = manufacturing and general overhead + advertising costs other than on working media + fixed promotional cost
(e) adspend = working media spend
(f) promotional spend, other than fixed costs. Within this, identify price-cutting to the trade, price-cutting to consumers and others; review the value-adding or brand-building features of each item.
(g) contribution is found from
      (a) − (c) − (d) − (e) − (f)
   and the gross margin is then:
      contribution + (d) + (e) + (f), or
      (a) − (c).

2. Calculate and review the ratios below. Compare them with previous years, other brands and so on (see item 7):
   — contribution/revenue
   — gross margin/revenue
   — adspend/revenue
   — (adspend + promotional spend)/margin
   — adspend/(adspend + promotional spend)
3. Is adspend evaluated by these two criteria?
   — is it sufficient, that is, does it make the sales forecast credible?
   — is it affordable, that is, will pressure on the contribution threaten cuts in adspend?
   If it is not already evaulated in both these ways, consider the possibility of doing so.
4. If changes in adspend are under discussion, do you have a way of estimating their short-term effects on volume? Are long-term effects explicitly acknowledged?
5. In discussions on pricing, is the effect of advertising acknowledged, in that it maintains the perceived value and saleability of the brand?
6. In discussions on the promotional budget, is the effect of advertising acknowledged? Is the tendency of promotions to lower value acknowledged?
7. Are data available for your competitors, your category, and your industry about their adspend and the key ratios adspend/revenue, adspend/margin? And about promotional spend? Do you understand the trends affecting their budgets as well as your own?

Process

4   Recommended Process

> The point of focus for management should be on the process of budgeting, not simply the techniques.
>
> *Nigel Piercy (1985)*

Assumptions

Now we come to the heart of this book, where the advertising budget is determined. Chapters 1 to 3 have set the scene; Chapters 5 to 8 provide detail and examples.

The process recommended here may look slow and complex but, in practice, it moves along faster and more easily than it looks. In each particular case, the marketer selects only two or three key items among the many possibilities described. Concentrating on these, you will find that the budget decision usually comes down to a few business judgements.

It is assumed that you are working on an *established brand* in a *consumer market*. If not, see Chapter 6 on new products or on corporate and business-to-business advertising.

It is also assumed that the advertising budget under discussion is *worth serious attention*; for example, it is 5% or more of contribution. If not, the full process may not be worth while. See in Chapter 5 the sections on Inertia, Media inflation multiplier, Affordable, and Fixed amount. Each of these methods on its own is simpler than the approach described in this chapter.

It is assumed that a *future annual budget* is being planned, but modifications to a current budget follow similar steps.

Finally, it is assumed that you have already applied to your brand the suggestions made in Chapters 2 and 3, so you have reviewed the sort of advertising effects that you expect. Some of these may already be spelled out in the brand plan and in the advertising objectives or, if you are at an earlier stage, you should have at least the broad picture of what you hope to achieve. In addition, you understand how the brand's budget is made up.

Introduction

Note that the next four items proceed from internal company data to the external market. They are first described briefly, and they are expanded later. Each item requires you to review, and update if necessary, information on a particular area.

Brand Objectives

These are more than next year's volume forecast or the advertising objectives. The team working on the brand should see it from a company perspective. The marketing department has to have the managing director or chairman's input. How important is the brand to the company? What is its long-term future? What importance is attached to the volume sales forecast? How does the financial contribution made by the brand compare in priority with its volume?

Brand Budgets

You look back at recent, actual marketing expenditure on the brand and at what it has returned to the company. There will be a current, draft budget to work on, even if it is only the same as last year's. Management's vision and the brand objectives are translated by the accountant into numbers.

Marketing History and Forecast

Now the marketing director turns to the marketplace, where the company's view will be tested against reality. The category's behaviour must be understood and forecast. You need to know how your major competitors have planned in the past and how those plans fared. Thus you arrive at a view of how category and competitors are likely to act.

Advertising Effects

Here you put together, from what has been learned about the past, how you will predict adspend's probable results for the brand. Again, this requires marketplace experience: consumer research, a brand audit, experiments and so on. You need to be ready to answer such questions as: 'Is this amount of advertising exposure likely to have these results? If we spend more, or less, what results then?'

Looked at solely as a way of setting budgets, this checklist suggests a formidable amount of work. But budget-setting is part of normal company and brand management, and most of these four items should already exist. The brand manager and marketing director are involved with them every day. It is advisable for them to stand back occasionally and review what information they have. Some points may need special attention or updating. But most data that exist, and their interpretation, are already known and agreed. Where the brand is and where the company wants it to be, whether its contribution is satisfactory, data about the marketplace, evidence about advertising's effects — these are hardly novel items. These issues are repeated in some detail below so that you may check whether the work has previously been done thoroughly.

The four reviews complete the first of three steps. The second step is to obtain suggestions about what the budget might be. This is what the methods of Chapter 5 are for.

When suggested budgets are assembled, you start the third and final step. This is a system of checks and balances that may modify the advertising budget — and the rest of the brand plan. The intention is to end with the budget that meets company requirements in two main ways:

— the advertising budget is affordable and fits acceptably into the brand's budget
— the advertising budget is adequate to produce the effects expected from it in the marketplace.

Following this introduction is a detailed explanation of the three steps (1), which are summarized in a flow chart at the end of this chapter.

Brand Objectives

Review and understand what the company wants from the brand, both in the long term and immediately. Thus you start with the brand plan. This plan does not come out of thin air, nor does the draft budget of the next section. Most companies have a horizon of five years or so for outline planning. You have to concentrate on the year to come, but do not lose sight of the years ahead.

The plan should state the volume expected from the brand, and should make clear the priority to be given to volume or to contribution. The flexibility that can be exercised at either of these points may be critical.

The source of the brand's sales should be identified in the plan. The larger the target for advertising, the bigger the budget needed but, by concentrating on a smaller target in your media choice, you may be able to spend less. Decide whether the brand is on a maintenance strategy or needs conquest sales. The latter will increase the aggressiveness required from all the marketing efforts.

As was made clear in Chapter 2, the pricing and promotional policies, and other events in the plan, are also important in evaluating the advertising budget. If price is to move up, the brand will have to be made more valuable to consumers. If promotions are expected to increase, immediate volume might be secured, but the long term will require attention, and the efficiency of the promotions will need to be maintained. Some events planned for the product during the coming year may be specially relevant to the advertising task: the introduction of a new flavour or packaging, for example.

Relations with the trade must not be neglected. Although the plan may not spell out distribution or shelf-space objectives, you need to understand the position of the brand with wholesalers and retailers. Is this satisfactory, or does it require special attention?

Finally, the specific advertising objectives should be addressed. These will often be stated in the plan as short-term goals, within the year of the plan. This restriction may be too confining. Attention to only short-term effects on purchasers may lead to advertising being evaluated only as a direct stimulator of immediate volume. Accept the short-term objectives, but keep in mind the value of the brand, which probably needs to be maintained and which pays off in ways additional to the direct, short-term effect.

Example 1
The brand is to stay category leader, with the largest share and the top image scores on . . . A contribution rate comparable with the current year is acceptable. Advertising is to improve scores on . . . and to support distribution gains in . . .

Example 2
At a minimum, contribution is to be . . . Share should not fall below . . . but this is secondary to financial considerations. Advertising is to prevent further consumer penetration loss.

Example 3
The brand is to lead growth in the . . . sector. Breakeven on the annual budget is

acceptable. Advertising is to raise consumer frequency of use to . . . and to establish the brand as the most effective . . .

Brand Budgets

As was pointed out in the previous section, current and earlier brand budgets, as well as outlines for several years to come, will be available. But the most important brand budget to establish is the current forecast for the year we are planning. This should not be more than a draft at this stage: first, because the advertising section is not yet firm; second, because the effect of advertising on sales is usually not yet allowed for. However, to break into the system, a draft is essential. Its feasibility is examined later, in Step 3.

The budget must include first estimates of
— volume, price and gross revenue
— marginal costs
— contribution
— spend on other marketing activities (such as consumer promotions)

Trends in previous budgets, up to the draft we are examining, will be revealing. They quantify and put into context what is stated in the brand plan. Perhaps actual sales have recently been in decline; the increase asked for in the plan requires reversal of the trend as well as a gain. Perhaps the actual amounts spent on working media in previous years have been less than in the initial budgets for these years: the reasons for this could be important.

The ratios suggested in Chapter 3 should be calculated for the draft budget and for recent, actual budgets. These too should be examined for trends and for whether they feel right to experienced people. Too high a proportion on promotion, out of the advertising plus promotion total, for example, may show that list price reductions to retailers and other non-franchise-building operations have reached a dangerous level. What such a ratio should actually be is of course a question which is too brand-specific to have an easy answer. A study of the brand's history (see below) may help you decide the right ratio: perhaps it may equal the ratio in years when both volume and contribution moved satisfactorily. If margin/revenue is improving, perhaps because of lowered variable costs, or because sales are growing and fixed costs are taking a lower proportion, you have a better case for your media spend.

Marketing History and Forecast

'Find out the facts. Argument's daft. Find out the facts and then there's a chance you'll find out what to do' (John Braine, 1985).

While you concentrate on the history of your brand, you should also consider the category in order to see the brand in context. Look particularly at major competitors, both to see how they may affect your brand and to learn from them.

Whether or not you use the brand history review as a budget-setting method, you need a minimum number of facts about the brand's performance in the marketplace. The two vital areas are
— figures on volume and sterling sales, and on media spend: for the category, for competitors, and for your brand
— data (at least qualitative and based on judgement) on our progress in branding our product: its standing with purchasers, users and retailers, compared with competitors.

We are not yet using these data to look for regularities or analogies in the past, or to help suggest what the budget should be. We are assessing here how difficult the brand objectives are. We need to know especially, both as trends and forecasts:
— category volume sales, unit price and total adspend
— major brands' share of market and share of voice
— these brands' relative prices and images.

The minimum time frame for the historical review is the current year but it is better to have data for three, four or five years.

The brand plan and budget provide your brand's expected volume sales and adspend. These, compared with the category forecast, provide your share of market and share of voice. You evaluate the plan against the battlefield where it has to perform. Comparing shares of market and shares of voice across our brand and major competitors is often illuminating.

Suppose a competitor is expected to re-launch, or to spawn flankers, with heavy advertising support. Adspend that at first looked like a continuation of a successful share of voice suddenly seems inadequate. Or suppose that the category is evolving in a way that favours your brand's positioning. This may be just the time to drive for a major share increase. Next, suppose the brand share is already drifting down, perhaps for reasons which reformulation or repositioning will not change. You may decide that a lower level of advertising support, sufficient to keep the decay to a minimum, is the most profitable policy.

You may highlight problems which lie outside budget determination.

If a competitor's advertising-to-sales ratio is no higher than yours, but his sales are growing, for example, compare your product's performance with his.

The category volume forecast is essential. Many brands have neglected to give market share its proper weight. If the company is content with steady sales volume and does not appreciate the faster growth of competitors, it could be in for a nasty shock. With today's pressure on shelf space, it is easy for brands with declining share to lose distribution, even though volume has been satisfactory.

For a category with adequate consumer sales data or even shipments data only, regional or packing data would allow you to go into considerable detail. Similarly, consumer research data, both quantitative and qualitative, may be extensive. The objective is not to apply all of this detail, but to see, in broad brushstrokes, where the brand is now. Then you can evaluate where the brand is meant to go. Do you have a maintenance job, or is it a crisis?

Look particularly at brand awareness, penetration, and repeat purchase. The classic case for increased media spend is when repeat purchase is high (showing satisfaction with the product), distribution is adequate, but brand awareness and penetration are low. Conversely, high brand awareness, but low repeat purchase and poor distribution, indicate that you should save some of your advertising budget until more fundamental problems are corrected.

Do not neglect regional opportunities. At least occasionally, review your sales data by regions to see whether you could be over- or underspending locally.

Advertising Effects

Information on advertising effects is considerably harder to obtain than budget or history data. For many brands, the result of this review may be pitifully thin. Nevertheless, you should look for information on how advertising has affected, and is likely to affect, the brand. Without it, matching resources to objectives is risky.

It is here that you assemble the checks that will be used to test feasibility and to evaluate alternatives in the final step. It is essential that this job is done as thoroughly as possible. Even if the results are disappointing, one outcome of the review might be the resolution to collect better information for the future and so improve the process in the years to come.

The search should include, but not be restricted to, quantified sales effects of your own advertising. An analysis of historical data or experiments may have provided this information. If not, you should consider how to get it. Chapter 2 should be consulted for a detailed review of what to look for.

Do not neglect what at first may appear to be less directly useful information. In your brand image and trade research, look for evidence of advertising-led scores or movement of scores. Data about competitors can teach you as much as your own brand about advertising effects in your category.

History can tell you only about copy previously run. It is prudent to assume that new copy, for budgeting purposes, will perform no more than equally well. In other words, do not cut the budget just because copy development research indicates that new copy will do a better job. Prediction of sales-effectiveness is notoriously difficult and all new copy is thought to be better than old copy when it is first produced.

Several Methods

We have now reached the stage where some naive guides to budget-setting assume that we start. The work preceding this stage is, however, indispensable. The combination of the four previous reviews with the two following steps is the key to effective budget determination.

Putting together the results from several budget-recommending methods is itself sometimes called the *Total* method. It may be done somewhat informally, as is recommended here, because we allow a *range* of possible amounts for the advertising to be suggested; *affordability* and *feasibility* are checked later. It is sometimes suggested that the whole process follows a flow chart (2), and within a large company it can be worth while to be so formal.

Chapter 5 describes different methods. Review this list and use it as a checklist (use as many as you can), not as a menu (pick one). The most powerful methods, to be included if at all possible, are the Task method and the Brand History Review. If your company has the technical resources, Modelling should also be attempted.

Using several methods will give you several different recommendations. Record briefly the reasoning behind each figure; some will carry more weight than others. Record also what results are suggested if you should spend more or spend less.

Finally, settle on a first cut at the working media budget. This may be a single figure if the different recommendations happen to be close. More likely you will have a high figure and a low one. I continue as if there were one number only, but you may take the next step twice or more, until it becomes clear that either your high, or your low, or some intermediate figure, is the one to work with.

Estimate what this budget will buy, in media exposure terms. This means, of course, that media cost changes for the coming year are taken into account. Estimate what should be added to working media spend to give the total advertising budget. This includes, for example, production costs.

Checks and Balances

We now have for a base budget:
— the media exposure estimate of what the working media spend will buy, for example as TVRs
— the total advertising budget.

You next enter a system of feasibility checks and comparisons with objectives and constraints. Does the advertising budget meet the requirements of the draft brand budget? In turn, does this meet the brand plan?

Is the Plan Feasible?

This is the stage at which the review of effects is needed. Is it reasonable to expect the volume expected in the current budget, given the forecast of the environment and the resources available? Although a what-if model (see Chapter 7) is very helpful at this point, one is not usually available. Judgement will in any case be necessary, and the boldness to admit that a suggested plan is unlikely to work, when this is the case. From the volume forecast, and the draft budget which includes cost data, you may calculate the contribution expected.

The process set out here concentrates on the advertising budget. Similar steps should be gone through for other marketing activities. As was emphasized in Chapter 2, it is the whole of the marketing that affects sales and the value of the brand. For clarity, I have not repeated at each step: 'How will price, trade promotions, consumer promotions and other marketing decisions affect the results? How will advertising work with these activities? Will each activity planned maintain the brand's standing? Allow it to fall? Increase it? But you have to review the whole range of activities in order to set the whole budget.

If the Plan Is Not Feasible

The plan may look unfeasible at this stage. Either the volume, or the contribution, or the long-term targets may be unachievable. Something has to give, and it is best to say so at this point. There are then two alternatives: either company requirements or the advertising budget must be modified. Checking with the managing director and accountant is what budget meetings are all about.

There are four places where a balance most often has to be struck.

First is the choice between volume and contribution. A vague company priority requirement can suddenly become a very real decision. Are the last 100 000 cases, or the last £100 000 to contribution, the more important?

Second, priorities must be established between the short versus long term. Does management insist on a solution to today's problem, no matter what trouble is being left for its successors? Another way of phrasing this is: what is the importance of the brand's value, in consumers' eyes, against its immediate contribution to the company? Suppose that this value, as measured by attitude scores, is low and falling, but for no material reason, such as worsening product performance versus competition. In this case, for the long term, priority should be given to media spend. On the other hand, if value stands high, perhaps the brand can afford a higher price and margin.

Third, how confident is the team in the assumptions made about the effects from marketing activities? We are not looking for certainty, of course. Will the planned list price increase, without more advertising, really leave volume so little affected? Will the extra coupons not provoke competitive reaction?

Finally, other parts of the budget may be altered to provide the working media amount that is considered necessary. The two places to look at are:

— promotions: can advertising, perhaps direct advertising, do the same short-term job and have better long-term effects?
— price: can the margin be improved, leaving more to spend on advertising (the best combination of price and media spend changes is discussed in Chapter 7)?

When a decision is made to change an objective, or the budget, you start again at the feasibility checks.

The Plan Is Feasible

Suppose you are reasonably sure that the plan can deliver the required volume and contribution, and maintain value. Rather than settle on this budget immediately, ask yourself what would happen if you spent a little more or a little less. Can you improve things by a change? In particular, if you can still meet short-term goals when you spend more, remember that long-term effects are additional. You should invest when you can.

The work is not quite over even when the budget has been agreed. You have in effect set advertising sales objectives as well as deciding what to spend. This is true whether or not the Task method has been formally used and whether or not the brand plan originally specified sales objectives. Record also all the advertising objectives and then decide how to evaluate the advertising at the end of the year. Your advertising agency should be aware of this plan to make advertising accountable. A good agency will cooperate in planning the evaluation. Hopefully, when it is time to set next year's advertising budget, you will have learned something that will make it easier to determine what advertising can do for you. Check Chapters 2 and 6 for ways to see what advertising has achieved.

Chapter 4: Action Points

Recommended process to set the advertising budget

Review . . .

Long term and immediate. BRAND OBJECTIVES, especially advertising objectives	Current, draft, and recent actual BRAND BUDGETS
Category, major competitors and brand MARKETING HISTORY AND FORECAST	Evidence of ADVERTISING EFFECTS long and short term, consumers and trade

Review and use
SEVERAL METHODS
to estimate the working media spend, especially: Objective and Task
Brand History
Modelling (if available)

Estimate and add non-working media spend, to get the first RANGE OF ADVERTISING BUDGETS

Estimate what the media spend will buy

Check whether brand objectives and budget constraints are met.

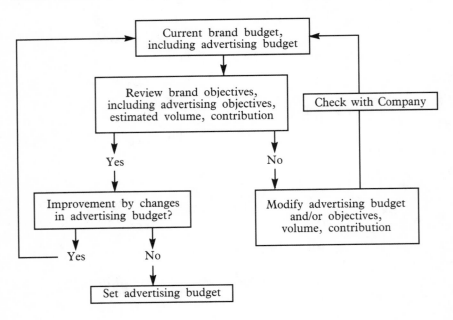

5   Methods

There is no formula for determining the ideal advertising appropriation.

Association of National Advertisers (1967)

This chapter is mainly a long checklist of methods which suggest advertising budgets, with a how-to description and at least one example of each. It also lists the pros and cons of each method.

Many observers have been amazed that advertising budgets are set every day, yet the methods described to outsiders seem so arbitrary and incomplete. This is because the so-called method is usually a small part of the real decision. Chapter 4 outlined the need to understand where the brand is, where we want it to be, and the resources available to promote it. This understanding is drummed into working managers and has enormous influence. Do we have growth objectives? Are we strapped for cash? Are we content simply to repeat last year with small improvements? The answers to these questions, plus last year's actual brand budget, tell us more about the likely advertising budget than any of the methods isolated in this chapter.

These methods provide input to the decision discussed in Chapter 4. They only propose budgets, they should never determine them. None of them should be used in isolation, though you may be tempted to do so. There is considerable overlap between methods which at first look distinct.

Advertising to Sales (A/S or Percentage of Sales)

The advertising-to-sales ratio is only one of several useful numbers about our budget and the budgets for competitive brands. Other numbers are the advertising-to-margin ratio, per case allowance, share of voice and share of market, and dynamic difference. Often we compare our own plans with those for other brands, using such numbers.

In this work, we frequently run into problems, both with the data and with definitions. A separate discussion of these difficulties is given, with case histories, in Chapter 8. In this chapter I assume that the methods recommended have been followed, and that data on advertising and on sales have been collected in a sensible way.

Definition

Sales revenue for the brand for next year is estimated, as described in Chapter 3, and a fixed proportion of this is allocated for advertising. Preferably, this ratio determines the working media budget, but the total advertising budget may be calculated. Sometimes the past or current year is used.

Example 1
The average price at which a case will be sold to retailers is expected to be £8. The sales forecast, based on the current trend, is 2 million cases. The proportion to be used is 7% (or A/S = 7%). The advertising budget is 0.07 × £8 × 2 million, or £1.12 million.

Pros

1. Easy to use, once the proportion is set.
2. Easily defended to top management: 'We must match competition', when our ratio is near the competitors' ratio.
3. Successful brands with high sales or targets get more support.
4. This method improves on the per case allowance (see below) by building in changes in our selling price. The advertising-to-margin method does the same, and further allows for changes in production cost. So this method is midway between the per case allowance and the advertising-to-margin methods.
5. 'It may encourage the manager to look at the relationship between advertising costs, selling prices and profits, when considering whether the "right" ratio is being applied' (1).

Cons

1. How is the proportion set? The method assumes that it is given. Often the proportion is from habit and custom, in effect an Inertia method. Or it is a competitor or industry average, not necessarily relevant to us. On the other hand, its implications may have been thought through at a higher level.

2. Each year, we must review whether the proportion should be updated.
3. As with other ratio methods, the effect of advertising on sales is ignored: with these ways of setting budgets, sales drive the advertising. Little account is taken of the contribution targets of the company, or of changes in the environment or of advertising's effectiveness. We may be missing opportunities or overlooking the real needs of the brand or over-spending.
4. Without a minimum level of spending being set, the method may give an unrealistically small budget. Instead, falling sales should sometimes be a prompt to increase adspend.
5. No account is taken of margin, so products with a high margin, on which advertising returns its investment more efficiently, get the same budget as products with a low margin.
6. Very large brands might do as well with lower proportions spent on advertising, which is not recognized when the same A/S ratio is used. 'A high share brand, with its more loyal buyers, requires a lower percentage of sales in advertising to maintain its franchise' (2).

Comment

Choosing the actual advertising-to-sales ratio to be used is obviously key. The choice may be made by comparison with competitors or industry proportions; see Chapters 3 and 8 for sources and examples. I list here some of the factors which have an influence on making our brand or company ratio above or below others.

Between brands, the following are reasons for high advertising-to-sales ratios:
— growth expectation, buying increased volume share
— high margin
— news to announce, new product, re-launch, fresh creative work
— low volume share (more on this below).

Between companies and industries, the following are reasons for high advertising-to-sales ratios:
— high margin
— large target
— price-inelastic category
— advertising-assisted growth in category volume
— high image content in branding
— less considered purchase, low-intent category
— frequent, small ticket purchase

— sales are made through intermediaries, few of them are to the end users
— standardized products, few differences between competitors.

Some of these comments are supported by the PIMS data base (3), but generalities on this subject can be dangerous. It is possible to speculate why the ratios are high for, say, cosmetics and cereals, but low for, say, petrol and spirits. This does not help much when you cannot change the category in which you are operating. It is best to study for yourself the history of brands in that category and in others like it.

In addition, care must be taken to distinguish the *associations* which such studies can measure from *causation* (which can flow either way or from some common third factor). Words like 'related', 'correlated' and 'linked' may be justified, while 'influence', 'affect', 'drive', 'powerful lever' or 'great impact' summarize an opinion, not a finding. Although generalities are suspect, however, individual published case histories suffer from self-selection.

The problem of proving causation is particularly acute when good companies tend to get everything right. This is like the difficulty of separating the effect of advertising for a single brand, when it has always been associated with other promotional efforts. The successful operator, as pointed out below, has a mix of good product quality, higher price, better sales, higher return on investment, and so on.

Two other breakdowns have shown strong associations with the advertising-to-sales ratio (1):

'Taking the averge A/S ratio of our (admittedly small) sample of products as 100, the ratio for relatively new types of product was 275, for established durables 120, for established consumables 60, and for commodities only 6. In the life-cycle analysis, products in their introductory stages had a ratio of 294, those in growth stage 60, and those in maturity 25: for products recognized as being in decline, however, the ratio was 102. This last is a particularly interesting finding, suggesting (on the assumption that the manufacturers in question know what they are doing) that greater marginal effectiveness may be derived from advertising when market trends are not on your side than when they are.'

The maturity products certainly had a lower A/S than those in decline: the actual percentages were 3 and 14 (4). Perhaps the maturity and decline stages are not distinct: product reformulation and relaunch have often revived brands with falling sales.

Brands with larger shares tend to have lower A/S ratios, so low-share brands tend to have higher ratios. This fact is part of a complex set of associated factors. It is often summed up as economies of scale or as diminishing returns, but there is more to it than that. Here is a list of

14 points about brand leaders, based on Leo Burnett experience and on some work with Nielsen (5). Brand leaders

1. . . . are more profitable than other brands in the same market, proportionally as well as absolutely,
2. . . . because they can charge a higher price,
3. . . . and have a lower proportional spend on advertising and promotion (but still higher absolutely than other brands),
4. . . . have a higher quality product,
5. . . . with more technical innovation,
6. . . . and more spin-offs, flavours, etc.,
7. . . . hence a better consumer image (which comes from both the product and the advertising),
8. . . . and more facings,
9. . . . higher distribution and stocking,
10. . . . with easier retail acceptance of new products, new terms, etc.,
11. . . . but probably similar levels of dealing with retailers: the higher consumer price comes from a higher list price, not less dealing, and a greater ability to cope with competitors' price-cutting.
12. . . . its consumer sales level coming from higher penetration rather than abnormally high frequency.
13. . . . caused partly by the generality of its positioning, as opposed to the consumer segmentation policies of smaller bands,
14. . . . and the manufacturer's management and staff are of higher quality, greater pride and loyalty, and better rewarded.

Finally, in comparing industry or competitor data with our own, be aware of definition differences.

Example 2
Standard sources report our sales as £14 million and adspend as £600 000: A/S = 600/14 000 or 4.3%. In the same year our revenue was £10 million and adspend £550 000, so our actual A/S is 550/10 000 or 5.5%. The same sources report for our competitors an average A/S of 4%. We decide to reduce our A/S to the same as theirs. Revenue next year will again be £10 million.

The point is that our actual adspend should not be £400 000, based on the reported A/S. It should be $0.04 \times (550/440) \times £10$ million, to allow for the bias in the reporting sources. This is £510 000.

Advertising to Margin (A/M)

Definition

Gross margin (see Chapter 3, where this term is defined) for the brand for next year is estimated and a fixed proportion of this is allocated for advertising. The working media budget may be calculated or the total advertising budget. Sometimes it is not margin but profit that is the basis, and sometimes the past or current year is used.

> *Example 3*
> Gross margin per case is expected to be £3.40 next year. The sales forecast is one million cases. The proportion to be used is 15%. The advertising budget is 1.5 × £3.40 × 1 million, or £510 000.

Pros

1. The method is easy to use, once the proportion is set.
2. It is easily defended to top management: 'We must match competition'.
3. Successful brands that are making large contributions, or have ambitious objectives, get more support.
4. Margin is more relevant than revenue or unit sales, since it allows a brand with lower production cost, but the same price and turnover, to spend more on advertising (see Chapter 7 for why this is appropriate). Hence this method is preferred to advertising-to-sales ratio or per case allowance.
5. Rising prices are built in, so we go some way to coping with media inflation. Further, advertising at the time of a price rise, justified by this method, is often advisable.
6. Provided other deductions from gross margin have been properly allowed for, so that contribution is safeguarded, the budget should be affordable.

Cons

1. How is the proportion set? The method assumes that it is given, often from habit and custom, in effect an inertia method. Or it may be a competitor or industry average that is not necessarily relevant

to us. On the other hand, its implications may have been thought through at a higher level.

2. Each year, we must query whether the proportion should be updated.
3. As with other ratio methods, the effect of advertising on sales is ignored: with these ways of setting budgets, sales drive the advertising. Little account is taken of the contribution targets of the company or of the changes in the environment or of advertising's effectiveness. We may be missing opportunities or overlooking the real needs of the brand, or over-spending.
4. Without a minimum level of spending being set, the method may give an unrealistically small budget. Instead, falling sales should sometimes be a prompt to increase adspend.

Per Case Allowance (also, Case Rate)

Definition

Unit volume sales for next year are estimated and a fixed sum for advertising is allowed per unit. The unit need not be a case, and sometimes the past or current year is used. The working media budget, or the total advertising budget, may be calculated.

Example 4
This example includes the way the fixed sum was agreed. Last year we sold one million cases and spent £3.5 million on working media. The total category sold 6 million cases and its advertising expenditure (converted from ratecard to estimated actual spend) was £25 million. Hence our case allowance was £3.50 and the total category's was £4.17. Competitors were estimated to spend £4.30 per case. This is from $(25-3.5)/(6-1)$.

Taking into account expected media cost increases and category spending, plus our need to be more aggressive, it was decided to raise our case allowance from £3.50 to £4.20. Category volume is expected to be the same as last year, but we are aiming at 25% share or 1.5 million cases. The working media budget is £4.2 × 1.5 million, or £6.3 million.

Pros

1. The method is easy to use, once the fixed sum is set.
2. Successful brands with high sales or targets get more support.

Cons

1. How is the fixed sum set? The method may assume it is given, although a more constructive approach was followed in the example above. Often the amount is from habit and custom or at most adjusted for media cost inflation. It may be an industry or competitor average, not necessarily relevant to us.
2. Each year, we must query whether the proportion should be updated.
3. As with other ratio methods, the effect of advertising on sales is ignored: with these ways of setting budgets, sales drive the advertising. Little account is taken of the contribution targets of the company or of the changes in the environment or of advertising's effectiveness. We may be missing opportunities or overlooking the real needs of the brand, or over-spending.
4. Without a minimum level of spending being set, the method may give an unrealistically small budget. Instead, falling sales should sometimes be a prompt to increase adspend.

Other Allowances

Definition

The units used in these calculations may not be cases or tonnes but the numbers of people (in a demographically or usage-defined target) in various geographical regions, retail outlets stocking the brand, or a similar measure. A fixed sum for advertising is allowed per unit.

Example 5
Last year our product was stocked in 100 outlets. Our working media budget was £500 000. So per store we spent £5000. This year we expect to increase the number of outlets to 130. Working media is therefore 130 × £5000 or £650 000.

Pros

1. This method is sometimes used to allocate the media spend by region at the same time as setting the total.
2. When category usage opportunities, or actual sales, are patchy, advertising can be concentrated where expected sales are likely to be highest.

3. When distribution is patchy, advertising can be concentrated where the product is on sale.
4. When penetration of category usage, or our distribution, is changing, the budget changes in proportion.

Cons

1. The way the fixed sum is determined may take little or no account of company targets.
2. Low spend regions get little chance to be developed. Below a minimum, advertising may have to be cut. National advertising may not get proper consideration.
3. Changes in the environment, such as media cost inflation, may not be taken into account.

Inertia

'If it ain't broke, don't fix it' (*Traditional*).

Description

Literally, the budget is the same as last year's. Sometimes, the budget is different but some aspect of the media plan is the same. Thus this method can overlap with the media inflation multiplier, which is described next.

Example 6
Last year we spent £1 million on magazines, achieving a cover of our target of 80% with a frequency of 4. The budget this year is again £1 million, and we are prepared to see frequency drop, since it is known we will buy about 8% fewer insertions.

Pros

1. Simplicity is an advantage of this method, and it is often used when advertising is a small part of the marketing mix.
2. If advertising is having its expected and economic effects, this is likely to be true in the following year.

Cons

1. If media inflation is ignored, this method leads to steadily reducing effects.
2. Little account may be taken of company objectives, of changes in the environment, or of advertising's effects. We may be missing opportunities.

Media Inflation Multiplier

Description

This is used in combination with another method, often inertia. A budget as agreed up to this point (such as, same spend as last year) is multiplied by the estimated increase in media costs. This multiplier may be defined in several ways. An average cost per thousand for the relevant target is often used, then the multiplier is the ratio of next year's forecast cost per thousand to this year's actual. An identical schedule to last year's may be costed, then the multiplier is the ratio of the cost estimate to this year's actual spend. The second way clearly means more work but is not likely to be much more precise than the first.

Example 7
This year's working TV budget is £1 million. Cost per thousand in our target next year is expected to be 10% up. The budget is 1.1 × £1 million, or £1.1 million. The number of TVRs to be bought is then expected to be the same as last year.

Pro

The consumer effects of advertising depend on its exposure to the target. If these effects have been satisfactory, we should repeat this good result because we will repeat the number of opportunities to see the advertising.

Cons

1. The inflation rate used may not match other changes in the annual budget, and the contribution change may not be taken into account.
2. The assumption that media owners should automatically be

compensated for raising costs is made by few advertisers.
3. At times of sharply rising media costs this method may remove the incentive to improve media efficiency in other ways. More on this below.

Comment

When TV costs change (and year-to-year alterations can be large), should the adspend always change? The answer depends on why the cost changed. Sometimes the research tool itself has altered so that the rating numbers are different though we believe viewing behaviour is the same. Even if the price we pay for commercial transmission is identical, and real advertisement exposure is the same, the reported cost will alter. It is wrong to use this as a reason for altering the advertising budget.

If ratings genuinely fall, and the main purpose of the budget is to buy a certain number of opportunities to see, then we have to increase our advertising spending.

If increased prices charged by the TV stations are the main reason for a cost change — and demand for TV time may allow them to do so — the advertiser is in a dilemma. Protests do not solve the problem. He attempts to increase the efficiency of his plan (see Chapter 6). Mainly, he has to start again on budget-setting at the new price. It is particularly important to forecast how competitors will react. If all brands in a category reduce their ratings, then the harm to share may be negligible. If the others increase their budgets to meet media inflation, and he does not, he will lose share of voice.

Competitive Comparisons

Definition

Advertising spending of our competitors is studied, either in total for our category or for identified key competitors. It is usually only reported expenditure that is considered, but details of media planning may be included. There are then many ways to match competition.

The most common way requires us next to establish our share of market. This may be in pounds or units; it may be as sales are now, or as they are forecast for next year. Then set the budget that makes our share of voice equal to this share of market. The recommended choice is for share of market to be in pounds, and to use the forecast for next year. Thus we build in an allowance for change, such as a planned sales increase. Share of voice is usually also in pounds; the difference between reported spends (for competitors) and actual (in our budget) must be allowed for.

An alternative is to match a particular competitor, often in the media exposure he achieves. This becomes the task against which the budget is set.

Example 8
Our brand has 10% share of market, which is expected to continue. MEAL (unadjusted) reports that the category spends £30 million, which is expected to increase by 5% next year. It is estimated that actual adspends are 90% of those reported.

Actual category adspend next year is estimated at $0.90 \times 1.05 \times £30$ million, or £28.4 million. If our share of voice (i.e. of adspend) is to equal our market share, then our adspend should be $0.10 \times £28.4$ million, or £2.84 million.

Example 9
Our brand's marketing objective is to grow to a share equal to the market leader's. His adspend, on a trend basis, is expected to be £2 million next year. Our adspend should be £2 million.

Example 10
Our Brand B is declining in share. The marketing objective is to stabilize share. The market leader, Brand A, has steady sales. Other data are in Table 1.

Media costs are expected to be the same next year. Our adspend per share point is set at £42 000, like Brand A's. Hence, to maintain a share of 30%, our budget is $30 \times £42\ 000$, or £1.26 million.

Table 1   Comparison of Brand B's Adspend
with Market Leader Brand A

Brand	Sales share (%)	Adspend (£000)	£000 per share point
A	36	1500	42
B	30	900	30

Comment

You can imagine total sales in the category being divided up, by the brands next year, in proportion to the amount of advertising seen by category purchasers. Although this over-simplifies, it is an attractive idea. There is a certain glamour, for a large brand and especially for the brand with the largest share of market, in being a large or the largest advertiser. To maintain such a position, especially for its effect on the trade, is sometimes a marketing objective. For both these reasons, share of voice is considered critical by many advertisers. They monitor competitors' adspend carefully.

When our brand's share of voice equals its share of market, then the ratio of its adspend to sales equals the market average. Thus this version of the method is the same as the advertising to sales method (if the definition of sales is revenue) or per case allowance (if the definition of sales is units), provided we look for equality with the category average. The pros and cons of these methods then apply.

Note that when our adspend is a significant part of the total category's, changes in our adspend alter the total. This affects the calculation of share of voice.

Example 11
We spend £2 million, the competitors' total is £4 million, so the category total is £6 million. To get a 40% share of voice, the sum for our adspend is not $0.40 \times £6$ million = £2.4 million. It should be $40/(100 - 40) \times £4$ million = £2.67 million. This is because the competitors' £4 million must be 60%: in proportion, our spend must be 40/60 as large.

Pros

1. The method is easy to use.
2. It is easily defended to top management: 'We must match competition.'
3. Successful brands with high shares or targets get more support.
4. The method directs attention to competitors' advertising activities.

Cons

1. The method assumes that competition is spending the right amount, or alternatively, that market share does follow share of voice. These assumptions may not be correct, so the method can lead to either over- or under-spending.
2. As with other ratio methods, the effect of advertising on sales is ignored: with these ways of setting budgets, sales drive the advertising. Little account is taken of the contribution targets of the company or of the changes in the environment or of advertising's

effectiveness. We may be missing opportunities or overlooking the real needs of the brand or over-spending.

3. Without a minimum level of spending being set, the method may give an unrealistically small budget. Instead, falling sales should sometimes be a prompt to increase adspend.

4. Large brands might do as well with a lower proportional share of voice and small brands might need more. See the comments on brand leaders under the Advertising to Sales method, and the Share of Voice, Share of Market section.

Task (also, Objective and Task)

Definition

The task method of setting advertising budgets, or budgeting by objectives, starts with the marketing and advertising objectives. It then defines the work needed to achieve the objectives. The cost to do the work is the budget that is set.

Some of the earlier methods can be turned into tasks, for example, by using a desired market share in the advertising-to-sales ratio method. However, the task is usually defined in more direct terms. These follow from whatever objectives are set in the brand plan, either sales or share goals or values of intermediate measures such as awareness, image dimensions and so on.

Example 12
This repeats Example 1 of this chapter, with £8 as our average price per case and the advertising-to-sales ratio to be used set at 7%. However, instead of forecasting sales at 2 million cases on a trend basis, an aggressive target of 2.5 million cases is set.

The advertising budget needed to achieve this (if the proportion used is to be trusted) is $0.07 \times £8 \times 2.5$ million, or £1.40 million.

Example 13
A US telephone company plans to increase the number of installed phone extensions in its residential market by 15%.

Part of the advertising budget is designed to pay for bill inserts and a programme of local newspaper and radio ads. This push is intended to produce identifiable revenue and judgement is used to estimate the amount of advertisement exposure needed to achieve the goal.

Note that, in giving this example (6), its author points out that advertising is not an isolated expense. 'It should be planned to coincide with, to aid and abet the plans your company has made to improve its revenue and satisfy its customers.' He adds that, 'Marketing and management have an obligation to give clear cut ideas of the company's future plans to their advertising people. Only then will management receive an objective, task-oriented budget they not only can understand, but of which they can heartily approve.'

Example 14
Analysis of tracking studies over more than 40 brands was used by Foote, Cone and Belding, Chicago, to develop a general relationship between the number of advertisement exposures and increases in unaided brand awareness. Media plans at different spend levels were first assessed to choose a daypart mix that maximized the effect expected (see Table 2). This table can be used to 'help set realistic advertising goals. If, for example, the advertiser's goal was to increase unaided brand awareness by 17%, but he could only afford a budget at the 2X index level, he'd better find a way to get more money for advertising, or reduce his goal' (7).

Table 2   **Advertising Budget and Change in Unaided Brand Awareness**

Budget ($M)	Forecast % increase in awareness
X	10
2X	14
3X	17
4X	18
5X	20

Source: Ref. (7).

Pros

1. Money is put against specific, and hopefully measurable, goals. Advertising is seen as an activity that produces results. Not only the budget but the whole advertising plan is affected by this approach. The benefits are felt far beyond the budgeting exercise. The whole team pulls in one direction when it is clear to all exactly what has to be achieved. This applies to copy as much as to spend. Further, this method encourages campaign evaluation. Everyone will want to know whether the goal was met. Accountability is implied.
2. The cost is checked for affordability, as it should be, later in the process. We may then detect unreality in the objective: there simply

is not enough money made available for advertising to do what is expected of it. This can apply also to copy: advertisements, which were written with an unrealistically grand notion of how often they will be exposed, may not actually be seen by consumers often enough to work in the way intended. It is an advantage to raise these possibilities before the event, and if necessary to replan. 'Modest budgets and ambitious goals are irreconcilable. Ambitious budgets for modest goals are inexcusable' (8).

3. The more clearly defined the role of advertising for the brand, the more appropriate is this method. If you cannot use the task method, check to see why. You will probably find something wrong in your strategy.

'What has emerged from our work is that it is the task approach, deployed against the background of an appropriate model and within the framework of the company's overall marketing and financial requirements, which offers the most efficient method of determining advertising budgets with the maximum cost-effectiveness and the minimum of prodigality' (1).

Cons

1. Athough correctly emphasizing the outside world, the method may ignore affordability internally.
2. How much advertising is needed to complete the task is still to be determined. This may not be easy to do and is commented on below.
3. The goal chosen may be a surrogate for our real objective, but selected partly because it is measurable; and partly because we hope that, if it is achieved, the objective will be met. We may be wrong, and the link may not exist. Then we not only set an incorrect budget but, what is worse, an incorrect advertising objective. See the next two examples.

Example 15
This published case history (9) shows the effect of a copy change. The conclusion would be the same if it had been increased weight behind the new advertising. The objective was to persuade housewives that a brand of fresh cream was of better quality than competitive brands. On image dimensions, the brand 'rocketed up'. Research reported that the cream was seen as thicker, creamier, and so on. Sales were accurately monitored by a retail delivery system in which unsold product was returned after a certain time on the shelf. Sales showed no improvement.

How could this be? The image improved on what seemed to be relevant dimensions but this produced no change in behaviour. The answer was that the image dimensions were not seriously held. Housewives were ready to replay the advertising claims, but not to act on them.

The conclusion must be that surrogate measures for sales such as image changes (here, that the brand is creamier, etc.) can move without sales necessarily following. We may *hypothesize* that we have found relevant image measures. This is not the same as *proving* that they predict sales effects.

Example 16
Example 15 showed sales unaffected by image improvement. The converse is also true: sales can rise without image changes.

Hofmeister Lager (10) 'lacked front-of-mindness' and 'had a weak image profile compared to the other leading brands' in 1983. The mechanism by which sales were expected to be pushed up was the creation of a new brand image, to raise its profile in the marketplace. George the Bear was the campaign credited with increasing Hofmeister pub sales by 25%, while standard lagers rose only 9%. Hofmeister's distribution rose a mere 1.5% and its price actually increased in relation to competitors.

Yet, 'when we turned to the quantitative data, we were surprised to find that there had been no significant shift in Hofmeister's consumer standing'. Investigations suggested this was because non-drinkers of the brand, who were reluctant to rate it, swamped the scores of regular drinkers. Further, drinkers are aware that product differences are small: 'mainstream lagers are much of a muchness in product terms, and the low temperatures at which they are served usually mask any differences that may exist between them'. Thus the relevance of product image scores such as 'lots of flavour' or 'good quality' is questionable.

Effective Frequency

'How much is enough?' is the question behind the concept of *effective frequency* (11). This is an influential tool in the US but is much misunderstood and warrants a digression.

We put together two ideas. The first is the distribution of the number of advertisement exposures produced by a schedule. Whether this is for TV or for print, a media planner can estimate how many people in the target audience will be exposed at all, and how many once, twice, and so on. It is essential to specify over what length of time this distribution is obtained, and to be clear about the definition of 'exposed'.

The second idea is the response function. This is a theoretical construct, though occasionally it can be observed. It gives a weight to each number of advertisement exposures. The weight is zero for no exposures and increases as the number of exposures goes up. The weight is proportional to the response or sales effect at this number of exposures. It represents the value to the advertiser of reaching people this number of times.

If we know both the frequency distribution of exposures, and the response function, then we can calculate a value for the schedule. It is just the sum of the number exposed at each frequency times response at that frequency. This way of using these two ideas is an indispensable tool in the computer evaluation of different print schedules. It is used in computer programs that write schedules.

There is one particular way of specifying the response function: zero up to a particular number of exposures, and one thereafter. For example, none, one, two and three exposures count for nothing, but four or more count one. In this case, the value above is the four-plus of the schedule: the proportion of the target exposed four or more times. Four is then the effective frequency. Clearly, this is a simplification. In the real world, it is unlikely that three exposures have no effect, while both four and, say, ten have the same effect.

The step function just described may be taken further, by calling all exposures over a certain number excessive or even wasted and so worth nothing (12). The response function is now a step both up and down: for example, a zero response except between three and ten exposures. Again, this is unlikely to be exact: how can ten exposures have value and eleven have none?

There is nothing wrong with simplifying a sensible procedure in order to make it operational, provided the violence done to the underlying ideas is not terminal. In this case the sensible procedure is the use of a smooth convex response function, the simplification is a step function.

But criteria such as effective frequency, or even the advertising-to-sales ratio, or the per case allowance may be used in two ways: first, as a way to split a budget over time, or to allocate it regionally; second, as a method to suggest a total budget. It is very important to distinguish these uses.

The first use of such criteria may be a practical rule book technique to carry out the allocation. At this lower level, after the main budget decisions are made by senior people, such rules are not statements about advertising's effects, but practical tools for administering a complex numerical job, done by less senior people. For media planning after the budget is fixed, simple operating rules such as 'in any burst, the four-plus cover must be at least 30%' can lead to reasonable results. This particular one forces the TV planner to get adequate reach: the buy cannot all go on cheap time to maximize TVRs.

But when these criteria are used to set budgets, we *are* implying a statement about advertising's effects and must take much more care. So when a concept like effective frequency is used not just for allocation, but to set the budget, you are advised to inspect the logic carefully. An example will show the difficulties.

Example 17
A research study concludes that X is an 'effective frequency', to buy X costs £Y, hence £Y is the correct advertising budget. A research study often quoted is by Colin McDonald (13). This has been simplified to 'We need two exposures of our advertising between purchase occasions'. Because the average purchase frequency in a category is known, the total number of exposures is quickly calculated as are total TVRs and so the budget.

As baldly stated as this, the reasoning in patently absurd. It implies that a budget for a once-a-week purchase should always be at least four times that for a once-a-month purchase. It ignores copy: the budgets for 10-second and 60-second spots would be very different. It ignores brand share: the budgets for a 1% share brand and a 10% share brand would be the same. It ignores competitors' advertising.

Some of these points are made in the IPA appraisal of one of the attempts to update the McDonald finding, and to re-write the rules deduced from it. Jeremy Elliott (14), however, usefully adds the need to distinguish what the brand's objectives are. If it is on a maintenance strategy, he suggests that it needs 60 to 80 TVRs per purchase interval. If the brand is on a change strategy, it needs 120 to 140 TVRs.

More fundamental is the fact that a McDonald analysis is one-dimensional: only the number of opportunities to see in a purchase interval is used to explain brand switching or retention. In fact, the relationship between interval length, weight of purchasing by the individual, price of the brand and so on is more complex than this implies (15).

Although media planning and buying may be fairly safely controlled with the help of the effective frequency concept, it is a potentially dangerous aid in budget-setting. It may certainly be used in the task method, but not as a mechanical procedure. To choose the desired frequency calls for experienced judgement, plus careful specification of what frequency over what period and why.

Zero-based Budgets

The task method is often linked with the *zero-based* approach. This attractive idea, which also has much currency in the USA, states that nothing should be taken for granted in budget-setting: the inertia, same-as-last-year method is specifically rejected. Instead, a bottom-up approach is used, each part of the budget being explicitly justified, the justification often being the task to be achieved by advertising. Other methods may be used, so zero-based is not so much a method itself as an attitude.

The danger with the zero-based approach is that we may assume sales will continue as last year, in the absence of advertising. Any spend on advertising has to prove itself by additional return, as a short-term investment.

It is certainly worth considering what might happen if we had no advertising: what effects on volume, on contribution, on consumer image, on the trade by year end, and so on. Examples are quoted in Chapter 8. It is, however, better to use a fairly secure base to project from, for example last year, than to imply that the zero-based situation is actually known.

How Much to Achieve the Task?

We turn now to the problem of matching resources correctly to the objectives. The task method sometimes just turns one question into another. Suppose we agree on this objective: 'Make 20% of non-users aware that . . .' To use this to set a budget implies that we know that £1 million will make 10% aware, £2 million will make 15% aware and so on. How often can we say that?

The answer is, sometimes. We may have relevant history of our own or information from some generalizable source. Some new product models, for example, contain previous experience in the form of a connection between cumulative TVRs and brand awareness. Example 14 similarly solved this problem.

More often, the task method is a way of allowing common sense or intuition to get to grips with the problem: the task becomes understandable. We have to put ourselves in the position of our target individuals, whose attitudes and behaviour have been described to us by research. We have to imagine them exposed to our commercial. How will they react? Again, research may feed our intuition.

Thus, when we are discussing the budget, we should also have in mind what it will buy. Only when we think in terms of people seeing advertisements, and of how they might be affected, do we get the full picture.

Suppose the target is housewives; we have agreed that the spot length is 30 seconds and the cost per hundred is £200 000. Then each million pounds we spend buys us on average five opportunities to see our commercial. We can now turn what is almost an abstraction — do we spend £1 million or £1.2 million — into something more concrete. Are we satisfied with five opportunities to see? Or do we need six?

Such alternatives can be made even more real when we have the ads in front of us. The target will have not just six exposures, but one opportunity every two months to see *this* commercial. Suddenly, what seemed like big money is put into proper perspective. What was just an accountant balancing a column of figures becomes exciting selling to our target consumers.

Note that after we have used one set of media costs, part of the budget may later be allocated to other media, or the main medium may be changed. There can be different lengths and sizes of ad. The ads may not yet even be written. The approach can nevertheless be used with our current best estimates.

We may also consider different schedules explicitly. 'Without the last £250 000 we could not afford print', or, 'We'll have to drop the :30 and run it all in :15s.'

In some cases, exploring the media options may uncover restraints that help set the budget. There may be, for example, only certain publications and ad sizes available in time for a print campaign. Or legal and other requirements may determine limits to what we can do.

Affordable (also, Residual)

'Shake the budget and take what's loose' (*Traditional*).

Description

The budget is set up as described in the first part of Chapter 3, starting from a sales forecast. When the revenue has been reduced by other costs, we divide the remainder between the advertising budget and other items. A great deal is left to the characters of the protagonists. A process of theatre and bargaining settles the division. A brand champion is needed, who can debate on equal terms with those who support other uses for the money.

> *Example 18*
> Company rules dictated that 30% of total retail sales were a required contribution. The sales director estimated sales at £10 million. Production cost and overheads were £5 million. Contribution had to be 0.3 × £10 million or £3 million. Thus £2 million remained for advertising, consumer promotion, retail promotion, research and development, consumer research, and so on. By rule of thumb, the advertising and promotion budgets were declared equal. R&D and the other items were settled at £1 million. The total advertising budget was £500 000.

Pro

By definition, the advertising budget is affordable in that the major items in the total budget are not threatened by it.

Cons

1. No account is taken of advertising's effects on sales or of changes in the environment. We may be missing opportunities or overlooking the real needs of the brand or over-spending.
2. Without a minimum being set, the method may give an unrealistically small budget. Instead, falling sales should sometimes be a prompt to increase adspend.

Brand History Review

Description

Record and examine the brand's recent history. Do this within the relevant category, if possible, and also for major direct competitors. Include volume sales and share, sterling sales, prices, advertising activity and other marketing activities. Events such as product formulation changes, flavour additions, new packaging, new positioning, major distribution gains and losses should all be recorded.

Without actually modelling (see below) you will see averages, trends, and perhaps associations. These help you understand the dynamics of the category and the part played by advertising. This view may allow you to estimate the effects of different spends. Then this suggests the budget, either directly, or using the Task method.

Comment

Brand histories are mentioned at several points in this book. In Chapter 2, various effects were described, some of which can be seen and measured only when we look at history. In Chapter 4, we examined where the brand is and has been, in order to evaluate how difficult it will be to achieve the company's objectives. In later methods (Share of Voice, Share of Market, Dynamic Difference and Modelling) history is looked at in special ways, to quantify any regular association there may be between adspend and sales.

In this section, we look generally at history for such associations, without using any special techniques.

Example 19
The case history, Ten Years of Franchise Building, in Chapter 8, is used here. It allows us to say that, during years 7 to 10, Brand A made about $12 million profit, when advertising and other promotional spends were at $6 million, and $16 million profit when they were at $7 million. There is some growth trend to be allowed for here. Now suppose we are in year 11. In a debate as to whether the $7 million spend should be cut, this information is a powerful argument not to do so. Falling below $6 million is even more unwise.

Example 20
Between 1975 and 1979 our brand happened to have spent on advertising different proportions of the total advertising and promotion budget. See Table 3. The variations were due to inventory situations and various marketing pressures. Success, both in volume and share, was associated more with the balance of advertising and promotion than with the actual spend. The 1980 total was set at the 1979 level adjusted for media inflation: £1.65 million. The proportion for advertising was as in 1975 and 1979: 75%. Thus the advertising budget was 0.75 × £1.65 million = £1.24 million.

Table 3 Sales, Advertising and Promotion History

Year	Cases (millions)	£000 on			% on	
		Advertising	Promotion	Total	Advertising	Promotion
1975	17	825	275	1100	75	25
1976	11	1050	625	1675	63	37
1977	13	950	425	1375	69	31
1978	14	875	600	1475	59	41
1979	17	1150	350	1500	77	23

Example 21
History gives its clearest lessons when there has been a deliberate experiment. A simple example is an area test, when advertising is introduced in some TV regions, not in others. This was the case for Mazola, a cooking oil (16). The brand spent £340 000 in 1983 and £476 000 in 1984, in four TV regions only: London, Southern, Tyne Tees and Central. In all the advertised regions, Mazola gained share, +12% on average. In the rest of the country, it generally continued a previous share decline, averaging −12%. Price and distribution were looked at, but varied little across regions. With such results, it is not surprising that TV support for the brand was continued.

Pros

1. Sometimes the regularities observed allow volume sales estimates, however crude, at different adspends. These can be converted to contribution estimates (see Chapter 3). Hence the outcome of alternative budgets can be evaluated.
2. Realistic understanding of what has actually happened can correct false expectations about future plans.

Cons

No regularities may be seen, or those seen cannot be trusted, because other explanations are possible. The data you would like to have may be too costly. The method therefore cannot be relied on always to be available or reliable. Other factors, associated perhaps by chance with adspend, may be the real causes of the pattern that appears.

Ways of Using Brand Histories

The method is a contrast to zero-based budgeting. Instead of starting from the assumption of no spend, we start from the reality of actual, recent spending. Thus, for established brands (that is, not new products but those for which we have a history), setting the advertising budget is more a matter of adjustment from a known position than starting from scratch (17).

The budgeting process is a series of mid-course corrections which keep the brand's performance in line with company objectives. Changes are needed as these objectives are modified and as the environment for the brand alters. If there is an overriding company cash requirement, marketing budgets may be cut; everyone accepts that the brand is being temporarily milked and put at risk. When the cash flow permits, the resources are put back so that the strength of the brand is restored. Or when we know a competitor will launch a rival to our brand, the company may decide to meet this pressure and retain share by increasing adspend. The brand fights back since we have decided that volume matters more than contribution at this time.

We are able to manage the brand in this way because we know pretty well where the brand is now and has been in the recent past. If we are setting the budget for 1990, and the time is September 1989, then we have a good idea of 1989 actuals. We know what our marketing activity spends were and what they bought (so much adspend, so many rating points).

The first question is, has 1989 been satisfactory? The second is, what will change in 1990? The answers to these questions are a major part of determining the budget. They are also, of course, part of normal brand management.

The evaluation of 1989 uses criteria such as the following: Did the brand's sales volume and market share behave as planned? Was the selling price (to retailers, allowing for discounts) as expected? Were costs controlled? Were revenue, contribution, and return on assets satisfactory?

Next, we use forecasts on the 1990 environment, as described in Chapter 4. What will happen to category volume and prices? What do we expect to have to pay for media? Our own costs have also to be estimated.

It is important that we have a feel for how the category will behave. It may be sleepy, with low A/S ratios and a high level of margins. The best course may be not to disturb this. Or perhaps we ourselves, or a competitor, will go for share growth with product innovations and a high marketing investment. If a competitor is likely to attack in this way, our budget should allow for a counter-attack.

Most often, the budget for next year will be set by assuming we react passively to relatively small changes. We follow category prices, we pay media owners the new rates and buy the same total ratings. We enjoy the same growth in category volume as other brands. The plan is as it was in the previous year, with minimum necessary adjustments. In particular, the advertising budget is the same as last year, adjusted mainly for media inflation. Then we consider alternative budgets and what effects they may have. An example is described in Chapter 7.

The comments above have described the routine followed in most companies. The budget for the brand, including its advertising, is arrived at by adjustment. Satisfactory performance is continued; unsatisfactory performance means big decisions have to be made (about the product itself, the advertising strategy and so on). Although placed here as one of the methods, this process is more familiar as brand management.

Note that it is always useful to compare the decisions that you have made, and what happened to your brand, with other people's decisions and results. Do not assume that you should copy them. By studying competitors you will get some new ideas, the norms can be illuminating, and you should understand better how your category behaves. You should concentrate on your direct competitors. Relate their decisions to what you know about their situations.

Remember, as discussed under the advertising-to-sales method, that comparative data necessarily come from industry sources, which probably do not use the same definitions as in your budget.

You will see, as a by-product of this work, the media your competitors chose, commercial lengths, timing and so on. These may suggest questions about your own media plan.

You have to decide how fine the detail should be in these records. The numbers soon multiply if you use short periods and many geographical areas. You will always look at annual national data. So the examples here are at this level, and I do not discuss finer breakdowns. Several years' records should be acquired, in order to see movements.

Remember that there is a chicken-or-egg problem for the analyst who uses annual data. Suppose the advertising budget has been set by a fixed advertising-to-sales ratio. Then, as sales vary, so does adspend. Looking back, you see an association between the amount of advertising and sales, but the company's policy, not advertising's effects on sales, could have caused this association. 'If sales go up, advertising is almost invariably increased (normally the next year); and if they go down, it is reduced (generally immediately). This procedure means of course that the prime determinant of the amount spent on advertising . . . is the sales of the brand' (18).

Although we are not going as far as modelling such data here, it is worth discussing ways of summarizing and presenting them. It is easiest to show these with a fuller example.

Example 22

To keep this example relatively simple, suppose we study only one competitor in the category, Brand C against our Brand B, and only one year. These two brands are the only advertised ones. We have their TV ratings total by year and their TV spend at ratecard. Annual sales are given in tonnes and in sterling at the consumer level. For the most recent year we have data, as in Table 4.

Table 4   Sales and Advertising for Two Brands and Category

	Brand B	*Brand C*	*Others*	*Category total*
Sales, tonnes	14 000	6 500	22 500	43 000
Sales, £000	80 000	36 000	113 000	229 000
TVRs	8 000	4 000	—	12 000
TV spend (at rate card) £000	4 000	2 000	—	6 000

Table 5   Key Shares and Ratios Derived from Table 4

	Brand B	*Brand C*	*Others*
Share, tonnes (%)	32.6	15.1	52.3
Relative price			
(category = 100)	107	104	94
Share of voice (%)	66.7	33.3	—
A/S (%)	5.0	5.6	—

From these numbers it is easy to obtain volume shares (or shares of market, sometimes abbreviated to SoM), relative prices, shares of voice (or of ratings or of media spend, sometimes abbreviated to SoV) and advertising-to-sales ratios. These are given in Table 5. The way to derive three of these numbers is obvious. Relative price may not be as clear, so this is now explained.

Average price in the category in £000 per tonne is 229 000/43 000 or 5.33. Brand B's price is 80 000/14 000 or 5.71. Thus, relative to the category = 100, Brand B's price is 100 × 5.71/5.33 = 107.

In practice the intermediate step of calculating the individual prices is not necessary, although they may be interesting figures in their own right. We can go straight to Brand B's relative price from:

$$100 \times 80\ 000 \times 43\ 000/(14\ 000 \times 229\ 000) = 107$$

Table 5, or rather one like it in your own category, is very informative. It tells us how much of the category is being sold unadvertised (here, about half) and at what price (the relative price of unadvertised brands is well below that of those advertised). Our share of voice is much higher here than our total sales share (though a little lower than our sales share of advertised brands since 100 × 14 000/(14 000 + 6500) = 68.3%).

A brand leader typically has an above-average return from each of its individual marketing activities. Its high share often derives from high product quality supported by advertising. There is always a cheap end to a category, but our brand is not competing there: we command a higher price. In fact, we are able to get a price higher than the other advertised brand. Our advertising achieves a higher share of voice, but at a lower advertising-to-sales ratio. Our profits are therefore likely to exceed our competitors, giving us more to spend on R&D and keeping our quality ahead of competitors. This gives us claims of superiority which we can in turn exploit in our advertising. These are all examples of the brand leader points made at the beginning of this chapter.

Share of Voice, Share of Market

There are special ways of handling data about brand shares which deserve separate descriptions in this section and the next. In Chapter

8 more detail is given about the definitions, and more examples. The techniques are all ways of plotting share data that in many cases make clear the regularities in the category. Then a proposed budget for our brand provides a new point on such a plot. You can see whether the strategy looks typical for the category, or unusual (if so, you need to explain why). You may also use the average relationship to suggest an adspend for your brand's situation.

Example 23
Plots or maps for a real category are given in Figures 1 and 2. They help you to see where our brand stands in comparison with others. The first figure shows share of market against relative price: there are five main brands and 'all others'. Of the named brands, three are at above average price. Figure 2 shows share of market against share of voice and identifies these brands as the advertised brands. Drawing a line through the origin in Figure 2, roughly through the centre of these three, identifies Brand B as the one with the largest advertising-to-sales ratio (to the right of the line). Figure 1 shows it bears the highest price. Brands D and E are unadvertised. Other brands are only lightly advertised.

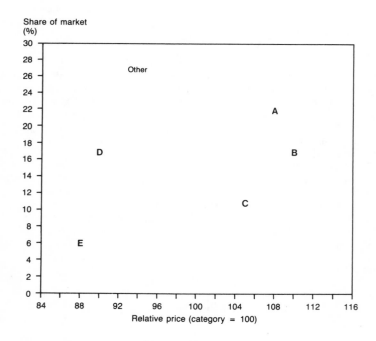

Figure 1   Shares of Market Against Relative Prices.

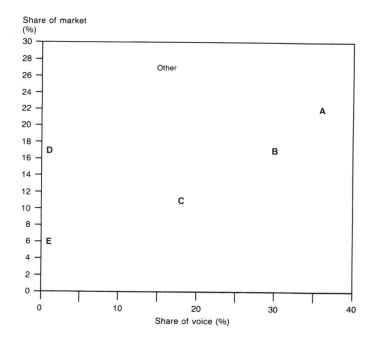

Figure 2   Shares of Market Against Shares of Voice.

Suppose you manage Brand B and a cut of one-third in adspend has been proposed. Share of voice would fall from 30 to 22% (100 × 20/90, since the total falls from 100 to 90). This would move you back to a position near Brand C, and Brand A would become even more clearly the most heavily advertised brand. This is a dangerous position for Brand B, given its price prominence in Figure 1.

A brand with an advertising-to-sales ratio above the category average also has a share of voice above its share of market. Earlier, some of the likely characteristics of such a brand were described. When you examine your category, keep an eye open for the reasons why each brand is a high or a low advertiser. Any one of these may help you discover a useful regularity in advertising spending.

It usually leads to a clearer analysis to consid
brands separately. These may include privat
brands, some of which may have very limited dist
are priced differently from the advertised bran
advertisers to carry the burden of maintaining c

brands being launched may also be separated, since these usually advertise at a relatively high share of voice.

The size of the brand's market share is also strongly associated with the amount by which its share of voice differs from its share of market. As mentioned before, large brands can spend proportionally less. The following example demonstrates this, and there is more in Chapter 8.

Example 24

A striking demonstration of the importance of market share is given in the results of a survey by John Philip Jones (19). The original data were about brands in 23 different countries, so the conclusions are international. The categories considered here are all packaged goods and contain at least four advertised brands (in fact, the average was nearly six). In no category was there a single dominant advertiser. There were 666 brands in the analysis reported, and 117 categories.

First, the brands were grouped by the size of market share; the first group was for the brands with the smallest shares, only one to three percentage share points; the largest brands were in a group of between 28 to 30 share points.

For each group, the average share of market of the brands was subtracted from the average share of voice. As you would expect, the small brands advertised at a share of voice well above share of market, in fact about three times as large. The large brands' share of voice could be five points or more below their share of market.

Figure 3, which is drawn from these data, is called a Jones diagram. It plots SoV–SoM against SoM and demonstrates remarkable regularity. It may be used to suggest an advertising budget if you wish your brand to have a typical share of voice, rather than an average one. Enter the chart with your share of market and read off how much you should add or subtract to get a typical share of voice. For example, a brand with 5% market share typically has $5+4 = 9\%$ share of voice.

The average relationship suggested in this example is usually made up from five different types of brand strategy. See Figure 4, which shows where, on a Jones diagram, such brands fall:

— *unadvertised:* when SoV is zero, SoV−SoM is a diagonal downward-sloping line against SoM
— *token advertising:* when SoV is very small, this may indicate that the manufacturer is milking the brand, or sustaining it at the minimum level at which the trade will accept it as advertised
— *launches:* SoM is small and SoV−SoM is large, which indicates that the advertiser is going for volume growth
— *large brands:* when SoM is large, it is normal that SoV−SoM is negative, and that the brands make profits larger than average
— *rest:* brands which fall into none of the types above are struggling where the competition is hottest.

Share of voice (%) minus share of market (%)

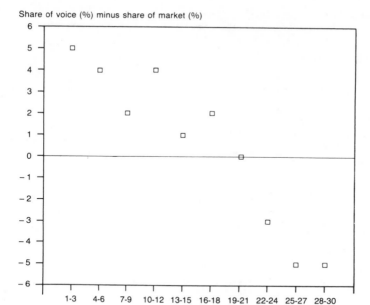

Figure 3 **Share of Voice is Above Share of Market for Small Brands, Below Share of Market for Large Brands.**

Source: Jones (1988).

Dynamic Difference

Description

This method presumes that you have brand histories, as described in the previous section, but over several years and preferably for several brands in your category. For each brand, each year, you have its share of market and share of voice. The work below is often done among the advertised brands only, so shares in this group have to be worked out.

Calculate for each brand, and for each year except the first:

— Y: share of market this year minus share of market last year (change in share of market),

— X: share of voice this year minus share of market last year (this is the 'dynamic difference').

Mark these points, on an XY scatterplot, identifying the brand and

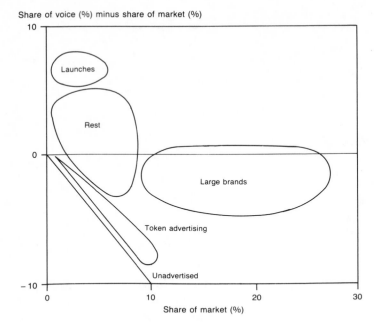

Share of voice (%) minus share of market (%)

Figure 4   Five Spending Strategies for Brands: Positions on a Jones Diagram.

year. Looking at the points for a single brand, ask yourself these questions:

1. Whereabouts on the overall plot do they generally fall? Are they generally above the Y-axis zero (so that share of market is increasing)? Are they to the right of the plot (share of voice above share of market)?
2. Do you see any association of large dynamic differences with share of market increases? Could you draw by eye an upward-sloping line through the points?

Looking across the brands, note:

1. The general positions: brands spending aggressively, the brands losing share of market and so on.
2. If lines can be drawn through the points for single brands, can we say their slopes are roughly parallel? If so, we may adjust the lines by eye to be parallel. Then the plot may be read as follows:

Where the lines cut the Y axis is the 'natural' sales growth (or decline) rate of the brand, which it would experience if its share of voice were to equal its share of market (or it had an average A/S ratio). The growth (or decline) is because of product quality, perceived value, price effects, and so on. Thus the plot indicates what these other aspects of the brand are worth. The slope of the lines tells us what increase in share of market we can expect for a given change in share of voice.

Interpretation of this plot summarizes the general positions of the brands and brings out which are the exceptional years (for which we may know other reasons). Hence we get some insight into the spending strategies and fortunes of the brands. The plot may also be used to evaluate a plan for next year. We know this year's share of market and can make an estimate of next year's category volume sales and advertising spend. The plan gives us our brand's volume sales and advertising spend. From these we derive the X and Y for next year and put this point on the plot.

1. Does the new point lie among those previously observed for the brand? If so, and other things are equal, the plan looks feasible.
2. Does the new point lie far from those previously observed? If so, do we have a good reason for the previous pattern to be broken?

In this way, alternative budgets can be evaluated and among those that look feasible we may make a choice (based on volume and contribution estimates compared with company objectives).

Comment

This technique was developed by Moroney in Unilever in the 1960s. A fuller description is in (18). It was published in the US (20) under the name *Marketing Advertising Patterns*. It is possible that the method works less well these days, when price changes and promotions play a larger role, than it did a couple of decades ago. It has been replaced, in a sense, by the demand curve described in Chapter 2. Both are a plot of sales, or of changes in sales, against an activity. It is worth experimenting, in your own particular category, with several different plots in order to see whether you get sensible, regular patterns (see also the previous section and Example 5 in Chapter 8).

Example 25
To continue Example 22, the advertised brands' shares over three years gave Table 6. By subtracting the previous year's sales shares, we get Table 7 for years 2 and 3. Thus the 'dynamic difference' for Brand B in year 3 is its share of voice in that

Table 6   Share of Market and Share of Voice for Two Brands

	Brand B		Brand C	
	Share tonnes (%)	*Share of voice (%)*	*Share tonnes (%)*	*Share of voice (%)*
Year 3	32.6	66.7	15.1	33.3
Year 2	30.1	48.1	17.2	51.9
Year 1	29.0	54.5	16.9	45.5

Table 7   Derived from Table 6 for a Dynamic Difference Plot

	Brand B		Brand C	
	Change in share of market	*SoV −SoM*	*Change in share of market*	*SoV −SoM*
Year 3	+ 2.5	36.6	− 2.1	16.1
Year 2	+ 1.1	19.1	+ 0.3	35.0
Average	+ 1.8	27.9	− 0.9	25.6

year (66.7%) minus the share of market in year 2 (30.1%): hence 36.6%. These points are plotted in Figure 5.

Obviously, from only two pairs of points in our simplified example we are not going to see real regularity. But we quickly note that Brand B has grown about one or two share points a year. It grew more in year 3, and Brand C grew in year 2, both when their share of voice was highest above their share of market.

As was pointed out above, even at zero dynamic difference (share of voice = share of market), some brands grow while others fall. In our example, Brand B clearly has a two or three share points a year advantage over Brand C. This comes from having more flavours, or superior positioning, or a better distribution, or other qualities. Further, we might estimate from Figure 3 that a brand gains one share of market point when its share of voice goes up ten points. Investing another 1% of the total advertising spend in the category gets us one-tenth of a point in share of market.

Example 26
Figure 6 uses real data (20). Now that we have data for as many as 14 years, there is more credibility in the association we see than there was with two years given in Figure 3. The brand grew at about 1% a year when the dynamic difference was +4. It declined at as much as 2% a year when share of voice fell below sales share.

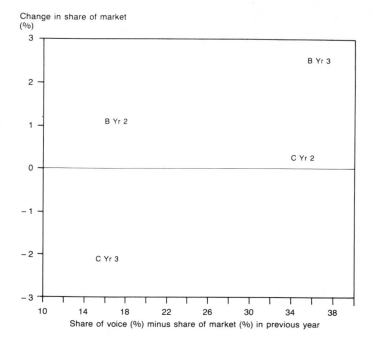

Figure 5   Changes in Share of Market Against Share of Voice Minus Share of Market (Dynamic Difference).

Source: Table 7.

One exception stands out. In year 3 our share of voice was clearly low, but instead of share falling as was normal, the brand grew by half a share point. Clearly, the reason for such growth needs investigation before we can say we understand all this brand's movements.

How does such information help in setting an advertising budget? Suppose we decided to advertise in year 15 so that our share of voice equalled our current sales share of market. Figure 6 suggests that it is reasonable to expect steady sales. If we increase adspend to get share of voice to, say, 5% above share of market, then we might hope, given recent history, for about 0.5 or even 1% share of market growth.

Suppose the plan called for adspend that we believe will be 10% below our share of market, and also forecast no change in share of market. Such a point would be very unexpected on our plot, throwing doubt on the wisdom of the planned advertising budget. Unless we are repeating something like the extra activity found for year 3, there is an argument here that a larger adspend is necessary.

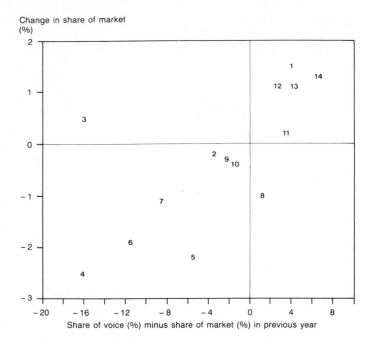

Figure 6   Changes in Share of Market Against Share of Voice Minus Share of Market (Dynamic Difference).

Source: Peckham (1974). Key: year number.

Pros

1. Considered purely as description, this plot adds a dynamic element to the static maps recommended in the section above (though these may also cover several years). Hence we improve our understanding of the category.
2. Unrealistic plans may be rejected and a more reasonable plan may be constructed. A budget that is achievable, and in line with company objectives, is more likely to be set.
3. The exceptional points may indicate the effect of other marketing activities, so we learn about more than advertising effects.

Cons

1. Few regularities or none may be seen. This means only that brands

in the category do not behave in the simple way that a well-behaved dynamic difference plot would support. We get such a plot when share of market change is related to share of voice, and other factors are steady or have little effect.
2. Other factors, associated perhaps by chance with adspend, may be the real causes of the pattern we see.

Modelling

Modelling is a technical operation which is not recommended for amateurs. It starts with the same data as are collected in the Brand history review. Then one or more mathematical equations are written which fit the sales observations, given the data on advertising and on other factors (price, for example). These equations are a model. Picking the equations, and estimating the values of some of the terms in the equation (the parameters), is modelling. The IPA commissioned a booklet (21) to give advertising people a general understanding of modelling. A model may be enshrined in a computer program, or it may be pencil-and-paper work. In this section, models are not described in detail.

Once a successful fit has been obtained, the model can be used. There are two sorts of application. *What-if* models spell out the implications of any decisions you decide to input, using the assumptions built into the model about the effects of advertising. *Prescriptive* models tell you what to do.

In chapter 7, some of the equations possible are described. I comment also on how they may be used — or misused. It is the exceptional advertiser who has access to sound modelling advice in his budget-setting. This section — and Chapter 7 — should be skipped by many practical people.

Pros

1. Sometimes the best outcome of using a model is that you have to consider the assumptions and the input. Leo Bogart has suggested that it is a learning device which forces you to think the problem through, rather than a means of explaining phenomena, or of deciding what to do (22). A model also suggests ways of summarizing history which can be valuable. Even when you reject the solution offered, you are clearing your own mind. All budgeting

methods do this to some extent, but an explicit model is most likely to draw out the implications clearly.

2. Suppose the following conditions are met. You do understand the assumptions and accept them as reasonable. The modelling has given a good fit (it has explained much of the observed variation, and has estimated key parameters rather precisely). You are satisfied that the decisions you input into the resulting what-if model are compatible with the conditions under which it was built (for example, the adspend is not beyond current experience). Then combining the model with your knowledge of the brand budget does help the advertising budget decision. It spells out the likely effects on sales, hence also the effects on contribution. As in poker, it does help to know the odds, although this does not ensure that you will win the game. Company priorities will settle the advertising budget.

Cons

1. Whether or not the model-supplier spells it out, a model rests on a theory about the real world. This theory may be wrong, or it may not apply in your case. The biggest omissions in the theory behind most models are that advertising has only short-term and direct effects, and that the manufacturer's objective is only short-term profit. Chapter 2 explained that advertising can have other sorts of effect: ignoring them can lead to misinterpretation of history and under-spending. Ignoring volume objectives can have even more serious results: a good bottom line for a year or two, then all the horrors associated with declining volume.

2. In the Dynamic Difference section, I pointed out that causality was unproven (that advertising caused the sales change). The same point applies to most modelling. All we can observe is association. After that, we essentially make a leap into the unknown. There are ways to reassure ourselves, but not without technical expertise and never giving complete certainty.

   The fundamental problem is the existence of other factors affecting sales (such as price). In the dynamic difference technique (and other simple associations) these are largely ignored. Unless odd points (like year 3 in Figure 4) draw themselves to our attention, we may forget that other factors exist. But they are always there and, at the extreme, these factors can so confuse the picture that we cannot see an advertising effect. At the other extreme, they may be positively associated with advertising decisions. For example, we advertise heavily when our price is low. It often makes good marketing sense, to coordinate our marketing activities. But it can invalidate the conclusions indicated by a naive model. We may see the association of heavy advertising and high sales share. We may attribute it all to advertising, while really it was the price which caused the added sales.

'The better the marketing the harder the modelling' is true in several ways. The coordination of activities, or their simultaneity, increases their effectiveness synergistically but raises the problem just stated.

The difficulty described in the next paragraph arises even when continuous advertising is the best policy, which is often the case. New products that are flankers or spin-offs usually perform better than average, but are harder than average to research and to model.

3. A handicap in modelling is when advertising has been rather continuous over time. I do not mean that we advertise identically every month, but that, taking one month with another, there has been little variation in our ratings. There is then no chance of seeing short-term advertising effects. Even if they are there, all we observe is a constant effect. We are back to the fallacy of 'sales unaffected by advertising'.

Example 27
In Figure 7, based on real data, are the sales shares for our brand for two successive years. Each point shows whether it is for year 1 or year 2. For this brand there was, unusually, very little price variation or promotional activity. The sales share in each four-week period is plotted against the adstock (23) for the brand at that time (recent and cumulated, decayed TVRs: think of it as current advertising pressure).

In year 1, advertising was virtually continuous and adstock varied very little. In year 2, a different media plan was followed and there were two heavy bursts, followed by several off-air periods. With year 1 data alone, it was hard to see any advertising effect. Only at the high and low adstocks of year 2 did the relationship become visible.

4. A model is more likely than most methods to *look* infallible. To output on computer paper, or on a screen, by itself adds authority to the results. When this happens, other methods are undervalued and discussion is stifled. In particular, the model is usually about short-term effects. Long-term effects, although they may matter more, can get overlooked, because the short-term effects get all the attention. Conversely, the whole process may seem so hard to understand that the model itself is rejected unused. It is hard to strike a balance, to use the results just like the output from any other method — as input to the final decision.

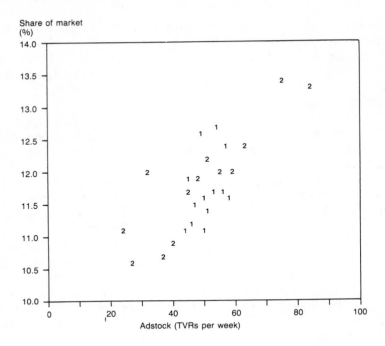

Figure 7   Four-weekly Shares of Market Against Adstock.

Experiments

'Most national advertising is done without justification. It is merely presumed to pay. A little test might show a way to multiply returns' (*Claude Hopkins, 1923*).

Advertising experimentation is another large and technical subject. Use specialists if possible and do not expect quick, cheap or decisive results (24).

The attraction of experiments is that they counter one of the objections to modelling: causality as a problem is met head on by our altering advertising weight deliberately (25). We try to keep constant, or to allow for, other marketing activities. The households that have received an advertising upweight should buy more of the brand. The difference between purchases by those at the higher weight and by those at normal weight is ascribed to the increased adspend. The experiment may not be of upweight but of downweight.

Description

The main method is the area test where the heavyweight is applied to one or more TV regions. In the UK, the best known method of analysing area tests is AMTES (Area Marketing Test Evaluation System), supplied by Abbey Management Services (26). Examples (as in *Advertising Works* case histories) are most convincing when a copy change has been tested (other marketing changes can equally be the subject of experiment), but we are concerned here with advertising weight.

With systematic recording of the results of a number of experiments, some generalizations become possible. For example, Beecham have summarized the results of using AMTES on 18 advertising weight tests and 21 copy tests, between 1973 and 1980. The weight tests included both upweights and downweights. Though the sizes of the advertising weight changes were not given, it is likely they were mostly plus or minus 50%, or double weight. The copy tests were all expected to show improved sales due to new copy. The results are given as estimates of the percentage changes in sales (compared with a control area where the original weight or existing copy was run).

Sales Change, Percentage, from Weight and Copy Tests

	Below −10%	*−10% to 0*	*0 to +10%*	*Over +10%*
Number of weight tests	1	6	4	7
Number of copy tests	1	8	4	8

This table suggests that the sales effects of major advertising budget changes can be of the order of 10% or more in sales (compare with Figure 1, Chapter 2). Copy effects are of the same order of size, emphasizing the importance of brand positioning changes or creative work. However, copy changes are notoriously difficult to evaluate in advance, and some changes expected to produce increases had the opposite effect.

Electronic test markets have been available for years in the US. In that country, under controlled conditions, the heavyweight is applied by cable (in the case of TV) or another device to a selected set of households in a panel. For example, services are supplied by

BehaviorScan, AdTel and ERIM. No such service is sold in the UK. Specially-designed test services, mainly for new products, are available, but are generally unsuitable for weight tests.

The result of an experiment may be to set the budget directly. For example, we have been wondering whether to spend £2 million; a test of £2 million equivalent locally pays out within a year; the budget next year is £2 million. The help may also be directional. Perhaps £2 million did not reach payout, but we decide to go to £1.5 million nationally and to continue the local test. Note that payout sums are usually on short-term effects only.

Up to this point it has been assumed that the experiment is a one-off, to answer a particular question, as is usually the case. It is much less common to run a programme of continuous testing, perhaps combined with modelling. Such an approach is central in direct marketing (see Chapter 6). It is also applicable to packaged goods, though it requires management commitment and time. Therefore, continuous weight testing is very rarely done, although 'as part of an overall long term program to develop sales-response and profit-maximization models' (27), a lot can be learned on the way.

Much is claimed for weight testing, but the results are often disappointing, for the reasons explained below. I do not recommend it as a routine solution to the budgeting problem.

The three examples which follow are American, since they illustrate the variety possible between test areas (the Americans have more than we in Britain do), the disturbing effects of store activity (we do not have so many data on this), and the combination of experiment and projection.

Example 28
For a food product, spot TV was bought in three cities at a weight equivalent to double the national rate. After a year, the results were as in Table 8. Note the

Table 8 **Consumption of a Food Product in an Upweight Test: Consumption Indexed on Year Ago**

Test	
Kansas City	114
Omaha	99
Des Moines	103
Control	
Remainder of USA	98

variation in consumption among the test cities. This is normal. It shows the need for robust designs and an understanding of what else has changed. As a result of this test, a 30% upweight in adspend was agreed. There was no good reason for this number, other than judgement.

Example 29

The numbers in this example are from an upweight test that was run in Jacksonville/Orlando, Kansas and Seattle. There were five control cities. ScanTrack data were available for 13 four-week periods before the test; which lasted for nine more four-week periods.

In contrast to the last example, where no other explanatory factors were measured, seven were looked at. Five were found to make significant differences in sales in the test area, compared with the control area. The first was the relative price of our brand. The others were whether the brand was on display in a store and how many major advertisements in local newspapers were replaced by a store. These two factors were recorded both for our brand and for two major competitors. The actual increase in our brand's sales was 6.4% in the test area, compared with control. However, all five of the significant other factors contributed to this improvement. That is, we were also at a slightly lower relative price in the test area, one competitor had lower display there during the test and so on.

After proper allowance was made for these effects, the conclusion was that the upweight brought us +3.7% extra sales. The extra contribution was more than the media cost added and the policy tested went national.

Example 30

This example (28) combines modelling and an experiment. AdTel was used to transmit 2695 GRPs to one group of 439 households, 39% more than to another group of 616 households that received 1932 GRPs. This test covered 36 weeks, and there were 32 previous weeks of data. A model of advertising's effects on sales was fitted to the data from the first 20 weeks of the experiment. This was successfully validated on the 16 weeks of hold-out data. The model was then used to predict theoretical maximum sales effects, which would result from an extremely heavy spend. Two numbers were then available, for each of three different spends over 36 weeks, as shown in Table 9. Such numbers obviously help the marketer to decide whether to move adspend from normal to heavy or beyond.

Table 9 Predictions of Sales Results, Based on an Upweight Test

	Adspend		
	Normal	*Heavy*	*Maximum*
Percentage of households buying at all	52	56	62
Ounces bought, per household	17	21	38

Pro

Especially when experiments are accompanied by consumer surveys, which help us to understand why the observed changes take place, we can learn a lot from a series of such experiments. We really need to run more than just one or two experiments to see the effects at different levels of adspend under different circumstances.

Cons

1. Experiments rarely affect the trade (our own representatives and retailers), so effects on them are not reproduced. This is specially important for downweights which, if reproduced nationally, might alter the brand's distribution and stocking.
2. Because experiments cost money, and are undertaken when the company is anxious to know the result, they are often stopped too early and there is no opportunity to see long-term effects.
3. Experiments with only one, or even two, test areas are easily disturbed by competitive activity and by catastrophes (distribution changes, for example). But it is hard to run an experiment with a much larger number of test areas. You would also have more faith in the results if you could cover a more representative cross-section of the country. Try to measure contaminating variables (as in Example 29) and to allow for their effects. All this advice on design and analysis results in cost and delays, though it can improve the reliability of the results considerably.
4. A good review of the problems in using experiments to help set budgets (29) points out that:
   — brand shares seldom change dramatically; in fact stability is normal, and effects take time to show
   — measurement errors or natural variation, even without marketing activity, can be as large as the changes we hope to cause
   — changes in share of voice, even for major upweights, are small; that is, to double weight from say 5 to 10% is a big actual change but a small one relative to all advertising in the category
   — factors other than advertising affect sales, and some are not measured
   — reducing weight may have a different size of effect from increasing it.

For these reasons and others, media weight tests are often disappointing. The review quoted above reports that only one in twenty US tests is conclusive. Some of these failures are due to over-expectation, such as an upweight of only 25% and a search for as much as +10% in sales within a few months. Some are due to poor execution, such as media upweights not reaching the target. But 'this is not to suggest media weight tests will always be ineffectual': they are most likely to give useable results for new products, or where there are few competitors, or where there is normally a low level of advertising.

Comment

The largest problem with weight tests is that the short-term effects of changing weight are often relatively small, and the long-term effects do not show through by the time the test has stopped or conditions change for some other reason. It may well be that the 5% market share brand that increases share of voice to 10% will increase its sales to 6%. This could be an economic return. But it may take more than a year to climb to this sales share.

By the time results are available, which may be a year or more after the decision was made to test, the problem has often changed. We may have improved product or copy, or a competitor may have made alterations, so that the new conditions are not those in which we ran the test. More drastically, a change of management priorities may have set a new budget anyway. A large proportion of tests are dropped before they have been completed; regrettably, many were set up only to postpone a decision or to protect the decision-taker.

Any test involves uncertainty in reading the results. This may be because of random sales variation or because of the effects of our, or our competitors', marketing activities. If we have not allowed for extraneous effects, the test may show an unbelievable result, or one that does not reach significance. It is advisable to pre-analyse the kind of data that will be used to read the test, and to check whether the design is sensitive enough to read the expected result.

The likelihood of reading a reliable result increases when the size of the advertising weight change is large and the test runs for a long time. As a general rule, the weight change should be 50% at least. A test should be planned to run for at least a year (though results from copy changes emerge earlier); better, two years.

Fixed Amount

Description

Management establishes a fixed amount to be spent, or the number of TVRs or magazine pages, etc. Portfolio management may be in this style, for example, 'For products turning over less than . . ., no advertising. For products over this rate, the budget is . . .'.

Comment

In this extreme form, the method is open to every objection. It is included here to make two important points. These in fact rescue the method from absurdity. Just as with the per-case allowance, and some other methods, remember that there are two levels of management involved. At the lower level, say brand management in a large conglomerate company, they are handed-down rules and actually do determine the budget: there is no discussion. At a higher financial and strategic level, determining the actual fixed amount, case rate, effective frequency, or ratio, has been the subject of debate. Several methods may have been used to help set the rule and the numbers are evaluated by their impact on company objectives and affordability. This way of operating is not itself a method: some other process is used to arrive at the fixed amount.

Next, especially when there are many brands to control, management does not want to start from scratch each year with the question, how do we do this? So it is common to have an operating procedure that settles the question quickly and cleanly. Everyone involved then knows the part that he has to play. Arguments are avoided. These are not negligible advantages. A firm decision, even if slightly wrong, is often better than a long drawn-out discussion. Especially when the whole subject seems so uncertain, why not settle the matter somewhat arbitrarily? Of course, when this happens, it is necessary to review the procedure at a high level from time to time. This may involve only a few people and is itself a lot simpler than a zero-based, detailed operation for each brand, every time.

Example 31
At the highest level in the company a competitive comparison is used to set a fixed number of TVRs. This is intended to equal the most that any competitor will put behind his brand. It is estimated from a study of competitive brand histories. A second fixed number is set. This is a maintenance level, intended as the minimum

that will convince retailers that the brand is being advertised seriously. This is agreed in discussion with senior sales staff who know their customers.

Brands are allocated to a high budget, low budget, or no advertising, on the basis of

— importance to the company
— current turnover
— planned growth.

Pros

1. The method is simple and time-saving at lower levels.
2. It is easy to administer. Changes to such budgets might improve total performance, but at a real cost in added complexity.

Con

The method is only as good as the process used to set the amount or guidelines.

Ten Per Cent Reserve

Chapter 3 described the use of part of the advertising budget as an unofficial reserve. The following is a formal method.

Description

After a budget has been agreed, 10% (or some other proportion) is added. This is a reserve that may be drawn on in an emergency.

Pro

Provided that it is an addition, the reserve helps the marketer to meet unforeseen problems. If none arises, it may nevertheless be spent, adding at least to long-term effects.

Con

Sometimes the reserve is not added to a sensible budget but held back from it. This defeats the attempt to set a realistic budget. Experienced managers bluff and argue for 10% more than they expect to receive.

Comment

Specific advertising reserves are not recommended. General reserves, or sources to borrow from, are good practice, provided they are genuinely allocated to general needs. When the unexpected does happen, the marketing director should have available ways to make the most of opportunities. The budget itself should be what we really expect to spend.

Surveys on Budget-setting

At least 20 surveys have been carried out, in the UK and US, on the methods used by advertisers. They have offered conclusions on how budgets are set, as well as commenting on the differences over time, between types of business, and between countries (30).

Some of these surveys were done as academic exercises, with small samples and limited resources. These restrictions cause problems, because considerable time and experience are required to find out how, even in a single firm, the budget decision is actually made. Such depth cannot be expected when an MBA student carries out a telephone interview. Nor can much light be thrown when the results from one sample of 25 firms is compared with another sample, using a different technique, of 40 firms.

These surveys tend to paint a simplified picture: you get the (false) impression that each method is mechanically applied and the negotiations and compromises are omitted. In fact, budgets are invariably talked up and down according to the pressures and personalities involved. The methods used, as pointed out above, are only starting-points. The most which you should expect from such surveys is a listing of some of the methods, with a rather weak indication of their popularity. In no way should this be used to decide what is likely to work in your case.

Surveys which were much larger than usual have been carried out by Dr James Lynch and Dr Graham Hooley of the University of Bradford Management Centre (31). Both these surveys recognize that no single method is likely to be used in isolation from either other methods or the wider complexities of any commercial budget-setting process. In the study reported in 1988, over 1300 replies were received from what proved to be a representative sample of British business. While this survey was not specifically confined to advertising budgeting, it asked respondents 'Which . . . methods are used regularly by your company to help set advertising budgets?' A summary of responses is contained in Table 10.

Table 10   Methods Used Regularly To Help Set Advertising Budgets

	Total sample (%)	Company size [a]		
		Small (%)	*Medium* (%)	*Large* (%)
What we can afford	50	56	48	49
Objective and task	49	29	49	59
Expected sales (%)	20	14	22	21
Last year's sales (%)	8	8	9	7
Experimentation and testing	20	20	18	21
Match the competition	8	8	7	9
Totals	155	135	153	166

Source: Ref. (31).

[a] Company size definitions: annual turnover
    Small   :   below £5 million.
    Medium :   between £5 million and £25 million.
    Large   :   above £25 million.

From a detailed analysis of all the responses to the survey, Lynch and Hooley drew the following conclusions:

1. Most respondents report the regular use of more than one method in helping to set advertising budgets: budget-setting is a process involving many contributory factors.
2. The 1988 report confirms the trend noted in 1984 towards the wider use of more complex techniques. Thus, regular use of 'Objective and Task' is reported by almost half the respondents and 'Experimentation and Testing' by one-fifth.
3. As might be expected, larger companies tended to report the use of a wider range of techniques than did smaller ones, reflecting greater

expertise in the marketing function and their generally larger advertising appropriations. There was also evidence from the analysis by industry type that consumer goods marketers tended to report greater use of more advanced techniques than those in other sectors. This again reflects the typically greater role advertising plays in the consumer goods marketing mix.

General findings from a number of these surveys follow:
— Advertising budget-setting is 'largely an art. This is, most firms are "budgeting by ear". For many of them, however, this is not arbitrary decision-making, but reflects considered judgement based on experience and the reported impracticality of more sophisticated budgeting methods' (30).
— It is common to use *more than one method*.
— The *task* method (or 'Objective and Task') is used increasingly with a variety of ways of determining the task.
— The *advertising-to-sales ratio* is common, more often of anticipated sales, but quite often of last year's sales.
— *Per-case allowance*, or a budget based on unit sales, is also common; again more often of anticipated than last year's unit sales.
— *Affordable* is a frequently quoted method, though it is hard to believe that it is not a criterion always applied.
— *Arbitrary* methods are quite common, presumably meaning the person answering the survey did not know how the budgets are set.
— *Modelling* is rare, used only by a sophisticated few.

Chapter 5: Action Points

Review the methods described in this chapter and pick *all* those relevant to your situation. This means that you have the time, data, and skills required to apply them and that the thinking behind them is in tune with your company approach. Remember that you have prepared for this choice with the action points in Chapters 2 and 3 and that the results will be combined and used in Chapter 4.

Pros and cons are given under each method and are not repeated in this overview.

Advertising-to-sales ratios or A/S; Advertising-to-margin ratio or A/M;
Per-case allowance; Other allowances

All ratio and allowance methods need a way of determining the right
ratio or allowance to use. They are better as implementation methods,
down the decision line, and used to alter the budget when other factors
change, than as budget-setting methods. If a sensible study has been
made of competitors and of history, useful suggestions may emerge
about the right number to use.

Margins provide a better input than do sterling or case sales.
Expected sales for the year to come should be used (despite some
circularity in the argument), rather than previous sales.

In special cases, like regional expansion, 'other allowances' may be
relevant.

Inertia or 'same as last year'

This method is to be used seriously only when you have little
information, time, or interest. As a starting-point, last year is sensibly
used in the brand-history review method. Be sure to remember media
inflation: it is better to buy the same advertisement exposures than just
to spend the same amount.

Media inflation multiplier

This should always be taken into account, especially when using the
methods above. Do not think of the budget only in pounds, but also
record what it will buy.

Competitive comparisons

Always be aware of what your competitors are doing. As a method of
suggesting budgets, this method still requires you to decide what sort
of matching to use.

Task

As a management tool, I strongly recommend that you determine explicitly what the advertising has to do. It is often hard to take the next step — costing this job. The method should, however, be used even if the precision of the budget suggestion is low.

Affordable

The implication is that you should spend as much as you can or that the task is so large that you know in advance you will have to reduce it to what you may reasonably spend. This often applies to new or rapidly-growing brands. Remember that all suggested budgets should in any case be checked later for affordability.

Brand history review; Share of voice, Share of market; Dynamic difference; Modelling

All of these methods review the data that you hold about your brand, competitors, and category. It is very wasteful to ignore what history may teach you, so a review should always be made. Be ready, however, for regularities in budget effects being difficult to see.

The third and fourth of these methods are merely special cases of the first two, only to be tried when the data look promising and — in the case of modelling — when you have access to the expertise needed.

Experiments

These are not generally recommended, unless you have the time and expertise. In simple situations, or where you can measure and allow for other factors that complicate sales, or in direct marketing, the method is very powerful. Be sure that your case falls into one of these groups before you commit yourself to basing a budget on experiments.

Fixed Amount

Any or all of the above methods may result in a sensible suggested budget, which is then passed on down the line for implementation as a fixed amount. For managing a portfolio of many brands, this management technique may save, in time and by reducing complications, more than it risks losing by inefficiency.

Reserve

Do not allow a fixed advertising reserve. The budget should be what you decide to spend. General marketing reserves are sensible, and sometimes the advertising budget is used as a place to hold them.

Finally, I repeat that none of these methods determines the budget. The process in Chapter 4 does that.

6   Special Cases

Portfolio of Brands

Which Brands to Support

Suppose the marketing director is reviewing plans put forward by a number of brand managers. He may treat each brand quite separately, or he may look over all the brands, not only to compare the advertising budget for each but also to allocate a total media spend across them.

Allocation is legitimate, unless it is of a fixed and arbitrary amount. It is inefficient to set a total without considering what would happen if the total were larger, or smaller. However, the job is often done in two stages, and in this section we change the amount on each brand but not the total.

Companies usually follow one of two policies. In the first the brands appear to the consumer to be quite separate. In the second policy, there is an umbrella of some kind: just the manufacturer's name will do, or a slogan saying, in effect, 'Another fine brand, making life better, from . . .'. Similarly, a brand itself can appear in new flavours and new packages, even in new formulations: 'Now in pink . . . now in an easy-to-open jar . . . now an alcohol-free variety . . .'. Each of these may rely on the parent brand, or may be separately supported with advertising.

There is no doubt that coming from a respected source is a great help to a smaller brand or sub-brand. It may be possible to save on the advertising budget in this way. The trade-off is of course that the special claims and position of the small or new product get lost. This is a creative problem, not simply a budgeting difficulty.

One of the first tasks in reviewing a portfolio of brands is to consider whether you can combine, if possible, several of its constituents. Or, alternatively, not to advertise separately some of the brands, but to rely on the umbrella for their protection. Occasionally, the company may decide to support only a very few brands. When there is a strong family resemblance, the choice of a few 'pillar brands' to support many small ones may be creatively effective. When the brands are distinct in character, so that the consumer does not see them as substitutable or appreciate that it is really a range which is being advertised, this can be a dangerous policy. Neglected brands have a habit of declining, if only for trade reasons. Without minimal individual advertising, survival of the small brands may be put at risk.

We should be able to group a portfolio of brands into:
— major, individually advertised brands
— groups of brands, advertised jointly
— token advertising for some brands
— unadvertised brands.

We are left with the question: How much of the advertising support should be given to the advertised brands or groups (treating a group as one)?

Company objectives for the brands are often dictated by what is seen as their natural, inherent growth or decline, which the company believes it can influence but not turn round. This means that success is reinforced. More simply, 'Some brands are growing, some are not. Some brands are management favourites, others aren't. That's what determines budgets.'

Organizing the Budget Data

A practical way to organize the data is to make the following table across the brands:
— revenue, or total annual sterling turnover
— margin, or total gross marginal revenue (revenue less production cost)
— adspend, or media budget.

For example, information on three brands is given in Table 1 in this chapter (Brand B was the example given in Chapter 3).

Next, calculate the ratios of these entries, as in Table 2. These ratios are the ones introduced in Chapter 3, except that adspend/margin was given there since it is a more common accounting ratio. Its reciprocal, margin/adspend, is suggested here because the larger this number, the better the case for more adspend, and often this is a more natural way to think; but either ratio may be used.

Table 1   Budgets for Three Brands (£ million)

Brand	Revenue	Margin	Adspend
A	40	20	2
B	20	8	1
C	10	5	2
Total	70	33	5

Table 2   Key Ratios Derived from Table 1

Brand	Margin/ revenue (%)	Adspend/ revenue (%)	Margin/ adspend
A	50	5	10.0
B	40	5	8.0
C	50	20	2.5
Total	47	7	6.6

Using the Key Ratios

We can now evaluate the current budgets, using these two tables and our knowledge of the brands' objectives. B gets the lowest adspend. Is this correct, especially because C produces less revenue and gets twice as much adspend? In fact, B's advertising-to-sales ratio is only one-quarter of C's. Should we perhaps switch round B's and C's budgets? But B has a smaller margin than C: it is more expensive to produce. Could this be the reason that C gets so much more adspend? Or is it perhaps to establish C's product superiority in a rapidly growing sector? We may be spending now to recover the investment once the brand is well established.

Note that the method of a fixed advertising-to-sales ratio would give each brand 7%: it would not consider favouring C, despite its better margin than B or its market situation. Such an inflexible position should, of course, be rare: C's brand manager would argue against it.

Finally, A is the largest brand, producing more than half the company's gross margin. It is normal for very large brands, with their economies of scale, to get less than their share of total adspend. A's brand manager might argue that this has gone too far, putting at risk the major earner, and ask for at least a 6% advertising-to-sales ratio.

Margin/revenue and adspend/revenue are figures in normal use. Their ratio, margin/adspend, is not as common but turns out to be critical. Margin/adspend is obviously large if the margin is large (meaning that production is relatively cheap). It is also large if the advertising-to-sales ratio is low. More detail is given in Chapter 7. It turns out that *the larger the margin, in proportion to adspend, the better the case for more adspend* (other things being equal and increased contribution being the criterion). If we had the advertising elasticities for the brands (see Chapter 7) these should multiply margin/adspend before the ratio is used to rank the brands for possible adspend changes. *The larger this number, the better the case for more adspend.* Like all modelling conclusions, these must be treated with caution. The brand's situations and objectives, as described above, are also important and may take priority.

In this case, the main questions suggested are: Does Brand A get enough adspend? Does Brand C get too much? This depends on the other evidence we have about the brands' situations and the sales effectiveness of their advertising. At this stage we can say only that C may be overspending and that A, with a better margin than B, might get more.

Contribution is not necessarily the only criterion. If the brands are in a category where there is a common unit of volume, we might want to increase total volume. It is shown in Chapter 7 that instead of margin/adspend, we should use units/adspend for this purpose. That is, if other things are equal (we do not know anything about elasticities, for instance), we should rank the brands by units/adspend to see which has the best case for more adspend. If we had the advertising elasticities for the brands, then elasticity × units/adspend should be used to rank them.

Action points

This section assumes that there are several advertised brands to consider. Decide whether their advertising budgets are determined separately, or whether an allocation may be made across the brands. In the latter case, decide first which brands, or groups of brands, are to be advertised. Construct a table of key ratios, as Table 2, as well as assembling the facts about each brand. Make the comparisons suggested in this section, in order to help your judgement as to whether each brand is receiving relevant support.

Note that formulae in Chapter 7 suggest allocations. 'Managing

Four Brands', in Chapter 8, also discusses allocation.

New products

This section discusses how to set an advertising budget for a new product. The new product may be based on a genuine breakthrough, which is a novelty in the marketplace. Or it may be a me-too, following a competitor. Third, it may be a line extension. We cannot expect all of these types to behave in the same way.

Both the second and third products are, in some ways, like established brands. How to handle their planning and budgeting is somewhere between the really new case, and the way recommended in the rest of this book. Therefore, I concentrate here on the breakthrough product. I assume that it is being launched for the first time. The launch may, of course, itself be a regional one.

New products differ from established brands in three obvious ways:

1. The company has no history to go on for this product. It has to rely on laboratory consumer research, not marketplace experience.
2. Retailers need to be persuaded to stock and display the product. This means they have to decide that some other product gives way. There has to be a good reason for a retailer to take an unproven product.
3. Consumers are also unfamiliar with the product. The image and history of use that accompany established brands are not available. Consumers may be unaware of a need for the product or even what it is for.

The brand's marketing plan is therefore hard to write. It is not an adaptation of last year's plan or of actual history. For this reason, manufacturers rely heavily on general experience with other new products. This may be their own experience, or details gleaned about other roughly similar cases, or is based on the information available from research and advertising agencies. US companies usually have more launch experiences than UK companies, and the modelling examples I quote are American.

So the plan is often based on what the manufacturer knows about a few recent examples or what an agency can generalize from previous cases, although not all of them are obviously relevant. In these collections there are often strong patterns: in some ways, all new products start equal, so that it makes more sense to look at such averages than it does for going brands.

The money for the new product may be additional, coming from the company's general resources. Overall payout is not often expected in the first year. Sometimes, other brands in the company suffer in the launch year, as their budgets are cut back to provide funds. In this way the company's total advertising spend is kept roughly constant. The first policy — additional money — was used in more than half the cases in a survey carried out by Leo Burnett USA about its clients' practices.

The Process for New Products

The process recommended in Chapter 4 mostly still applies. Some parts have to be skipped, and some of the methods that suggested budgets in Chapter 5 require special consideration.

The brand's objectives will include the positioning of the new product: how do we want it to be seen by the trade? By purchasers? By consumers? Thus the main work is to establish this position, to reach a specified level of distribution, and so to sell the volume forecast. These sales separate into the important first trial purchases and then repeated purchases following trial as the brand establishes itself in buying reportoires. Often the result of trial is consumer disappointment. Then consumer sales, which looked encouraging to the manufacturer for a period or two, fall off in later periods. Typically, a high proportion of first year's sales come from trial.

The effects of advertising that we expect are therefore:
— to communicate facts and images to purchasers and consumers
— to help get distribution, which is often a major problem for new products and is a specific media objective: merchandising the advertising plan to retailers is a powerful aid
— to stimulate the trial purchases
— to sustain repeat purchases.

Methods

Of the methods available to suggest budgets for established brands, some are obviously inapplicable for new products: inertia, media inflation multiplier, brand history review (that is, for the brand itself) and dynamic difference. Some can be considered under the general heading 'Fixed amount': ratios and allowances may be included in this way. Experiments are a special case, because we are considering here the original decision on what to spend, but I give one example below of an extension from regional launches. The task and competitive comparisons methods require norms and are considered below under 'Models'. There is also one new method: twice the market share.

Thus there are only five methods available:

1. Fixed amount
2. Experiments
3. Affordable
4. Twice the market share
5. Models.

Fixed Amount

If we have a regular series of launches, we soon establish norms. Other people's launches also provide norms. These may be applied as a ratio or per case allowance based on expected sales, but a media plan or TVR level is more often taken as the fixed amount.

Pro
The method is simple to use once the norms are established.

Con
There is a trade off between building up norms, which implies rather standard media plans, and experimenting with new media ideas. The experiments may be more relevant to the individual product, but then comparability is lost.

Example 1
Nabisco regularly launched two or more new crackers every year and used very similar campaigns. 'We start with a six-week burst. For the first three weeks we buy 135 GRPs and then 75 to 85 for the next three. We drop coupons in the second week. This is the best time for us because it ties in well with displays in stores. [To distribute coupons] we either use newspaper supplements or *Reader's Digest* in combination with ROP or the women's service books and *TV Guide*' (1).

Example 2
A collection is kept by Leo Burnett USA of launch case histories. Most of these are of packaged goods. There are currently 63 examples where consumer surveys were carried out six to eight weeks after launch. At this time the cumulative ratings were recorded. The average was 1200. The top quintile averaged 2500. At 14 to

16 weeks, there were 39 surveys. Cumulative ratings then averaged 1700. The top quintile now averaged 3200.

These numbers give a feel for the number of ratings used early on in typical American packaged goods launches and in heavyweight launches. To calculate equivalent budgets we have to extend the ratings at current costs and commercial length.

Experiments

If your brand is going into the marketplace for the first time, you cannot be helped by previous experience, but you may deliberately run a number of different budget levels in regional launches in order to help a later, national decision.

Pro
Careful testing obviously improves the chances of the new product's success. Some in-market experience is very desirable.

Con
Experiments take time and alert competitors.

> *Example 3*
> When Kronenburg beer was first introduced to the US, it was test marketed in Washington DC and in Miami. Both campaigns were in TV, radio and print, but the Washington plan was at $4 million national equivalent and the Miami plan at $2 million. At the higher rate, 'sales really seemed to take off', and that helped the national launch decision (1).

Affordable

Many marketers believe, in my view correctly, that you get only one chance with a new product. If you fail, it is almost impossible to try again because of trade scepticism. There had better be a real, extra product improvement the second time, if you are forced to launch twice. It is better to succeed the first time.

Therefore, every resource possible should be put behind the launch. These activities should be coordinated, so that one activity supports another. It is usual to front-load, that is, to spend a high proportion of the budget early (though not before distribution is satisfactory). This helps to establish repeat purchase as soon as possible, and generates the all-important trade confidence in the product. The budget should err on the side of generosity, not caution. The higher efficiency of advertising during a launch (see below) points the same way.

'Above average ad spending on a new product can help to hedge financial risk and increase the probability of reaching breakeven. The greater the new product investment relative to the equity [risk] capital in the firm's financial structure, the greater the need to reach breakeven sales volume quickly.

'If the new product is substantially better than other products and is first in the marketplace, the advertiser can reap big rewards for a longer period of time by saturating the market and staking out a large share' (2).

Twice the market share

Peckham (3) argued, using American data, that there is a relationship between share of advertising and share of market for successful new products. In his analysis, share of advertising was calculated as the average over each bi-month for two years. Share of market was taken as the percentage of category in the last of these bi-months. Only products which were genuinely new were included, not line extensions or changes in packaging or formula. They had a demonstrable and unique consumer advantage. They were launched with good promotional support by skilled sales forces. The data for this first analysis were from the 1960s.

The products differed in the ratio of share of advertising to share of market. For some, this was close to one; for others, two or more. On average, the ratio was 1.7. 'Importantly, share of advertising is not an in-and-out affair, but is consistently maintained over an entire two-year period.'

Discrepancies from the average ratio were for believable reasons. For example, six of the brands succeeded at relatively low share of advertising to share of market ratios. Five of these turned out to be 'the first brands in their respective fields to adequately exploit a demonstrable, believable consumer plus over other brands then on the market'. Conversely, brands requiring larger ratios to succeed, say up to three, had 'minimum consumer plus characteristics — relatively minor degrees of difference from other brands then on the market.'

Thus, to do equally well, you must spend more to launch an average product than you need for a good one, or at the same spend, the good product will do better. 'If product differences are minor or perhaps difficult to develop into an effective copy story, you will probably find it necessary to increase your advertising by 50% or more'.

The data from the 1960s have been checked with later experience. In both 1971 and 1978, the ratios had hardly changed (4): successful new brands' spend on media advertising was such that share of advertising again averaged 1.7 times share of market. For products where the share of voice was high, so was the final share of market.

The explanation given of the relationships observed might today be questioned. Comparative prices, and other marketing activities, might also be studied before settling on a recommended ratio. More important, some self-selection is going on. The products with the best chances of success (seen in consumer research and early trade acceptance) may have also been given the largest budgets. Nevertheless, frequently-used rules have been developed from these observations:

> Estimate the share of market at the end of the second year. Set the budget so that the share of advertising obtained in Years One and Two combined is twice the estimated share of market.

Note that the rule is often actually applied over *one* year rather than two. That is, if the year-end sales share aimed at is X, the advertising share over the year is set at 2X. Note also that spending at a rate above market share should generally lead to share growth according to dynamic-difference experience. It also implies a higher than average ratio for advertising to sales, which is reasonable, given the extra work advertising has to do at the time of a launch.

Pro
These rules are simple to use and often lead to a sensible budget.

Cons
1. It is often difficult to decide exactly into what category a genuinely new product fits.
2. Moreover, the category itself may have an unusually low rate of advertising, resulting in too small a budget.
3. No account is taken of the task advertising has to do when the rules are applied strictly. If the task is hard (a proposition difficult to communicate, for example, or a product with no relevant advantage), then the budget may be too small. The range of results noted above, and the reasons for it, are important.

Example 4
We aim at 5% share of market. Category spend, apart from our brand, is estimated to be £30 million next year and £33 million the year after. Competitive spend is therefore £63 million over two years. To get 10% (twice 5%) share of total spend, we must budget to spend £7 million over the next two years.

From this rule comes another, which is applied not to share of voice, but to the advertising-to-sales ratio or the per-case allowance (2):

Estimate the sales rate after the end of Year Two. Fix a ratio or allowance which will be used for Year Three onwards. This gives a quarterly adspend rate.

Use *three* times this quarterly rate in the first quarter of Year 1. Reduce adspend regularly each quarter, until it reaches the Year 3 level, so that in the first two years the total is double the final rate.

Example 5
We expect to sell 2 million cases a year when the brand has settled down after the first two years. The per-case allowance for advertising is then expected to be £2. The quarterly adspend rate is therefore set at 2 million × £2 × 1/4 = £1 million for the third year.

In the first quarter of the launch, the budget is three times this or £3 million. This is reduced in each of the next eight quarters by 2/7 of the final quarterly rate.

Thus, in the first year, we spend 3 + 2.72 + 2.43 + 2.14 = £10.29 million. In the second year we spend 1.86 + 1.57 + 1.28 + 1.00 = £5.71 million. In later years we spend £4 million.

In the first two years together we spent £16 million, which is double the later annual rate.

New Product Models

The description given at the beginning of this section of the effects we expect from advertising easily translates into specific tasks. Generating awareness and inducing trial are two jobs particularly well suited to the task method. This approach depends on having usable, expected relationships between the TVR levels set and their results.

When data are available on a number of launches, such as awareness, trial and repeat purchase rate, it is not difficult to fit them with a model. Many models therefore exist (5), and many successes are claimed for them. The underlying assumptions are not always obvious, and it is hard to get validity checks, so it is not easy to be sure of the models' reliability and generality. However, these models are often the best guide we have to the effects of changing marketing activity. Most of them can be used to investigate the predicted results of different advertising schedules, including different adspends.

A new product model can be used to predict year-end sales at different levels of adspend. The results can be costed, to show the changes in contribution as well as in share. The decision on how much to spend can be helped directly. The model also can be used to estimate the sales elasticity of advertising which in turn is used in a what-if budgeting model (this is explained in Chapter 7). We are also able to compare the elasticities for launches with those for established brands. In our experience, new product elasticities are much larger: 0.60 or even higher values are common, whereas 0.25 is high for going brands.

Because models spell out the larger return expected from advertising for new products, bigger budgets may be set than would otherwise be the case: 'In the introduction of [Totino's pizza], we estimated its advertising elasticity by computer models. This made it possible for the Pillsbury Company to set advertising strategy from a knowledge of the expected results which, in turn, gave management the confidence to use much higher levels of advertising for its frozen pizza product category than had been used in the past' (6).

Example 6
A new food product was required to reach 5% share of its category by the end of its first year. From consumer research, this was believed to be achievable only if trial levels were high, say 20 to 25% of category users. The advertising agency used its new product model to estimate that in this case the relation between GRPs and trial was as follows:

GRPs	% trying the product
500	7
1000	15
1500	20

Thus 1500 GRPs was agreed as the minimum and $5 million were required to buy the schedule suggested.

A model that allows for changes in several variables obviously gives a wider range of alternatives.

Example 7
The forecasts in Table 3 are from the Hendry System (7) and look at alternative adspends and price in a particular case. Only some of the published results are given in the table. The real decision, as with established brands, is not as simple as maximizing contribution. We need to balance a larger immediate return against establishing a sounder long-term base. The first scenario (low media spend and high price) gives the largest profit but a low sales share. The third scenario (high media spend and low price) gives a lower contribution but a much higher share.

Table 3   Three Strategies for a new Product, with Share and Profit Forecasts

Adspend ($MM)	Price (cents/unit)	Share (%)	Gross profit − adspend ($MM)
3.2	95	8.5	15.2
8.6	89	11.6	13.0
10.7	86	12.6	11.4

Example 8

The Leo Burnett new product model gave as its central forecast year-end sales of 12 000 tons. This forecast assumes 2200 GRPs, which cost $10 million. Gross margin was $1900 per ton. Sensitivity analyses showed that the advertising elasticity was 0.57. That is, 1% additional adspend gave 0.57% increase in sales. The cost of this much extra advertising is clearly $100 000 (one per cent of $10 million). After production costs, the additional revenue would be

$$12\ 000 \times \$1900 \times 0.57/100 = \$130\ 000.$$

Thus additional adspend pays off even in the short term. It also increases year-end sales and so establishes the product on a firmer base for the second year. As it happened, the marketer was considering a reduction in GRPs. This analysis persuaded him that, far from saving money, the cut would increase the year-end financial loss on the new product. It would also seriously endanger the sales volume. In fact, the 15% budget cut being considered was estimated to reduce sales by a thousand tons. The cut was not made.

Example 9

John Philip Jones (8) quotes the case of Brand Q which had two tasks. First, it was neck-and-neck with competitor R for brand leadership. In fact, in 1975 both had equal market share, at 18%, and equal share of voice, at 11%. But Brand Q's manufacturer was also trying to launch Brand G, which clearly took funds from Q. Despite high investment spending for five years or so, and no less than 8% share of voice in 1979, Brand G had then reached only 3% share of market.

The manufacturer fell between two stools. He failed to establish Brand G satisfactorily and made only small profits there. At the time, Brand Q, probably because of lowered management attention as well as reduced advertising, lost two share points. Jones calls this a 'classic case . . . a disappointing new brand G funded in the main from a large and successful brand Q, which is now also suffering from this unproductive syphoning of expenditure'.

This deplorable practice is particularly common when a manufacturer diversifies. I have seen projects in the new and risky field, with which the manufacturer is not familiar, take media spend, attention, and ultimately sales from the old but reliable profit earner.

Survey of Methods Used

The methods used to suggest budgets for new products occur with different frequencies from those for going brands (discussed in Chapter 5). In a survey of its client practice, Leo Burnett USA found the following distribution of methods, in percentages:

Fixed amount determined by previous own launch experience	21%
New product model used to evaluate alternative spending levels	20
Similar to competitive launches	18
Affordable after required payout plan	18
Task, to meet volume objectives	13
Task, to meet media plan or brand awareness objectives	5
Per case allowance	5

In the same survey, it was found that in over half the cases the new product was allowed more than one year at a budget level above what an established brand would normally command. That is, the launch took more than a year.

Action Points

I assume that the product is at its initial launch, without in-market experience (if you have this experience, use the Brand history review in Chapter 5). Review the way advertising is planned to help the brand meet its objectives: there are suggestions in this section. Turn these into specific tasks. Decide which of the following methods are applicable to help suggest a budget:

1. *Fixed amount*, using previous experience of your own or of your competitors.
2. *Experiments* may be planned during the launch, in order to see the effects of different media spend levels.
3. *Affordable*, which states that every possible pound will be raised to ensure the new product's success.
4. *Twice the market share* and similar rules of thumb set out in this section.
5. *Modelling*, specifically with a new product model. This turns the

tasks agreed above into media spend, or answers what-if questions about the likely effects of different budgets.

Remember that the new product is likely to have only one chance and that advertising usually has a greater effect per pound during the first few months than at any later time in the product's life.

Direct Marketing

'At midnight on July 18 1987, Cable Value Network, a Minneapolis-based cable home shopping organization, sold $173 000-worth of 30-inch, 14K gold chains in 20 minutes. By Friday of the following week, jewellery sales had reached nearly $19 million' (9).

The quotation above comes from a world different from the one in which most TV advertisers live. Details of two other real direct-response campaigns can be found in *Advertising Works*. The scale of the two is very different. In the first (The British Film Institute, 1981), the investment and direct return were both under £20 000. The second (National Savings Bank Investment Account 'Save-by-Post', 1983) invested £400 000 and brought in over £50 million.

If you are a direct marketer, this section has nothing new for you. It is written to point out the main differences between direct and traditional advertising. The traditional advertiser can learn from direct mail, telephone selling, catalogues and the like. Much of what is said applies also to business-to-business, but that is covered more particularly in the next section.

Direct marketing has been called non-store marketing. Its essence is that sales are not made through a retailer, who changes the price of the product to consumers and adds other marketing activities of his own, although some direct marketing assists the flow through retailers.

It follows that the offer made to the consumer is totally under the control of the marketer. The price he sets, the description of the brand, delivery and so on are his responsibility alone. It also follows that the consumer's response is known to the marketer. There is no pipeline, filled by the marketer's deliveries to the trade and emptied by retail sales to the consumer. Most important to the marketer, he gets all the money that the consumer pays: there is no retailer margin. This has influenced the rapid growth of this sector of advertising.

In addition, of course, are 800-numbers, freephone, freepost, post codes, ACORN, PiN, MOSAIC, databases of many kinds and all the computerization which makes a lot of direct marketing possible; and the apostles who spread the gospel that 'MaxiMarketing is the new direction in marketing in which the prospects who are potentially your best customers are identified, located, persuaded, motivated, converted, and cultivated in a way that maximizes sales and profits' (10).

All these differences add up to another real distinctiveness of direct marketing: the sales effects of marketing activity are measurable. Not only *can* they be measured (with far higher precision than when the retailer intervenes), but the measurements are routinely *applied* to decisions.

Direct marketers are ingenious in finding new ways to use media of all kinds; some they have created for the purpose. They also key responses so that the efficiency of each medium is revealed. Direct marketers are much more open about their techniques than traditional marketers are. Of course, we hear only about successes, but that is normal. Read *Direct Response*, the monthly magazine of direct marketing, or visit the Direct Marketing Fair. For British examples, see the documentation of the Montreux Direct Marketing Symposia for brief case histories from Europe as well as from America. These demonstrate the learning that is possible.

This determination to experiment and to measure is the key lesson for the traditional advertiser. He should look equally hard for ways to uncover the effects of advertising, and so to help budget setting.

Example 10
Two publications are being considered for a couponed advertisement. A new product is to be put on sale and will return £20 per unit after delivery and other processing costs. This is called the allowable margin or allowable cost. If the actual advertising cost per response is below the allowable cost then you are in profit. For the publications considered, we have the circulation and space cost for an insertion:

Publication	Circulation ('000)	Space cost (£)	Cost per thousand circulation (£)
A	1000	3000	3
B	750	1500	2

In packaged goods space buying, we would go on to consider the readership profiles, the reach and frequency of various combinations of the publications, and so on. Such numbers are used by media planners for a direct campaign, but only as directional and provisional. We can now calculate what percentage of the circulated households need to buy in response to the advertisement, in order for us to break even. This figure is

$100 \times$ space cost/(circulation $\times$ £20)

or (C/000)/(10 $\times$ £20)

and is 0.015% for Publication A, 0.010% for B.

Next we consult our records for the history of response for similar products advertised in these publications. These may tell us that, although Publication A has the higher breakeven, it also has a response rate record so far above B's that we are much more confident of a profit from advertising there.

What should the budget be? It is determined initially by a managerial decision: 'Let's use A only and see how it goes', or 'Two ads in A, one in B, to try the water.' Thereafter, results for this product are analysed in a continuous programme of comparative testing. What about Publications C and D? Is A still the most effective? Is the space size and position used the most efficient? Would broadcast support make our print advertising more productive? And so on.

Another way of stating the formula given above is that, at breakeven, the value to you of an order will equal the total cost of your activities, per hundred, divided by the rate of response per hundred. In a direct mail shot, for example, the 'hundred' is a hundred mailings sent out, and the cost includes design, printing, addressing, postage and so on.

Naturally, response must be correctly defined. It is not enough to get a reply; what you need is a sale. Indeed, it has been said (11) that large numbers of replies are nothing to get excited about, since they can threaten profitability. This is because of the cost of handling every lead, many of which do not eventually lead to a sale. 'The most notorious medium for producing loose leads is television, using a telephone response mechanism.' A case is quoted for holiday tour operators converting only 3% of such leads into sales. On the other hand, the Automobile Association (AA) has sold insurance by phone, from leads produced off the page and with TV support. This is because for this product the explanation of the offer by a knowledgeable person is very helpful in making the sale.

You will easily see the extension of Example 10 into copy testing and into budget size testing, just as the tour operator and AA examples are about media choice.

The budget-setting itself is no different from the procedure for any business decision. Because it is about the future, risk is still involved. Direct marketers do not know what the ideal budget should be, but they get closer than the rest of us. The monitoring process corrects the budget size continuously.

The decision on where to start, before you have any results, can be tricky. Experience is the best guide, but you can never be quite sure how relevant this is in a new case. Sometimes you have to go directly to a major decision: 'Testing advertising media, especially big national ones, is far more risky, expensive and difficult [than sampling from a list]' (12).

For example, Abbey Life Assurance decided to support their salespeople with a major PR, advertising and direct campaign (13). This used data collected from a specially commissioned consumer survey, which disclosed that three times as much was spent by respondents on alcohol as on life assurance. Such facts were circulated in newspaper advertisements as well as by direct mail.

The plan could not be tested, because 'without the national campaign, the results would not have been conclusive'. In this case, £300 million life cover was written in a month, compared with £100 million in the same month of the year before. The conversion rate, incidentally, was very different from the 3% quoted in the tour operator example above; it was near 70%.

Of the methods reviewed in Chapter 5, the ones direct marketers use most to suggest their advertising budgets are: task, brand-history review and experiments. It is no coincidence that the first two of these are also recommended as the most powerful for traditional advertisers. Experiments are, as has already been pointed out, so much easier for the direct marketer.

Thus 'The budget should be prepared on the "task method", meaning that recommended cost estimates should be provided for achieving the objectives stated in the plan. Possible budget shortcuts and abridgements should be included if it is possible that the task-based budget is in excess of management's expectations. However, the task-based budget should be stated, even if it is unlikely that the necessary monies will be appropriated. Where there are alternatives, their effect should be clearly expressed' (14).

This advice continues, very pragmatically: 'It is a mistake to end a marketing plan with the cost of implementing the plan, for many executives scan the last pages first. The final wrap-up should restate the sales and profit expectations, to keep the final focus on what is to be gained, not on what investment is required.'

Modelling was the third main method suggested in Chapter 4 for traditional marketers. Direct marketers use this technique instinctively. They understand very well the two main principles which maximize short-term profit:

1. There are diminishing returns to large amounts spent on advertising.
2. The budget should be increased to the point where the profit from

resulting sales just matches the last advertising pound spent.

They can, at least in theory, identify where the advertising investment will pay off best: publications with a traditionally cheap response rate, parts of a mailing list most like previous responders and so on. Thus they can say where the first million media pounds should be spent, where the second million and so on. With each bundle spent goes an estimate of the return. Often the marketer works outwards or down from the group he thinks best, so determining a response function as he goes. TV and radio time may be bought on a guaranteed response basis, so the budget is flexible, depending on how well the station does.

Instead of being an aid to sales, as traditional advertising so often is, advertising is the heart of the business in direct marketing. Production costs, and the media spend, usually take higher proportions of revenue than traditionally. Because it is central, direct advertising is subject to the same sort of business disciplines and flexibility as any major business acitivity. It is not on the sidelines; it is the football.

The equivalent of production limitations may also help determine the budget. If a campaign is producing too many leads for the sales force to follow up, or if the warehouse is empty, then advertising stops. This happens rarely with traditional advertising.

There is often no discussion of long-term effects. Clearly such effects exist, whenever later advertisements have a common theme, use the same brand name or house name and so on. Such considerations affect copy: it should increase efficiency to be consistent, to reflect theme advertising elsewhere and so on. But these ideas rarely influence the budget: direct marketing expenses are expected to be paid back quickly. As usual, the start of a new brand may be an exception. A new record club or catalogue may need to establish itself with more announcement advertising, to educate its potential customers, and more expensively than it expects later. You do not become a Littlewoods overnight or without investment.

In the financial field it has been argued (15) that the reassurance which branding provides is in fact an essential ingredient. This can, of course, be tested when a list is used. In one case, half a mailing received a proposition from an established life company, half received the identical proposition, but from a major bank. The bank received twice as many responses. The perceived value of the branding can even be seen as worth some of the cost. A direct-response advertisement can be thought of as a corporate advertisement — with a coupon.

'Say you spend £100 000. If you get £120 000 back you've succeeded, if you get back £80 000 you've failed. Or have you? Looked at another way, £100 000 worth of corporate communication has generated £80 000 of direct income, thus costing only £20 000. It seems like a good deal.' There is striking similarity here with the point in Chapter 3 that consumer goods advertising may actually be economic even when the direct, short-term return is below breakeven, because of indirect and long-term effects. It is pleasing to find this argued in the hard-headed direct field.

Note that 'paid back quickly' does not mean 'within a week', even when overall payback is required. The response initially measured may require careful evaluation. First, it may have to be reduced, to allow for the real income we are expecting. The potential purchaser, who responds by returning a coupon which requests a brochure, may not buy from it or from the salesman who subsequently calls. Leads have to be reduced to conversions, as has already been pointed out. Second, it may have to be increased, for a similar reason. The new annual subscriber to a magazine may generate revenue additional to the first subscription, from renewals, and from response to other mailings. Third, the response first measured may have to be increased to allow for later response. In a fast moving business, the media buyer may have to place space orders before the results from previous insertions are all in. The most recent advertisements, whose outcome is used to evaluate the schedule, may not yet have pulled all we expect. For example, four weeks after a monthly magazine carried an advertisement we may have received only 55% of the final number of replies, though 90% from a first-class mailing and all the phoned-in orders from a broadcast spot. With experience, factors can be added for seasonality, special days and so on. These delays and variations in immediate response apply also to traditional advertising, but our measuring tools are usually too coarse to calibrate them.

Recruitment or job advertising is a special case of direct advertising. The results are simply the applicants the advertisements produce. Hence all the advice given by specialists in direct advertising still applies. There is one additional angle. In most direct work, the firm which is making the offer has some importance, but it is limited. When a firm advertises for workers, however, it is definitely selling itself. Depending on the state of the job market at the time, it may indeed have to sell in a very competitive way. Hence the advertisement is not just the simple announcement of a vacancy. The actual appearance of the advertisement will influence more than the immediate response; it will build up an image of the firm in the minds of every reader, some of whom are suppliers, competitors or potential employees in the future. Hence the element of image may have a definite role.

There are rules of thumb in this field as well as the task method. For example, the budget may be between 10 and 15% of the annual salary (16), or half the fee charged by an employment agency. But the biggest determinants are experience and a judgement on the difficulty of filling the vacancy. The importance of record keeping and the analysis of this history are obvious. A clear and helpful book (17) on the subject includes a brief chapter on response analysis, and this sets out the summaries which you require.

Business-to-business and Corporate Advertising

Most of this book is written for manufacturers who sell their products to a mass consumer market. Even these manufacturers sometimes have targets other than the consumer to influence. They may wish to speak to the financial community or to environmentalists, for example. Their trade advertising to wholesalers and retail buyers, in support of their representatives, *is* business-to-business advertising.

Manufacturers who sell to other businesses operate in a different way from consumer marketers. Corporate advertising is different again. This section comments briefly on the special problems all these advertisers face in setting their advertising budgets.

There are no exceptions to the disciplines of setting objectives and of defining what advertising has to accomplish. The marketing plan has still to be drawn up; targets and media have to be agreed. Thus the process of budget-setting starts in the usual way. The main differences from most media advertising are as follows:

1. Advertising plays a smaller part: some advertising-to-sales ratios are very small. Total industrial advertising spending is nevertheless a significant part of total advertising, and some ratios are comparable with packaged goods (see below). Comparisons with competitors are less common, since the data are often unavailable.
2. The advertising budget is in clearer competition with alternatives: PR, lobbying, visits by representatives, telephone selling, direct mail, trade shows, and so on. The effects of many of these activities can be seen more clearly than the results of advertising.
3. There may be less spent by business-to-business advertisers on finding out whether the advertising objectives were met. It is sometimes difficult to define success, so measurement of advertising's effects is more rarely attempted.
4. It should not be thought that an important difference is that business

decisions are totally rational while consumer decisions are not. There is evidence that industrial buyers, stockbrokers, and so on are influenced by values in much the same way as are housewives.

When the advertising objective is to help representatives in the field, the three main aids which advertising gives are as follows: leads, announcements, and support and comfort. These three headings may help in drawing up the advertising objectives.

Leads

A couponed ad in a trade magazine is aimed at direct response, very little different from the direct marketing to consumers discussed in the previous section. The representatives follow up these leads, so it will be unclear how much of the final sale is credited to the advertising and how much to personal selling. Nevertheless, the cost per lead is an important figure. The principles of direct marketing apply.

Announcements

Advertising may well be the most economical way to transmit news of new products and other changes and details.

Support and comfort

The representatives are not calling unannounced. They are reassured that they get some direct help from a head office which often seems far away.

The objectives of corporate advertising may be poorly defined, although clear thinking about its targets and benefits is desirable. A particular problem arises when the need for a good corporate image is appreciated too late in the day. Advertising which starts after a crisis has developed may be unable to rescue a company in trouble. Convincing examples have been given by Bob Worcester, Chairman of Market & Opinion Research International (MORI) (18).

There may well be multiple targets, including, for example, employees, stockholders, the financial community, the trades in which the company operates, and end-users for the products of individual divisions. The objectives and the budget decision are often settled right at the top of the company. A good description of the balancing required to evaluate these complex situations is in an article (19) about the effect of the recession in the early 1980s on corporate advertising.

Often survey research provides a genuine measure of advertising's effects. If the object is to change attitudes, then a survey result is no longer a surrogate, provided that the research is done adequately. So a campaign intended to influence opinion about a company or an issue can be guided in the same way as a direct marketing campaign. 'Frequently it is easier to find out whether a corporate advertising programme is achieving its objectives than to determine whether product advertising is achieving its sales objectives' (20).

Again, Bob Worcester has given examples (21) of the sort of image dimensions measured by MORI and of the movements which are possible. Dunlop in 1976 had a well-established image, but 'research had shown it to be tied to industries which did not enjoy favourable reputations'. In a single year, after an imaginative campaign, the increases in Table 4 were recorded.

Table 4   Dunlop Image Profile

	Oct–Nov 1976 (%)	*Oct–Nov 1977 (%)*
Products are the leaders in their field	29	45
Products of the highest quality	34	40
Live up to their guarantees and promises	20	24
Imaginative, forward-looking management	6	10
Contribute significantly to the export drive	8	25
You can believe their advertising	21	25

Base: all adults who have heard of Dunlop.
Source: MORI.

Corporate advertising is also evaluated by the respect that the advertiser gets from his peers, the share price via City opinion, salespeople gaining entrance to prospects, and so on. The chairman, the finance director and the sales director evaluate largely by judgement the effects of their advertising.

Budget setting

The process summarized at the end of Chapter 4 still applies. There is nothing to be gained by omitting the four reviews suggested there: objectives, draft and recent budgets, market history and forecast, the evidence of advertising effects.

It is again useful to have several methods that suggest possible budgets. Chapter 5 should be scanned in search of input, but the methods most likely to apply are those which follow.

Since there may be little information to help the decision on how much to spend, the *Task* method is often used in a rough and ready way. The task is defined simply by the media schedule: so many insertions of such a size in this list of magazines, for example. The manager making the decision often has a sense of what is needed to do the job. One advertisement exposure a month in a key publication feels right, and there is little chance to prove wrong the manager who makes such a statement. The task method may, however, dig deeper into the objectives. This is when they are well defined, as leads for salespeople, or a score in an opinion survey, for example. Then history may be available on which to base a better estimate.

Corporate advertisers should be distinguished from industrial or business-to-business advertising. An excellent guide (20) includes, unusually, a chapter on budgeting. This recommends the task method, with one eye on the spend by similar corporations. It notes also that the seniority of the agency staff which is desirable, plus the relatively small size of the appropriation, often make it advisable to pay a fee to the agency handling a corporate account.

In some business-to-business situations, you may actually be in direct marketing (see above), when a *History review* and *Experiments* are also usable methods.

At the other extreme, the *Inertia* method plus a *Media inflation multiplier* may be applicable. In other words, 'We always run this schedule'.

Competitive comparisons often lead to the share of voice argument: 'To make the trade see us as big as Smith, we'd better spend as much as Smith does'. You should certainly know what your competitors, or firms of comparable size and situation, are spending.

The *Ratio* and *Allowances* methods are unlikely to apply to corporate advertising, but become possible when the direct support of salespeople or products is used as the criterion. It has been suggested (2) that a ratio of the field costs can be set: if salespeople are expected to perform X% of the selling job, then (100 − X)% of the total marketing budget should go to other tools, including advertising. The number X, 'for companies that rely on personal selling, . . . [is] typically in the 66% to 90% range.'

The third step in Chapter 4 is often quickly taken. Is the budget affordable, or is the bottom line threatened? This question seldom raises a problem. Is the advertising objective achievable with this spend? This question can rarely be answered objectively: we return to the judgement decision mentioned above.

Finally, experiments or analyses to measure advertising effects should be considered, so that we will be in a better position next year to answer the question. BP, for example, have published several papers on the evaluation of their campaigns, including the analysis of weight tests. Generally, less is attempted in this area than for packaged goods. However, experiments are not as impossible as is sometimes thought, even in business-to-business work. An American example follows.

An American Business-to-business Advertising Experiment

As noted above, a large proportion of the business-to-business marketing effort goes into face-to-face selling. Some manufacturers place only a few token advertisements in the relevant trade magazines. These manufacturers were the target of a research study, organized by the Advertising Research Foundation and the Association of Business Publishers. The report (22) should be read for the detail, but it is briefly summarized here.

Three typical non-advertised new products were selected (see Table 5). Controlled circulation trade publications were used for advertising these products, at three different media weight levels. The businesses receiving these publications were randomly divided into three groups.

Table 5   Design of ARF/APB Experiment

Product and price	Total advertising pages for low, medium, high cells	Advertising test period
Portable safety product	8	November 1984
	14	to
Less than $10	28	October 1985
Commercial transportation	0	February 1985
component package	18	to
About $10 000	36	January 1986
Highly specialized	2	August 1985
laboratory equipment	6	to
Between $5000	12	July 1986
and $10 000		

The first received only light advertising; the two other groups received copies with extra inserts bound in. Which business fell into each group was unknown to the manufacturers, so disturbing influences were impossible. Other marketing activity was controlled as much as possible. Thus sales and other changes could reasonably be attributed to the experiment alone. This was a massive test: $400 000 was contributed by sponsors; the magazine publishers absorbed the extra binding costs and charged only half the extra insertion costs.

The experiment was assessed in various ways. Sales were tracked for the three products, over time and for each cell in the design. Reader service inquiries were counted. Attitude and awareness information was obtained.

For all three products, sales by year-end rose more among businesses in the medium exposure cell than in the low exposure cell. Sales in the high exposure cell were larger again. Significant sales increases started four months after the first insertions. There were similar improvements in salespeople's leads from the reader inquiries. For two products, cost data were available, and profit improvements, after paying for the advertising, were demonstrated.

In the second year, when all advertising returned to the low level, sales among the medium and highly-exposed businesses continued at the level reached at the end of the experiment: buying habits seemed to have been modified.

Surveys of awareness and advertisement recall did not produce such clear results. Changes post-test were sometimes non-significant and inconsistent across the cells, though mostly positive results were found. The disappointing parts of this survey research are not unusual and carry an imporant message: indirect and surrogate measures are not reliable as an indicator of sales results. When both are available, use sales data. The clues we get from survey research may, however, help us to understand how the extra sales occurred: in this case, for one product, dealers clearly improved their recall of the advertisements while the gain among end-users was much less. Thus influencing the dealers was important.

The ARF/APB study is a model for research in a field where experiments are rare. Its findings may be projectable to a wider spectrum, given the diversity of the products involved. The two conclusions of most interest are:

— more advertising means more sales
— increased business-to-business advertising can result in higher profits.

Surveys on Industrial Budget-setting

In Chapter 5 I warned against surveys (usually with small samples) as a way of describing what methods are used to suggest advertising budgets. An exception is a mailed survey that 560 UK industrial marketers returned (23).

As expected, advertising and sales promotion were much less often ranked by industrial marketers as of overall importance (first or second) in obtaining business (6% compared with 27% for consumer marketers). But advertising and sales promotion matter almost as much to industrial marketers when new products are launched.

When methods used to suggest budgets were examined, there were clear differences between small and large advertisers. Four methods merged as important in themselves and more used by large advertisers. These are

Task

Advertising to sales (in fact, expected sales)

Experiments

Competitive comparisons (particularly, desired share of voice).

The affordable method was reported as used most often; although not reported, the inertia method was doubtless also often used.

Reference was made above to the problem of identifying and quantifying category sales. Often there are no data on competitors' sales so that, even when we know their media advertising expenditure and schedules, we cannot relate these to their turnover, let alone to their margin. The very idea of a category, or of a sales share, or even of a brand, may be alien to the way the advertiser thinks. A second problem is that a wider range of activities than in consumer marketing is funded from the budget called 'advertising'. For example, brochures and exhibitions play a larger part.

An attempt was nevertheless made to indicate what may be typical budgets and advertising-to-sales ratios for business-to-business advertisers. The exercise cannot be called a survey, but a collection of data was made by the Business-to-Business Committee of the Institute of Practitioners in Advertising, early in 1988.

A clear finding was that, from a large number of advertisers about whom information was sought, only a small proportion could provide any data. For 22 budgets, the range of sizes, for main media, including direct mail and all production costs, was from £15 000 to half a million pounds. These represented advertising-to-sales ratios between 0.2% and 6%. It may be surprising that, in as many as seven out of 19 budgets for which sales turnover was known, the A/S ratio was over

2%; a respectable figure, even for packaged goods. There was no indication that larger market shares were associated with smaller ratios, as is the case with packaged goods.

Stretching a small budget

The job advertising is expected to do would often cost more than the brand can apparently afford. This intensifies the search for efficiencies in the advertising plan. It also raises the following questions: Should we reduce the advertising objectives? If so, how? This section gets us close to the details of media planning, on which the advertising agency's input is needed. But, since the balancing of ends and means (see Chapter 4) is a critical part of budget determination, some alternatives are briefly outlined here.

The budget involved need not be literally small. The problem is just as real when millions of pounds are involved as when there are thousands. Indeed, it is particularly acute when a brand has habitually bought national and nearly continuous advertising, but now finds that this cannot be afforded. The point is that the budget is too small for the job that, it has been suggested, it should do.

We consider in turn:
   media choice
   target definition
   regional allocation
   time allocation
   and the advertisements themselves.

The place to start for all of these is at the advertising strategy and objectives. Who is in our prime target, how do we identify them and how can advertising be planned to reach them economically? The way we then spend less is to concentrate sufficient weight on our best prospects.

1. Media choice. This choice depends on the target definition and on the advertisements; all the aspects of the plan are inter-related. They are separated here only for discussion, but are not determined one at a time.

Often this decision comes in the form: Should we be in TV or in some other medium? Or, if in TV, on Channel 4 or TV-am? Sometimes a mix of media is indicated, for example starting a campaign in TV but continuing it on outdoor or radio. The answer may of course lie outside traditional media. Direct marketing or some form of promotion may be the solution in your case. Remember that the method you choose needs to add value, and should not simply cash in on the value your brand may now have, and perhaps reduce it.

2. Target definition. It sometimes pays to re-define the target in order to concentrate on its core. A smaller target, particularly one with special media habits, will cost less to reach. For example, we may have worked before with 'women and children at home', but change to 'women with children 0–4'; not 'adults' but 'men'. The biggest alteration is when we change to a new geographical definition, perhaps allowing geo-demographics to be used.

3. Regions. The simplest breakdown in defining our target is the geographical region, and when TV is used this means the TV region. Allocation of the budget over the regions is in any case a normal part of TV planning. Outdoor, radio, cinema, regional papers, direct mail and other media should also be planned regionally. Of course, when a brand is in distribution in only a few regions, advertising has to be regional.

Regional marketing for brands which have nearly national distribution is not as common in the UK as it is becoming in the US, but that is what we are now discussing. Should our marketing effort be national? Or is the best response to the budget problem to concentrate, or rotate over the years, our effort on the best regions? The definition of 'best' is the key. It depends on a combination of the brand's strategy, the 'importance' of each region (this term is defined later), the cost of reaching this region, and what competition is doing.

The strategy may emphasize maintenance, in which case it is the brand's sales already made in each region which determine its importance. Or it may be conquest sales which matter more, in which case it is either existing sales of the category, or the size of the population of buyers, which matter. One of these three ways of defining importance is normally selected.

When you have chosen the appropriate definition, you can calculate an index for the importance of each region. This is in comparison with the size of the region, measured by the buying criterion you are going to use. For example, if this is housewives, what matters is sales per housewife, or the proportion of housewives who are in your target.

When this is compared with the national average, the index is called the Category Development Index (CDI) if category sales are used, or Brand Development Index (BDI) if the brand's sales are used.

Next, index the regions by the estimated cost you have to pay to reach the target. This is not easy, when share deals mean that the cost itself depends on the allocation. Here the agency media department's advice is vital. Then divide the index for importance by the index for cost. The larger the result, the more it is worth investing in the region. Work from the top of this list. The region at which you should stop, and the actual allocation, are decisions which depend very much on the actual numbers in your case, and no general rule is given here.

However, it is worth considering McNiven's suggestions (6). Plot the position of each region on a graph. On one axis is the Category Development Index, and on the other is brand share.

'The natural variations in a business from market to market provide real opportunities for advertising productivity. In some markets, a brand may be well known and the market share secure; in others, a brand may have stronger competition and consumers may not know the product as well. These two situations require different advertising and marketing strategies. Matching spending patterns to each market's needs will yield more overall mileage.'

Where both CDI and share are low, 'write off markets of this type, they are not productive places to spend time and money.'

Market-building efforts should concentrate where CDI is low, brand share high. A competitive or share-building programme is required where CDI is high but brand share low.

Where both CDI and share are high, try to maintain your position: this is where profit is earned.

It is essential to understand why all these differences exist. This is as important as the actual numbers, since it could influence the choice of an allocation criterion. This means you should study carefully the history of the category and brand. Look for the association of high or low figures with natural causes; examples are the presence of strong local brands, distribution and other retailing difficulties, suitability of the product for local geographical and population characteristics and so on.

Thus commonsense corrections may be the real determinant of the regional allocation. The brand's sales may be low in the area where your main competitor has his factory and offices, for example. The difficulty is not distribution, but local loyalty. To allocate marketing and advertising money here in proportion to category sales (which may be high) would be foolish.

Example 11
In this case (24), there were two reasons why London and South got below average weight, thus allowing more to be spent elsewhere.

Knights Castile soap had in the South a lower than average proportion of 'most often users', which was the definition of the target. The North-west had a higher proportion. In addition, costs in London on ITV were considered to be high, so TV-am was used on its own there. Elsewhere a mix of these two channels was used. Table 6 shows some of the area decisions made.

Table 6   Brand Development Index and TV Costs Affect Regional Allocation of Knights Castile (only selected areas shown)

Most often users,		*Housewife TVRs, June & July 1987*	
index on all housewives		*Actual*	*Index*
London	88	324	34
South	93	252	27
North-west	115	1095	115
National	100		100

Note that some allocation methods use the importance of each region as the basis for settling how much money it gets, while other methods determine the ratings to be bought, not the money to spend. The attitude underlying the direct allocation of money is that the investment is being made in the region itself, not in its media. Media are expected to perform equally well across regions, or self interestedly. That is, growing the brand in their region is to their advantage since the media budget will also grow (when a 'reinforce success' strategy is followed). Thus media are expected to deliver good ratings, so low cost, in their own interest. When ratings are allocated, the attitude is different. It is accepted that media costs differ and you do not expect to alter them. Since it is advertising exposure which affects people, not the number of pounds invested, it is ratings which must be calculated to produce the overall best return from the brand. Note that rewarding more expensive regions with a larger share of the budget is an inevitable consequence of the ratings allocation. The long-term effects of this are questionable: expensive regions are rewarded and contractors who give you good value are penalized. The short-term result is that more pressure, in the sense of ratings, is put against the regions where you judge it is required.

A particular allocation that comes under this method is 'equal impacts' when individuals are given equal value. Then the TVRs are the same in each region. This is often chosen when there is little sales information. It is easily explained and used but is low in efficiency in most cases.

There are three other aspects to the regional allocation. First, its trade effect. It may be important to show a retail buyer that the areas where his chain is strong are getting good support. Or you may want such buyers to be exposed to the schedule as if they were consumers (which, of course, they may be, but the point is that they see the advertising naturally, and therefore more convincingly). This may mean extra money is given to London, even if the advertising presence there is only token, or in some cheaper part of the medium. Hence the attention which media planners pay to the news on TV, drive time on radio, and supersites. For similar reasons, poster sites may be bought outside your own factory. Second, for some products the margins or returns from each region may differ significantly. When short-term return has priority, this may influence the allocation. Third, the competitive presence in each region should be looked at. With a small budget, and on the share of voice argument, it may pay to concentrate in regions where the competitors are less strong.

Finally, the decision for this year is not the final one. You may drop a region for a year but return to it next year.

4. Time. Your agency will use the fact that media costs vary over the year. It can be worth adjusting the timing of your advertising, which itself had been indicated by market seasonality, or by your own marketing plans, in order to buy more advertisement exposures.

Example 12
Domestos was given new advertising at the end of 1987, the Big DOM campaign (24). Sales are lower in the South than in the North, so the relaunch was delayed in London and Southern in order to make use of lower TV costs at the beginning of the calendar year. Some dates are given in Table 7.

Table 7   TV Costs Affect Dates Chosen for New TV Campaign for Domestos (only selected areas shown)

Midlands, Anglia	October–November 1987
Tyne-Tees	December 1987–January 1988
London	January 1988
TVS	February 1988

5. Advertisements. The clearest way in which decreasing real budget size has affected campaign plans is the shift to shorter spots on TV. This increases the number of opportunities to see which can be afforded, though each exposure may have less effect. The debate on frequency versus impact has no general resolution. Each case has to be argued afresh. You have also to consider alternative and cheaper forms of production, which need not mean less effectiveness.

With these five ways of making the budget work harder, I have completed my suggestions to solve the immediate problem of having too little to spend. There are two closing comments.

Longer term, the reduction of media costs is obviously a solution. This is more easily said than done, but large advertisers are doing what they can to encourage more competition on TV, and in general to help new media to start up.

If, after all the reviews and economies, you still believe that the budget is too small to do the job, you may simply have to get more money.

The Ideal Campaign Evaluation

Five Stages

There are five stages:
   agreeing the strategy for the campaign
   planning the evaluation
   advertising and data collection
   carrying out the evaluation
   benefiting from the evaluation.

Campaign plan

This is not a book about campaign planning, so I am not trying to cover this subject in detail; clearly a good plan springs from the product, its position in the market, and the company's business objective. It depends on what consumers know and believe about the product. It often requires us to choose a simple advertisable product claim or position. A target must be defined, as the source of business, as a media choice criterion and as a mark for the creatives.

We also have to say how we expect our advertising to work. This implies a forecast of its effects and is the key to the planning of its evaluation. Is our objective to communicate some facts? To cause a change of attitude? Have we said how these are going to be related to sales? Only with the campaign's objectives in mind can you plan appropriate consumer research and so study the relation of advertising to its effects.

Evaluation plan

The time to plan campaign evaluation is while the media plan is being agreed. To ask for an evaluation after advertising has appeared is inefficient.

The best evaluations combine at least two types of data source. One starts with your retail sales or delivery data, plus consumer sales from some panel or survey source which is already known to relate reliably to the delivery numbers. For economy you will probably use syndicated industry data. These may need to be supplemented with specially-designed research. The second type concerns consumers themselves. You want them to tell you why they acted as the sales data show they actually did. Naturally they cannot literally tell you this: you must not expect the why question to be as precisely answered as the how-much question. You have to hypothesize, to penetrate the screen of self-justification and to allow for memory failure. These are the tasks of consumer research.

Broadly, there are two methods of researching consumers: quantified surveys and qualitative, open-ended research. Both should be used if possible — measures of average awareness, attitudes, usage and so on — and a wider trawl for what is going on at the personal level.

All this information should be collected about both the brand and its main competitors. The evaluation takes into account what else is happening in the category. This means that you also arrange to measure, as well as you can, all the factors that may affect sales. Competitors' media spend may be as important as your own. Price, display, and trade features all affect sales, and unless they are allowed for, you may misread the effects of advertising.

As well as this, you must decide whether you will analyse only naturally-occurring data or whether you will carry out a deliberate test. The design of the test depends on the media and the measurement system used because these determine how the target may be divided into groups that receive different treatments. The classic is a television area test because television may be imposed differently in content, weight and timing on different areas; sales data are often collected by these areas also. For other media and other sales measurements a variety of test methods can be devised. The ideal is both to analyse historical data and to put your current ideas to the test of the marketplace.

If an evaluation of previous advertising has already been carried out, you will have a model, either a simple unquantified one or the result of a full statistical analysis, of how advertising has affected sales (or other measures). This may be used to aid practical decisions (see below), but it is never final like a law in physics. It is only a working hypothesis, a way of presenting the facts that seems to make sense. As such, it should be tested. Do the relationships still hold? Should the numbers previously estimated be changed?

Thus the perfect evaluation uses a variety of data sources and methods. This provides a check that you are not being misled by any one source. You hope for a coherent picture to emerge, but you do not expect a uniform one.

Your data should ideally be continuous, forcing you to realize both the dynamics of the market and the fact that your effects decay. The combinations can be shown as a table:

Criterion		*Data*		*Design*		*Analysis*
Sales or behaviour	must be	Quantified		As occurs naturally		Inspection or common sense
			may be		may be	
Awareness, attitudes, and usage	may be	Quantified or qualitative		Experiment or test		Modelling

The campaign
As the campaign progresses, you should check that it is appearing as planned. Because continuous data should be used (panels or surveys for sales, tracking studies or groups for awareness, usage and attitudes) the results arrive regularly. There are also shipments and trade reactions to monitor.

Usually there will be dates set for formal reports; for example, when six months' data are available. As the data come in, the key figures should be inspected, for instance by plotting them. Thus trends will be observed as early as possible. For a new campaign, as a generalization, the results after two or three periods are often critical, whether these are four-weekly or bi-monthly. When advertising is specially effective, it often works fast. Like every rule, this has exceptions: the painfully slow building of a base may also be the way the campaign works.

The evaluation
The pieces of the jigsaw to be fitted together are the data from the

separate sources already chosen. Each piece has its apparent meaning: sales went up in the test area, more people scored the brand highly on a key dimension, and so on. But was the price lower in the test area? What happened to the scores for competitors' brands?

At this stage, you must be open-minded: real life is full of surprises. Honesty is absolutely necessary. When the analysis fails or when you cannot understand its findings, progress will be made only after you admit the problem. In our business, standards of self-criticism are not high enough. Advertising does not always work as you expected or with as big an effect as you had hoped or as profitably as you would like. Awkward discrepancies may be telling you that your assumptions were wrong.

Ideally, you should have a model which relates sales to advertising and other important factors, such as price, in a quantified way. It is, however, exceptional to have such a quantification. More often, your belief about how advertising works depends on a simpler demonstration. In any case, even when a full modelling method is used, its results should be put into a form where the result is intuitively obvious: 'If you can't see it, it isn't there'.

The way that advertising affects sales should be supported by the qualitative data. You need to explain first that people have been changed and then to show how this has altered their behaviour. Of course, with a maintenance strategy, it is resistance to change and to falling sales that you wish to demonstrate.

Use of the evaluation
Once you have a satisfactory explanation of the way advertising affects sales, plus an understanding of how it does so, obviously you are better placed to make decisions for the future.

The most important benefit is on the content of the advertising. Here, as usual, distinguish strategy from execution. Are the product qualities chosen to feature the ones that move consumers? If not, a change of strategy is indicated. If the strategy is confirmed, what fine tuning is suggested — that is, what improvements in execution? The advantage of having a satisfactory, agreed evaluation is that the team has a basis for sensible discussion. In practice, some campaigns are dropped or changed irrationally. Without a good understanding of the facts outside the office, how could it be otherwise?

After agreement on advertising content, turn to the advertising budget. You have estimated and ideally quantified the effect on sales of changing the amount of advertising consumers see.

It is a disadvantage already pointed out that most estimates of effect are based only on the short-term return and only on volume. The data collected during campaign evaluation can, however, contribute to the brand audit described in Chapter 2, and in this way the long-term and indirect effects can be examined.

Unless we evaluate in-market, the budget decisions to be made each year will depend very much on tradition, rule of thumb or individual whim. Evaluation sharpens our tools for shaping the future.

Detail

7   More About Models

The time is fast coming when men who spend money are going to know what they get. Good business and efficiency will be applied to advertising. Men and methods will be measured by the known returns, and only competent men can survive.

Claude Hopkins (1923)

The general reader should not attempt to go through all this chapter, which includes the results from mathematical equations. If these are obscure to you, then skip the detail. If you are not interested in models, then skip the whole chapter. The reasons for including such technical material in a book for general management were given briefly in Chapter 5. They are now expanded.

Major advertising agencies have for some years, even decades, hired operational researchers, management scientists, econometricians, statisticians and analysts. All of them do much the same job, though with differing levels of expertise, and with occasional disagreement. The pages of *Advertising Works* demonstrate one result: modelling has become an accepted, though still uncommon, method of campaign evaluation. There were 19 examples out of 75 case histories published in the first four volumes.

Other consultants are available to marketing management. In a few cases, these are from the company's own services, or suppliers who have set up shop as independent specialists. A few business schools and universities, or research and forecasting businesses, and even accountants, offer analyses. The quality here is more diverse. Anyone with a computer can run a regression and claim to be a modeller, or write a program which appears to link adspend with sales volume and profits.

Thus an increasing number of marketers are being exposed to modelling. Naturally they are interested in improving their decision-making. But managers who know a little are easily fooled by those who know a bit more, though not enough to get it right. When, for example, you hear the word 'optimize', my advice is to hold tight to your cheque book.

In this chapter I have tried to set out, without mystification or calculus, some of the equations and terms employed. I explain how they may be used to assist decisions. A brand man who is interested can work through some of this chapter with his own data, as far as it is available. The purpose is to give him a clearer idea of how far a model can be used, when one has been acceptably built, to help the budget decision.

In a model, equations have been written to represent what happens in the real world. The equations start by being general, ready to represent any situation (insofar as they can). Then some of the numbers, the parameters, are fixed, to make the application specific to this company and this brand. Finally, other numbers are varied, to see what happens; these are the variables. The exploratory process of choosing a model and estimating the parameters is called modelling. I do not explain how to model because I believe this is a specialist's job.

The modeller who works in marketing walks a tightrope. On the one hand, he strives for realism, for caution, for fitting data credibly. On the other hand, he soon learns that many elaborate models are not trusted, and so are not used; that over-caution is irrelevant when decisions are made anyway, though based on crude, back-of-envelope sums; that the information he needs is often too expensive or unobtainable.

I believe that the modeller has a contribution to make: he brings to the budget decision a way of combining facts and estimates and he displays their implications. The approach is not for everyone and its claims should be modest. When commonsense distrusts modelling, follow commonsense.

The chapter begins with the simplest ideas and only small changes to a feasible budget, for example, to media spend. This guides our direction: is it profitable in the short term to spend more or to spend less on advertising? Then larger changes are considered and finally the search for the optimum is discussed, which I argue goes too far.

I do not describe in detail elaborate custom-built models, or the proprietary programs available. If you are a client of OHerlihy Associates (1) or of the Hendry Corporation, then you do not need a summary. If you do not use such consultants, you should at least be aware that some services take this approach further than is outlined here.

Definitions

I start by setting out all the symbols we need in the equations. Fuller definitions and warnings about these values were given in Chapter 3. I assume we have a going brand which is actually achieving this volume at the given price and adspend.

U   Total number of physical units (cases, tonnes . . .) sold annually.

R   Total annual revenue, pounds, after fixed and listed discounts but before allowing for special retail deals and promotions.

$p = R/U$ Selling price per unit.

v   Variable cost per unit, pounds. This should exclude fixed costs of production, but include such items as raw materials, packaging and transport. This is for changes at the margin, that is, close to the current volume.

$V = vU$ Total variable cost, pounds. Note that using the definition of v above means this may be smaller than the figure given in normal accounting, since that may spread fixed production costs over every unit sold, irrespective of how many are sold. We have extended all the units at the marginal variable cost.

$(p-v)$ Gross margin per unit, pounds, which is our revenue less the assumed cost of production but before paying for activities such as advertising.

$(p-v)U = R-V$ Total gross marginal revenue, in pounds.

A   Adspend in pounds, or advertising budget less costs of production, research, and so on: the working media spend.

E   Elasticity, defined below.

a, u   Adspend may vary from A: a is the new amount in pounds, and u is the corresponding new number of units sold.

f   A small fixed sum, pounds, added to A, then $a = A + f$

Linear Model

Both the linear and log models use the same definition of elasticity. When A increases to a, the proportionate increase in advertising is $(a/A - 1)$. The resulting proportionate increase in U is $(u/U - 1)$. The sales elasticity of advertising is defined as the ratio of these. Thus

$$E = (u/U - 1)/(a/A - 1)$$

or the new number of units sold is given by

$$u = U\{1 + E(a/A - 1)\} \qquad [1]$$

In words, if A is increased by one per cent, then U increases by E per cent.

Equation [1] *is* the linear model, stated to apply even when a/A is not close to one. U, A and E are here parameters: the variable a affects the variable u.

Log Model

The log model looks at the new values in proportion to their old values, then takes logarithms. It defines elasticity as the ratio of these expressions. Thus

$E = \ln(u/U)/\ln(a/A)$

Another way of saying the same thing is

$$(u/U) = (a/A)^E \qquad [2]$$

Although it does not look like it, this comes to about the same as the linear model when the new value a is close to the old value A. Try some values with your calculator! You need a calculator which can raise X to the power Y: here (a/A) is raised to the power E. The usual spreadsheet notation is (a/A)^E.

Changes from Altering Media Spend

Changes in Volume

Consider the effect of a = A + f. Putting this value in equation [1] we see that the increase in volume is

$$fEU/A \qquad [3]$$

In words, the increase is proportional to f, to elasticity, and to the present number of units sold divided by adspend. This last phrase, units sold divided by adspend, is equivalent to units sold per pound on advertising. It turns out to be an important quantity when we are managing a portfolio.

Suppose we are considering allocating more money (or taking it away) across a number of brands, and that the brands operate within the same brand category, so that the units used are comparable. Because f is fixed, the volume return we expect depends directly on each brand's ad elasticity times U/A. In saying this, we ignore cannibalization: the fact that increases for one of our brands may cause decreases in another. This is one of many practical issues that the simple model discussed here does not deal with.

If we do not know the elasticities, but are willing to assume that they are similar across the brands, then the one with the largest U/A will return the most volume for the additional spend. We do least harm to total volume by taking adspend away from the one with smallest U/A. This is why the recommendation in Chapter 6 was made: rank the brands by units/adspend, when deciding where to increase media spend in order to improve the total number of units sold.

Changes in Contribution

Consider the financial return from spending f more on advertising. What we gain in pounds from the volume increase in expression [3], less the cost of advertising, is

$$fE(p - v)U/A - f$$

Because $(p - v)U$ is total gross marginal revenue, this can be written

$$f\{E(R - V)/A - 1\} \tag{4}$$

Again, looking across a portfolio, this contribution change will be greatest where

$$E(R - V)/A$$

is largest.

Where E is assumed to be similar across the brands, what matters is the size of total gross marginal revenue divided by adspend. Again, this is the reason for the recommendation made in Chapter 6: rank the brands by margin/adspend, when deciding where to increase media spend, in order to improve the total contribution.

Breakeven Ad Elasticity

What must E be, for expression [4] to be zero? It is easily seen that E must be $A/(R - V)$. At this value, the extra cost of more advertising is exactly balanced in the short term by the extra revenue, less variable cost, from the added sales. The extra advertising may of course also bring long-term and indirect benefits.

This elasticity is called the breakeven elasticity. It is calculated from figures in the current budget, that is, one which is actually being achieved. It is, in words, the advertising-to-sales ratio divided by (gross margin as a proportion of sales revenue). Thus the lower the current adspend, the smaller is the breakeven elasticity. The higher the gross margin — or the lower the variable cost — the smaller is the breakeven elasticity.

To make this idea concrete, consider the brand at the beginning of Chapter 2, which has a 5% advertising-to-sales ratio, and for which gross margin/revenue is 40%. Its breakeven advertising elasticity is 5/40 or 0.125. This is quite a small number, although typical. A measured elasticity of 0.15 may wrongly be thought to be low, particularly when compared with a price elasticity of, say, −2.00. But this is not comparing like with like and does not mean that advertising is ineffective or uneconomic. In fact, such a measured elasticity would be above breakeven.

The ratio of actual elasticity to breakeven elasticity is an important one. If it is above one, as above, since 0.15 > 0.125, then we can increase adspend (at least by a small amount), get more sales volume *and* increase contribution in the current year.

This happy state of affairs happens less often than the reverse, that is, the actual elasticity is below breakeven elasticity. This means that we can increase the contribution in the short term by cutting the advertising budget. A fall in sales and long-term effects are, however, additional results.

If actual elasticity is close to breakeven elasticity, there is little effect on contribution when we change adspend. Adding to the advertising budget gains volume and costs little. Cutting the advertising budget loses volume and saves little.

Whether actual elasticity is above, or below, or equal to breakeven, the following is true. Suppose we invest a little more money in advertising. Then the proportion of our investment which we get back is the ratio of the actual to the breakeven advertising elasticity.

Using Ad Elasticities

The example in Chapter 6 is now continued, with the addition of these ideas. Tables 6.1 and 6.2 are extended in this chapter's Tables 1 and 2 by adding volume sales and actual ad elasticities for each brand. Moreover, we assume that the brands do operate in the same category and that we are interested in our total share of category. The ratios previously calculated still of course hold, but we can calculate some new ones in Table 2.

Table 1   Budgets and Ad Elasticities for Three Brands

Brand	Units (millions)	Revenue (£ millions)	Margin (£ millions)	Adspend (£ millions)	Actual elasticity
A	10	40	20	2	0.06
B	5	20	8	1	0.10
C	2	10	5	2	0.20
Total	17	70	33	5	

Table 2   Key Ratios Derived from Table 1

Brand	Price £/unit: revenue/ units	Breakeven elasticity: adspend/ margin	Estimated elasticity/ breakeven elasticity	or	Estimated elasticity × margin/ adspend	Estimated elasticity × units/ adspend
A	4	0.10			0.6	0.06
B	4	0.125			0.8	0.10
C	5	0.40			0.5	0.04
Total	4.12	0.15				

The discussion in Chapter 6 now changes in two ways. First, with these elasticities, we need not assume 'other things being equal'. Does this alter the previous tentative conclusion, that C might get too much adspend? Its elasticity is well above the others'. Should A get more? It has the lowest elasticity. We consider these questions and then move to the second piece of new information: the volumes.

We should not compare the elasticities on their own. C's advertising is not necessarily 'twice as good as B's'. Note that C gets twice as much adspend as B, so a one per cent change (on which elasticity is based) represents twice as many pounds.

The comparison of actual and breakeven elasticities is legitimate. In practice, of course, we have to use estimates, not actuals. The comparison here confirms that C might be getting too much adspend, compared with the other brands, despite its higher ad elasticity. However, its strategy may justify this. C could be spending its way into a growing sector, not primarily planning for a large contribution. While C's actual/breakeven ad elasticity is the lowest, B's emerges as the highest. Far from A being the possible beneficiary of money moved from C, this could be B. By the previous criterion, margin/adspend, A and B were not so far apart. The fact that B's ad elasticity is larger now puts it ahead.

A final point on the contribution criterion is that in this example all actual/breakeven ad elasticities are below one. This is quite normal. We can increase contribution, in the short term, by reducing adspend, but this is not the only criterion to use.

Now we turn to volumes. These are not in very different proportions from revenues, because prices (revenue/unit) are not so different. By the criterion of elasticity × units/adspend, C is again lowest. But B is now further ahead of A than on the contribution criterion. The net is that A does not have a strong case for increased adspend. Its ad elasticity is too low. But A's adspend is unlikely to be cut, given that it is already low compared with revenue and margin. B does have a case for more adspend. Increased advertising would do most for both contribution and volume. It might take media money at the expense of C — if the total on advertising is fixed but depending also on the brands' individual strategies.

Note that the fixed costs that were part of the discussion in Chapter 2 have not yet entered the argument. It is not the actual contribution that matters here, but changes in contribution.

Is the Total Right?

Parts of the above discussion have implied that we are allocating a fixed £5 million across the brands, which may be realistic. The way that the company operates may well be to use a fixed advertising-to-sales ratio, here 7%, and leave marketing management to allocate the total across brands. The policy should be challenged. How do we know whether these three brands can operate in line with company volume and contribution targets with this sum?

There are two ways we can investigate this. The first is a bottom-up approach, in which each brand manager makes the case for his own brand. These cases are unlikely to be completely independent: company strategy should already have laid down different target priorities, creative objectives, timing and so on, so as to segment the category in the most advantageous way. The second way is to look at the total budget for all the brands together. Thus we evaluate the £5 million as a 7% advertising-to-sales ratio for the company. We know that for this 'brand' our actual elasticity is below breakeven: the weighted average of elasticities is 0.09 and breakeven elasticity for the total is 0.15. We return to the problem that often faces a single brand: do the volume targets and long-term benefits of advertising justify this overall budget?

Price Elasticity

This is not a book that discusses pricing in depth, but in general unit sales will also change when price is altered. This can apparently be observed more often than the advertising effect. But be warned that, when data show the brand at a low price, other marketing activities are often also favourable. Display and store advertising are often associated with low price, as was pointed out in Chapter 2. What we observe may be the effect of the combination of several promotional activities, not only price.

Reducing the price leads to an increase in volume sales (in most practical cases), so price elasticities are nearly always negative. This can make the discussion rather awkward: the convention is that a price elasticity of -2 is 'larger' than one of -1, the reverse of the usual meaning.

When price elasticity is larger than -1, then reducing the price means increasing revenue as well as volume. If we are not concerned about production costs (for example, when we are clearing written-off stock), then a revenue increase is also a profit increase. But if, as is usual, there are extra production costs incurred when we sell more, then we need to know the breakeven price elasticity. If the actual elasticity is larger than breakeven, then, when we reduce price, both volume and contribution increase.

The breakeven price elasticity is $-p/(p - v)$, or total revenue divided by total marginal revenue. Thus Brand B's breakeven price elasticity is -2.5, from 20/8. Note that $-$breakeven ad elasticity divided by breakeven price elasticity is

$$\{A/(R - V)\}/\{R/(R - V)\} = A/R$$

which is the advertising-to-sales ratio, as a fraction. Thus for Brand B, $0.125/2.5 = 5/100$.

If we assume that the current budget sets both price and adspend at the levels which give maximum contribution, then both ad and price breakeven elasticities will be at their actual values. The price elasticity may have been measured precisely in the field. If this is the case, then the ad elasticity is given by

$(A/R) \times -\text{price elasticity}$

Suppose for Brand B the actual price elasticity is -2.5, equal to the breakeven calculated from the budget. Then the ad elasticity (both actual and breakeven) is, with the assumptions above,

$(5/100) \times 2.5 = 0.125$

This is a sensible number, but sometimes the calculation leads to an absurdity, showing that there is something wrong with the budget, or with the assumption that we are near maximum contribution, or with the measured price elasticity.

Promotion Elasticity

Similarly, we can consider a change in promotional spending. This will have its own effect on sales, just as advertising has an effect. If we consider these effects to be independent (although this is unlikely), we can even say how much of a fixed advertising and promotion budget 'should' be spent on each.

Suppose we have P as the promotional spend, with its elasticity L. A + P is fixed. At the allocation for which A and P are such that contribution is maximized, we do not change contribution by moving a small amount of money from P to A or vice versa. For the log model, the elasticity does not change when the amounts spent on activities alter. Now, add f to A. We know the contribution gain from expression [4]. The loss from the reduction in P is the corresponding expression $f\{1 - L(R - V)/P\}$. For these to add to zero,

$E/A = L/P$

In words, the total A + P is divided between advertising and promotion in the proportion of their elasticities. Because Brand B divides A + P equally between advertising and promotion, this implies that another pound spent on each is thought to be equally effective on sales.

Beyond Small Changes

So far, we have been considering only small changes. These have given us summaries of the local conditions and priorities. They have brought together budget data and what has been learned from experience (the elasticities). It is obviously important to have such directions, to know what increasing the advertising budget, or decreasing it, is likely to do to contribution.

Some readers may not think of this as modelling. They want more than direction, they want to explore alternative real budgets. Some even want to be shown a destination: the optimum. These ambitious objectives can be met, if we make enough assumptions. We have been on fairly firm ground so far. As we leave local conditions, our conclusions become more precarious.

Continuing with Brand B as an example, the key facts are:

U	=	5 million units sold annually
R	=	£20 million revenue
p	=	£4 selling price per unit
v	=	£2.40 variable cost per unit
vU	=	£12 million total variable cost
p−v	=	£1.60 gross margin per unit
R−V	=	£8 million total gross marginal revenue
A	=	£1 million adspend
E	=	0.1 ad elasticity

We already know that breakeven ad elasticity is 0.125 (adspend/margin = 1/8). Thus estimated elasticity is below breakeven, in fact 0.8 of breakeven. Hence an increase in adspend will increase volume but reduce contribution in the short term.

The question we now answer is: What do we expect when we alter adspend by serious amounts, say between £800 000 and £1.2 million? Using the log model, equation [2], the new volume is

$$u = U(a/A)^E = 5(a/1\ 000\ 000)^{0.1} \text{ million units}$$

The contribution change is the change in volume times gross margin per unit, less the change in adspend. This is:

$$(u - U)(p - v) - a + A$$

These two relations are plotted in Figure 1. We return later to the question: how reliable are these estimates? For now, we see from Figure 1 that the two lines move in opposite ways. This is always the case when estimated ad elasticity is below breakeven: we have to choose between a volume increase and a contribution increase; we cannot have both.

To go further, the brand and company objectives must be known. We can imagine exchanges like these:

Q: 'Can advertising get me 50 000 more units? What will this cost?'
A: 'Yes, by increasing the adspend to £1.1 million. The contribution drop, or real cost, will be £24 000.'

Q: 'I am going to cut £100 000 from advertising, to increase contribution. What harm will this do to volume?'
A: 'You will lose about 50 000 units. You won't save £100 000; the improvement in contribution will be only £16 000.'

FIG 1

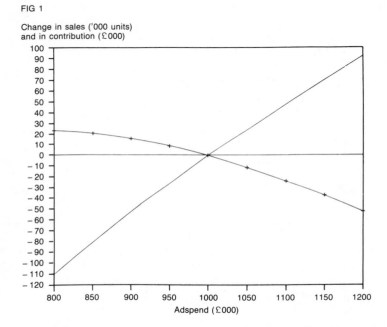

Change in sales ('000 units)
and in contribution (£000)

Adspend (£000)

Figure 1   Changes in Sales Volume, and in Contribution, from Changes in Adspend.

Key: —— = sales; + = contribution.

In practice, a computer program (2) should be available to answer such what-if questions and to provide other facts, such as the ratio of actual to breakeven elasticities. The figures just given were calculated in this way, but have been rounded off to prevent the illusion that such answers are very precise.

Changing Adspend and Price

Price elasticity may also have been estimated. Suppose that in this case it was -1.5. Breakeven price elasticity, using the formula $-p/(p - v)$, was given above as -2.5. Thus estimated is smaller (in absolute value) than breakeven. This means that a price increase, though it loses volume, will not lose so much that it is an unprofitable move. In addition, if the estimate was based on relative price, and if competitors followed us, we would suffer only a category volume loss, probably smaller than the calculated loss.

The last paragraph is moving outside the scope of this book. But it is worth pursuing the possibility that a price increase might provide enough contribution gain to pay for more advertising, which in turn will compensate for the volume loss. The criterion to inspect, in order to see whether this is locally possible, is: Is estimated ad elasticity, divided by the absolute value of the estimated price elasticity, greater than the advertising-to-sales ratio? If so, we can choose combinations of higher adspend and higher price at which we will sell more and improve contribution.

If these two (ad elasticity/$-$price elasticity, and A/pU) are exactly equal, we are at a stable optimum (3). In this case $0.1/1.5 = 0.067$ and $1/20 = 0.050$.

There is not that much difference in these key numbers, which implies that we do not have so much room for manoeuvre. Note that we are not considering more advertising having the long-term effect of making the product more saleable, such as justifying the higher price, or altering the price elasticity. These remain possibilities in the long term, but here we are talking about balancing the budget in the short term.

Again, a computer program is advisable to help explore such possibilities. With its use we will discover two interesting options:

A. Increase adspend to £1.2 million and price by 5 pence a unit. Volume remains steady, but contribution increases over £40 000.
B. Increase adspend further to £1.3 million and again add 5 pence a unit. Volume grows nearly 40 000 cases and contribution is steady.

Evaluating Next Year's Plan

If the budget for Brand B was being discussed mid-year, when we still had time for changes, the discussion above would have helped decisions about these changes. With a few more assumptions, we can also help decisions about next year. To do this, we need estimates of the changes expected in the environment.

Suppose we are discussing, as above, price and adspend changes. We need the following information, about the category or sector in which Brand B is sold, and about its budget:

Will the size of the sector change? Say by +2%.
Will prices per unit change? Say by +3%.
Will media costs change? Say by +7%.
Will our variable costs change? Say they will be the same.
Will our fixed costs change? Say these were £2 million but we add £200 000.

Further, we assume that Brand B will get the same share of category as in this year, provided it stays at the same price relative to the category and is supported by the same number of rating points. The adspend change is simply to keep pace with media costs. Finally, we use the log model and the same elasticities as before.

The first result is that we can write a feasible budget for Brand B, in the sense that the volume and contribution targets will be met at the level of the marketing activities supporting the brand.

This is not necessarily true for every proposed plan. Because of the pressures described in Chapter 3, a proposal may or may not be feasible. We continue the example by comparing the three budgets in Table 3. Since the promotional spend is not being varied in this example, it is included in contribution.

Table 3   Three Budgets for Brand B

		Next year	
	Current year	Feasible	Proposed
Volume (million units)	5.00	5.10	5.25
Selling price (£/unit)	4.00	4.12	4.20
Variable cost (£/unit)	2.40	2.40	2.40
Total variable cost (£ millions)	12.00	12.24	12.60
Adspend (£ millions)	1.00	1.07	1.00
Fixed costs (£ millions)	2.00	2.20	2.20
Contribution (£ millions)	5.00	5.50	6.25
Revenue (£ millions)	20.00	21.01	22.05

First, look at the feasible budget, in which we have merely reacted to the environment. We see growth in volume and in contribution. This is possible because the increase in media and fixed costs is smaller than the benefits from category growth and rising prices, while we have kept variable costs steady. The proposed plan is more ambitious. It takes a larger price increase, holds down adspend and expects a larger volume increase.

Such plans are often proposed in practice. Unless they are evaluated in the way suggested in Chapter 4, the results are inevitably disappointing. I exclude from this comment those cases where there are other, genuine reasons to believe in growth. A competitor may be going out of business, or we have a major improvement in distribution or in product quality; these are causes for optimism. I am considering examples where changes in only the marketing activities are suggested to back up the proposal. The outcome without proper evaluation is often enthusiastic reception of the plan, followed by gloom as the volume predicted does not materialize. The reaction may be to cut adspend in the hope of making the contribution forecast, accompanied by increased promotional spend to achieve volume. Traditionally, the next steps are the search for the guilty and punishment of the innocent.

It is better to review the proposed plan. We cannot do this simply on its differences from this year's budget. We need a forecast of the environment built in, and an achievable starting point. The feasible budget provides this. The two questions now are: Is the proposed plan achievable? If not, how near can we get to it?

The calculations to answer the first question can be followed through, using the methods already described. I jump straight to the result: the proposed pricing and adspend decision will result in sales of only 4.92 million units, not the 5.25 million suggested. Hence the contribution target is not achievable. What to do? We can try variations round the feasible budget, which attempt to reach the volume and contribution objectives. With a computer program the search is quite rapid. We learn that the two objectives are incompatible. The volume target is achievable with adspend approaching £1.2 million and by taking a price rise below the sector's. But contribution will then be below £5.4 million. Aiming at the contribution target is a hopeless task. This sort of realism is a real benefit when next year's plans are still in draft.

An 'Optimum' Adspend?

Returning to the current year, we left open the question, 'Can an "optimum" adspend be discovered?'

We saw in Figure 1 that, when the adspend varied between £800 000 and £1.2 million, contribution increased as the adspend dropped. Contribution was still rising as we went down to £800 000. Does it peak at some adspend smaller than this? Note that optimum is being interpreted as maximum contribution: a common view though sometimes a misguided one, as explained later.

We can indeed calculate what adspend should be, according to the log model, to give the maximum contribution. This is the value at which small changes in a do not alter the contribution. We know from the expression [4] that this is where a is E times the total marginal revenue calculated for this a. The log model says that volume at this value is $U(a/A)^E$, so marginal revenue is $U(p - v)(a/A)^E$. But $U(p - v)$ is marginal revenue at the old value of the adspend A, which is known. Hence the value that we seek is the solution of

$$a = (R - V)(a/A)^E$$

This is given by

$$\ln a = \ln\{E(R - V)/A^E\}/(1 - E)$$

For Brand B in the current year, this expression gives an a of £780 000. We were indeed close to the maximum contribution at the left side of Figure 1. Volume is there 4.88 million units, 2.4% below the current rate.

'Optimizing' Across a Portfolio of Brands

We use the expression

Elasticity × margin/adspend

to guide us to the brand in the portfolio for which an increase in adspend would repay most in contribution. Now suppose the brands receive such adspends that the total contribution is maximized, but total adspend across all brands is held constant. This means that the expression above is equal across the brands. If the changes are not too great from their present position, the changes in margin will be small. Hence adspend 'should' be divided roughly in the proportion

Elasticity × margin.

The data in Table 1 lead to the suggestion in Table 4. A similar argument on volume says that the division should be in the proportions given in Table 5.

Table 4   Suggested Allocation of Media Spend, for Maximum Contribution

Elasticity × margin (£ millions)		*£5 million, in this proportion*
A	1.2	2.00
B	0.8	1.33
C	1.0	1.67
Totals	3.0	5.00

Table 5   Suggested Allocation of Media Spend, for Maximum Volume

Elasticity × units (millions)		*£5 million, in this proportion*
A	0.6	2.00
B	0.5	1.67
C	0.4	1.33
Totals	1.5	5.00

These procedures can be refined, but this is not recommended. It is not even recommended that they are seriously used, although 'solutions' like them have been put forward. The reasons are given below. The most we should conclude is that Brand A has about the right proportion of adspend (if the total adspend is correct). Brands B and C should perhaps not spend such different amounts as now: the current plan says £1 million on B (which both criteria increase, the volume criterion most) and £2 million on C (which both criteria reduce).

'Optimizing' Across Regions

Allocating a TV budget across regions differs from allocating a total advertising budget across brands in a portfolio. Most importantly, share deals mean that the price paid for time depends on the allocation, and cannot be taken as fixed. On the other hand, it is unlikely that different advertising elasticities for each region will be estimated. It is very unlikely that the total budget will be changed. In the allocation across brands, media costs are assumed to be the same, but in the last section different elasticities were permitted. It is also possible that one brand may be seen to deserve more adspend without the decision to reduce correspondingly the spend on others. Since we are getting into the specialist subject of TV planning, no more is said here about this allocation though programs exist to do the job. Again, be cautious, when such programs are used, to see whether large sums of money are being moved for comparatively small and doubtful improved returns: The response curve is very flat near the optimum.

Elasticities Estimated and Expected

In deciding whether we should be spending more, or less, on advertising and evaluating the outcome by the short-term change in contribution, elasticities are obviously key. They are only the mathematical formulation of whether sales are affected a lot, or a little, but they have the great advantage of being numbers we can combine with those in the budget. Thus we get a feel for the likely effect of changes, both on volume and on the bottom line. Where does the number used for the actual elasticity for our brand come from? We can perhaps make estimates for this important figure from the recent history of the brand. But there are two reservations. First, even recent history may not be completely relevant to the conditions for which we are budgeting. Second, the estimates are very difficult to get.

There are two main methods. First, area testing, already mentioned as a direct way of experimenting with different budgets.

A test, if successful, reports its result in the form ' . . . a change of ratings of C% gave S% in sales . . . ' For example, '50% more ratings gave 6% more sales'. A simple calculation (assuming linear response) of elasticity is S/C, in this case $6/50 = 0.12$. If we are to use a log model later, a better estimate is

$$\ln\{(100+S)/100\}/\ln\{(100+C)/100\}$$

which gives a larger number, 0.14, because of diminishing returns. We have to start off locally at a steeper slope in order to reach the recorded increase at +50% in ratings.

The second way to estimate elasticities is by econometric modelling. This is modelling in the sense of trying out different fits to real data, as it fell. It is different from taking the model as fixed and trying out various what-if decisions with it, as we have been doing up to now.

As has already been stated, econometric modelling will not be described here (4). The reader is warned that some professionals are dubious about the validity of some of its findings (5). It has been described as 'like medicine in that the combination of a number of correct actions plus one mistake can kill the patient' (6). It cannot be done at all unless we have:

— data on at least some of the other factors that affect sales
— a schedule of past advertising that has in it some variation and that is reasonably independent of the other factors.

In other words, it is not enough just to look at our history of adspend and our history of sales, or to evaluate a burst of advertising that might have coincided with a price change.

Still, there have been successes in the modelling of sales, including the use of an advertising term (7). It is therefore possible that an attempt with your brand will be successful and will give you an estimate of the short-term effect of your advertising.

It is also possible to use elasticities collected for other brands, treating these as norms and making your own estimate of what applies in your case. Be reminded that an elasticity represents the effect of a one per cent change in adspend; if your adspend is less than the norm so might be the proportional effect.

Reactions to advertising, and so ad elasticities, vary considerably, across products and across campaigns.

Example 1
Six retailers cooperated in an American Newspaper Advertising Bureau experiment (8). An index was calculated for the relative effects of various newspaper ads, compared with the costs of producing and running them. The index is not the total return for a dollar spent in advertising, but allows us to compare the sales effects across stores.

Retailer	Relative sales dollars per ad dollar
A	20.34
F	5.22
B	3.69
E	2.36
D	1.94
C	1.11

The return is eighteen times larger for the best than for the worst.

The sort of factors that cause these differences between retailers include the values and prices of the goods offered, whether consumers knew about them beforehand, and so on. Another factor, the sales effectiveness of the advertisements themselves, also contributes to the differences. In this example a further factor, the effectiveness of the medium and of the media plan, is removed from the comparison because all retailers used the same medium.

Remember that, in other industries, and in earlier decades, advertising effectiveness may have been very different from our category today. In any case, because the range of observed values is large, we have to make a judgement about our position in this range; actually, this is not so hard to make when we have experience of the category and its advertising, and when we succeed in being unbiased. A collection of ad elasticities in the UK was published in 1980 (2). This suggested that for packaged goods:

— a significant proportion of campaigns had small elasticities, probably below breakeven
— the range from low to high elasticities was large: you may expect a high elasticity to be three or even five times as large as a small one
— a few campaigns can have major, immediate sales effect, but more often from a strategy change than from a budget alteration.

The following norms are based on this collection and on the fact that more recently published success stories (7) confirm the top end of this range:

outstanding	0.25
very good	0.20
good	0.15
average	0.10
poor	0.05

These values, and the log model, were used to plot Figure 1 in Chapter 2.

Does This Approach Solve the Budget-setting Problem?

It might seem that the problem has now been solved. We have methods and norms that give us advertising effects. We have equations that tell us the expected results of possible budget decisions; even the optimum budget. What more is there to do? The answer, unfortunately, is 'a lot'. The recommended way to use this approach is certainly not as simple as using a calculated optimum. We now go on to consider modelling critically, with four different objections. They are all variants of one: there is more to the budget decision than is contained in this over-simple model. Thus believing that there is an easily-determined optimum may wrongly stop us from looking more deeply (9).

1. Maximizing contribution, ignoring volume. There is a trade-off between volume and profit. The adspend which maximizes profit may lead to unacceptable volume. For example, for brand B we found that contribution was at a maximum when adspend was £780 000. What was not pointed out then was that contribution rose by only £24 000 despite our cutting adspend by £220 000. This was because sales fell 2.4%, to 4.88 million units. Is this acceptable? Only with company priorities in mind can we answer this question.

It might well be decided instead to spend £80 000 more. Contribution falls by less than £20 000. We gain 40 000 units. It may be worth our while to buy this volume, given also the long-term benefits.

In fact, it has been argued (10) that it is better to overshoot the 'optimum' than undershoot it. The difference in contribution from the maximum may be very small; remember that the response curve is likely to be flat. But the added sales and other results are very desirable. Higher and growing market share, a stronger consumer and trade franchise, may even have short-term advantages.

2. Longer term. The model described above is for only one year. It is quite possible that it may determine a very low optimum adspend. This would solve the problem as the model states it: short-term profit may often be improved by cutting adspend completely. The long-term result of not advertising may be quite different from the short-term result. Sales (to the trade and to the consumer) may be made now which are not possible when the reputation of the brand declines. This decline is a very possible effect of not advertising (see Chapter 8). Econometricians have attempted to model the long-term effects of advertising on sales, but there is no widely-accepted way of doing such analyses (11), and it cannot be generally recommended.

3. The indirect effects of advertising are not included. The argument so far has considered only the volume–adspend relationship and has treated the marginal return as fixed. In the real world, the balance between volume, adspend, brand reputation, and price is not so simple. Declining reputation (a result of not advertising) can harm the saleability of the brand, so that the price it commands can decline. We may not actually sell lower volume, but to maintain volume we sell at a lower price. The demand curve moves to the left: see Chapter 2. The marginal return falls and so does our profit.

In fact, each part of the marketing mix affects sales in a way which depends on other parts. Changing adspend may alter price effects, as has just been argued. It may also affect the efficiency of promotions, if the brand becomes less desirable.

4. The shape of the response function. The line in Figure 1 showing how volume changes with adspend is called a response function since it shows a response to different adspends. There has been considerable discussion in the industry about the shape of this function, that is, how sales in the short term are found to move with altered media spends. One problem is that competent measurements of the points on such a curve are rarely done. Another is that the detailed shape of the curve is not well-determined. Often in fitting a model, we are trying to draw a line through a cloud of observations. In practice, the most we know (and this seldom) is an estimate of the *slope* of the relationship.

There are two separate decisions here. First, what number should be used for elasticity? Second, what is the shape of the curve in Figure 1? We have used a log response, but the real shape could be different. The log curve is one often chosen by economists but that does not mean that it is true in any particular case. Suppose it were linear instead? Or negative exponential? Or a logit?

We may have some data, or guesses, on elasticity. We usually know nothing about the shape. It is fortunate that it is this way round, because if the changes we make are not too large, it is the elasticity which matters, more than the shape. If we make large changes, for example doubling the adspend, then the shape matters. In such cases the estimates also become very imprecise, because we usually have no relevant experience.

Sensitivity Analysis

A way to investigate the problem just raised is to try out different elasticities and different shapes. One of the advantages of modelling is that some what-if questions do have answers.

Suppose that the actual ad elasticity was not 0.10 but 0.15. Remember, we have only an estimate for this number. Still with the log model, Figure 2 shows the two response functions. Now consider Figure 3, which shows the resulting changes in contribution. It is very different. This is because the elasticity of 0.15 is above breakeven: increasing adspend also increases contribution. The 'optimum' adspend changes dramatically. Previously, with elasticity 0.10, this

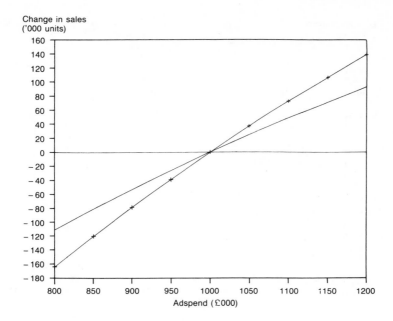

Figure 2   Two Different Sales Responses to Changes in Adspend.

Key: ——— = at elasticity 0.10; + = at elasticity 0.15.

was £780 000. At elasticity 0.15 it becomes £1 240 000!

Suppose that we evaluate changes of this size, adding or subtracting £200 000 from our £1 million budget. At these changes, plus or minus 20%, we are not moving too far from current experience. In addition to looking at two elasticities, we look at the linear model's conclusions as well as the log model. The two are wildly different if we move far from our present position. How different are they at moves of 20%? Table 6 answers this question. Again, in this table and in the next, the numbers are rounded off.

We work out the implications on contribution in Table 7. The change in adspend is one part. The other part is the volume change multiplied by the marginal return per unit, because income changes but so does production cost. Before commenting on these, I summarize what we have done. We want to evaluate some practical budget changes (up or down £200 000). We have two models to do this with; we want to know whether we would be led differently by the two models. 'Led' means 'which is indicated as the correct action: to increase or to decrease

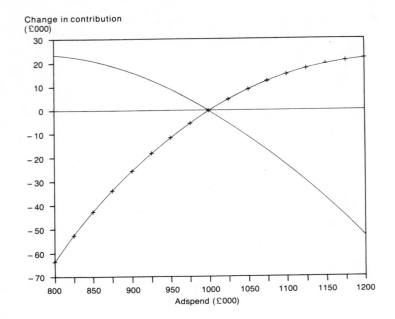

Figure 3   Two Different Contribution Responses to Changes in Adspend.

Key: ——— = at elasticity 0.10; + = at elasticity 0.15.

Table 6   Sales Responses to 20% Changes in Adspend

Volume sales change, 000 units, linear model	£1–£0.8 million	£1–£1.2 million
Elasticity 0.10	−100	+100
Elasticity 0.15	−150	+150

Volume sales change, 000 units, log model	£1–£0.8 million	£1–£1.2 million
Elasticity 0.10	−110	+ 90
Elasticity 0.15	−160	+140

adspend'. We have two criteria for this judgement: volume (Table 6) and contribution (Table 7). Finally, we are looking at two possible elasticities, in order to see how important this parameter is.

Table 7   Contribution Responses to 20% Changes in Adspend

Contribution change, £ 000, linear model		
	£1–£0.8 million	*£1–£1.2 million*
Elasticity 0.10	+40	−40
Elasticity 0.15	−40	+40
Contribution change, £ 000, log model		
	£1–£0.8 million	*£1–£1.2 million*
Elasticity 0.10	+20	−50
Elasticity 0.15	−60	+20

The tables tell us that in this case:

1. *The model that is used has a small effect.* We would be led the same way by either model. The actual numbers for changes are different, but, as percentages of their central values at £1 million adspend, the differences are small. The *largest* is the contribution change, when we drop to £800 000 at elasticity 0.15 (Table 7). The linear model says we lose £40 000 or 0.7% of £6 million. The log model says £60 000 or 1.0%. The difference is only 0.3% of the contribution.

2. *The elasticity that is used has a large effect.* The differences by volume (Table 6) are minor. In every case, altering elasticity from 0.10 to 0.15 means about 50 000 more units. This is 1% of current volume. For contribution, the differences are larger (Table 7). It is not only that we cross from plus to minus: that just emphasizes the size of the contribution change. The *smallest* percentage difference across elasticities is for the log model when we increase to £1.2 million. The elasticity of 0.10 gives £50 000 reduced contribution: 0.8% loss. The elasticity of 0.15 gives 0.3% improvement. The difference is 1.1%.

With models closer to the log shape (the linear is further from it than most), it would be even clearer that elasticity matters more than shape.

Allocation Across Brands

For similar reasons, the way described above of moving money between brands to get maximum contribution is not recommended. Again, large movements are suggested for small and extremely uncertain gains.

£5 million was divided across the three brands in Table 4 by a method which 'should' improve contribution. In theory, it is possible to increase contribution still further. But compare the three allocations by their actual adspends — and by the contribution calculated to be the result in Table 8. In the first 'improvement' we are moving £333 000 and changing adspends in proportions around 20%, to get a calculated £50 000 gain. This is bad enough; the uncertainties are greater than such changes warrant. It is worse to move a further £50 000 to get a calculated gain of less than £10 000.

Table 8   'Improved' Allocation of Media Spend for Maximum Contribution

	Originally (£ million)	By elasticity × margin method	Further improvement
A	2.00	2.00	2.02
B	1.00	1.33	1.38
C	2.00	1.67	1.60
Total resulting contribution (£ million) (margin less adspend)	28.00	28.05	28.06

Customized Modelling

The general discussion so far can be modified in particular cases. Some of the changes may be within the capacity of marketing management, some need specialized management science work (12). The model used may be made more relevant — or apparently so — in various ways:
 - the budget may be broken down by geographical regions: opportunities (hence response) and costs may differ between parts of the country
 - the compromises between volume (or share) and financial results, and between this year and later years, may be specified explicitly
 - specific regularities observed in this or similar categories may be built in
 - cannibalization (if we have a portfolio of brands), competitors' activities, or category growth effects (if the category volume shows changes) may be included
 - interactions of one marketing activity on another may be allowed for.

As one example, consider this specification of the Hendry Corporation's approach (13):

'Without going into the marketplace, we explore what would happen if one or more competitors were to change marketing forces on new or mature products.
'To accomplish this we use two different sources of data. We use historical panel data, first to identify direct and indirect "sets" of competitive products and, second, to determine the commitment consumers have for these "sets" from their switching rates. This identifies the importance of these variables. Sometimes survey data may be suitable for this purpose. The second source of data is financial data; i.e., sales, costs, wholesale selling prices, consumer purchasing prices, advertising expenditures and other marketing data. These data are used in addition to the switching data to answer "what if" questions.'

Part of the output is similar to that discussed above. That is, the model predicts relationships between adspend and price (as inputs) and market share and return (or contribution) as outputs. These are combined graphically on a strategy map. What follows indicates the kind of recommendation possible:

'The brand is overpriced. Reducing the brand's price to 107 would yield the same profits but would increase the share from 9.4 to 12. This, however, would not stop the decline but would, of course, slow it down. To stop the decline we need to achieve almost a 14 share. This could be done by increasing advertising from 12 000M to 17 000M and decreasing the price from 130 to 102, but at what cost in terms of profits?
' . . . to stop the decline through advertising and pricing alone costs 3600M dollars. A payback calculation indicated that this investment would take four to five years to pay back. At that time not only would the brand's share be higher, but the profits would be higher from then on.
'As a result of this work several things happened. The price rise that was planned never took place; instead a price reduction occurred. The advertising budget was increased and several product changes occurred. A test market was set up to evaluate possible changes in terms of how these will affect the decline rate.'

One of the methods used in customized modelling appears to solve the problem that the exact form of response is not known. The method is to have managers make estimates. Rather than attempting to fit a model to data, it is extracted from marketers' experience and intuition. The keys to success here are:

(a) the people interviewed must have enough experience and common-sense for their answers to be relied on;
(b) the questions asked must be pitched at such a level, and in such language, that their intuition can be applied. A fool may ask

questions a wise man cannot answer, but the wise man may not be quite wise enough to say so. Like all respondents, he is apt to give some response whether or not he feels really qualified.

Example 2
'We hold a day-long session in which we ask the management group such questions as: If we double local advertising aimed at market segment A and product B, what would be the effect on product B sales? We ask a whole series of detailed, judgemental questions and get the responses of different kinds of people in the company.

'Then we do some analysis and playback. We've asked the questions in micro, and we play it back in macro. What are the effects of these answers on estimates of sales, profits and share? We use them to develop tradeoffs, identify areas of consensus and determine measurement priorities.

'What we get out of all this is tradeoffs, identification of consensus, and identification of disagreement. These have implications for action. If their current judgement is a consensus, then they should reasonably be moving, at least directionally, as indicated by the model. Nobody would advocate going to an extreme; the managers rarely have that degree of confidence in their numbers. In some cases you find divergence between individuals. This tells where it would be desirable to have better information. The model thus provides guidance for setting up some measurements' (14).

Few of the elaborations in customized models alter the points already made, but they may provide additional input to the decision. It is recommended that this is all models should be used for. They can clear our minds about what advertising is supposed to do and how brands in our category behave. They should not replace judgement: if they seem to do so, make sure you understand on what assumptions their recommendations are based.

Example 3
The objectives of this example are to indicate what modelling does and how its output may be used; I also want to show the reader the serious difficulties which may crop up. It is presented as a series of conversations between a plodding but honest analyst and a bright but sceptical brand manager; I do not mean that these jobs always imply these characteristics. The two characters progress in this example from naivety to a more realistic attitude. Everything in this example actually happened, though in more than one company.

Stage 1. Manager: 'We agreed that you would look at our sales data and that you'd estimate the way in which volume responds to changes in our price and in the media spend. I have looked at the budget in the way you recommended, and I see that the breakeven elasticities for the price and for advertising are −2.5 and 0.15. I'm looking forward to hearing whether you think our real elasticities are above or below these, especially as I've been putting up the advertising spend and I need to explain to my boss what effect that has had.'
Analyst: 'Here are the plots I made, against time periods, of our volume sales and

share, our price and relative price, our distribution and our adstock. [The reader should note that this analyst was at least looking at the data!] You'll see that our volume has been climbing, so has our share. But you already knew that. Distribution has grown rather similarly. So I have calculated share per distribution point, in order to get rid of the distribution effect. Then I regressed this number against relative price and adstock. This should show the effects of price and adspend which you asked for.'

Manager: 'And?'

Analyst: 'Well, it's awfully good. First of all, the coefficient for price wasn't statistically significant. That means, it could well be zero. In fact, the estimate was actually positive, though of course it was small. You'll see that our relative price has actually been going up a bit during our share growth. I think this is because cheaper own label brands have got more share, so we look relatively dearer compared with the average. So my best estimate of price elasticity is zero. If you change the price, that won't affect volume at all.

'The advertising effect is very clear. You can see on the plots how the peaks of adstock correspond with these jumps in sales. The fit says that the advertising coefficient is definitely above zero. The elasticity estimate is in fact 0.3, twice your breakeven value. So you can put up the advertising weight and not only gain volume, but you will actually be better off as well.'

Manager: 'Sounds good, but let me think about it.'

Stage 2. Manager: 'The way you did the modelling is a problem for me. You said last time that you divided sales in each period by the distribution then. But doesn't this mean that you're assuming that the distribution effect is in direct proportion? Do we actually know that? Isn't it harder to get sales from the last few percent in distribution, because shoppers are anyway visiting other stores where we are already on the shelf, and making their purchases there already? And anyway, how did we get the distribution? Did advertising help?

'And you said I could change the price without an effect on volume. But it's not worth my putting it up unless I take an increase of 5% or so, and we haven't done anything like that for years. How do you know we'd get away with it?'

Analyst: 'Those are good questions. I suppose I'd better do a regression with distribution as an independent variable to see whether it is a proportional effect or not. I think distribution and advertising are positively correlated: I don't know what to do about that. And I'll look at the price data again.'

Stage 3. Analyst: 'You were quite right about the distribution effect. With the new regression, I get a better fit. Look, the R-squared is up to 0.8 now. The price effect is still not significant. But you're also right about 5% being outside our recent experience. The changes we've had in the last couple of years have usually been only 1 or 2% different from our average 125 index.

'Unfortunately, now I've brought in distribution as an explainer, the advertising elasticity has fallen. It's now 0.2, but this is still above breakeven.'

Manager: 'I've had another idea about distribution. It's really the two-litre size which has given us entry to more outlets. You remember that we launched it with that new campaign, behind which I put the bigger budget. Can we look at that size separately?'

Stage 4. Analyst: 'I've now done a regression with the distributions of the one-litre and two-litre as separate explainers. I get a much better fit; the R-squared is up to 0.9. I'm not using a price variable now, since we agreed that the range of variation we've had makes it not really relevant and the effect has not been shown to be significant. It is the effect of the two-litre which has really pushed up our total sales: look at these coefficients here.

'But I'm afraid that my latest estimate of advertising elasticity, which is 0.1, has now dropped below your breakeven figure. I think the reason for the higher number we got before is that adstock was up at the time the two-litre distribution was high, and the regression was telling us incorrectly that it was an advertising effect because the two-litre change didn't show up much in the overall distribution. My recommendation is that you cut the advertising. We'd be better off as a result.'
Manager: 'So are you telling me that you can't estimate the price effect so I'd better not change the price, and that I should spend less on advertising?'
Analyst: 'That's what it comes to.'

Stage 5. Manager: 'I've been thinking again about where we are now, and about your plots and averages. The situation is that our brand has a 25% premium over the market average, and this has been increasing slowly. We've successfully launched a new size and speeded up the rate of sales growth, which was pretty good before.
'I've been looking at the sales results in different stores and for weeks when we were above the price of our main competitor, and when we were below. We sell a bit less when we're above, but not much. The image data shows that we have a real perceived difference. I think a lot of that is because the advertising is telling people to look for the actual difference in the product. I'm going to take a 5% price increase. What do you think?'
Analyst: 'Well, that's a managerial decision. I can't really comment on the basis of historical sales data.'
Manager: 'And I can't agree that I should cut the advertising when I'm putting up the price. You say that we'd be better off. But from your present estimate of its elasticity of 0.10, compared with the breakeven of 0.15, I should get back £67 of every £100 I spend.' [This is in the proportion of 0.10 to 0.15.]

'Further, look at the price premium I have already, even before I take an increase. We're 25% above the market average, you tell me. Now if we had less advertising, or none, I'm sure I couldn't maintain that much of a premium. Suppose I could get only a 20% premium?'
Analyst: 'Then your revenue would be less by five over a hundred and twenty-five. That's 4%.'
Manager: 'And I'm spending only 5% of the present revenue on advertising. So if I get back four-fifths of that from the average price which I can charge now, and another two-thirds from the short-term lifts in volume, I must be doing well.'
Analyst: 'If you put it like that . . . '
Manager: 'I do put it like that.'

Chapter 7: Action Points

Modelling

Fitting a model to your data is not discussed in this book. Use a specialist.

What If?

With information about the brand's budget and some simple assumptions, it is possible to answer some important questions. You need to know how much your sales volume will change for small changes in your media spend, and what the shape is of this relationship, when changes are not small.

The first of these assumptions is usually the more important. It is the sales elasticity of your advertising: by what percentage does sales volume change, within a year, for a 1% increase in adspend? You will almost never have an exact value for elasticity, but you may get an estimate from modelling (see above), from an experiment or in-market test, from norms suggested in this chapter, or by guessing.

The questions you can then answer are limited to the short term, and are about the direct effects of advertising. Long-term and indirect effects are additional. What if you increase, or decrease, your adspend by moderate amounts (say up to 25%)? What happens to volume and to contribution? Is it profitable to increase adspend? If not, what is the estimated real cost, after allowing for the extra revenue, and the production costs of additional product sold?

A similar approach is outlined for promotional spend, and for price changes. The necessary equations have been set out to apply these methods. The management of a portfolio of brands, and the allocation of a brand's budget marketing activities or across regions, are helped by these equations. Once you have decided the priority between sales volume, and short-term changes in contribution, you can evaluate the priorities for spending your money.

When changes in the budget become larger (over 25%), then the assumption about the shape of the relationship between adspend and sales volume starts to be important. This is almost never known. The log model is often assumed and its consequences are explained.

Optimizing

Using a model prescriptively (having it tell you how much to spend on advertising) is not generally recommended. The difficulty with this use of a model is that its recommendation appears so authoritative that you tend to overlook its limitations. The optimization is usually based on one criterion only (usually short-term contribution). Thus effects on volume may not receive enough attention, let alone long-term and indirect effects. You may be encouraged to take drastic action without proper consideration of alternatives and overall effects. Nevertheless, and if great caution is used, the results of calculating an 'optimum' can be illuminating. The necessary equations have been explained.

8 Case Histories

Death of a Brand

'Shutting down two engines in flight is something you definitely want to avoid, especially if you fly a two-engine airplane' (T. Allan McArtor, Federal Aviation Administrator, 1987).

The brand discussed here no longer exists but was once part of a famous manufacturer's large portfolio. It had been adequately advertised, had a reasonable market share and was profitable. Econometric modelling had successfully measured both the short-term contribution of advertising to sales and the effect of price. Together, these two factors explained most of its sales variation (see Figure 1).

The size of the short-term advertising effect was below breakeven. This is quite normal. It means that reducing adspend will temporarily improve contribution. It was calculated that without advertising, but with a small price reduction, the brand should maintain adequate sales and return a larger profit. The decision was made: cut the advertising and lower the price. For six months the brand achieved the sales expected, delivering the profit planned.

Within a year, however, the model (of advertising and price effects) was failing to predict sales correctly. The brand's share started to decline and within two years was at a catastrophic low (see Figure 2).

In the post-mortem (literally, for the product was withdrawn), it was discovered why sales fell. The reasons started with the sales representatives. In detailing their brands, this one got less and less attention. There was nothing much to say about it: others were getting management attention and the representatives followed management's lead. The price reduction meant lower profits for retailers. Delisting began, but the problem was initially not serious enough to attract the marketer's proper attention. Distribution dropped and the brand was

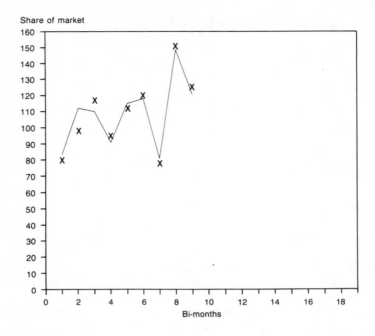

Share of market

Bi-months

Figure 1   Sales of the Brand are Well Predicted by Advertising Weight and Relative Price. Previous average share of market = 100.

Key: ——— = predicted; X = actual.

often out of stock. By the time these effects had been diagnosed, it was all over. Two years without advertising support was too long.

What are the lessons of this sorry story? It is an extreme example, in that advertising was not just reduced but withdrawn. The reaction was faster than is usual and the brand not large enough to be worth re-establishing. These are the mistakes the marketer realized too late that he had made:

— Representative and retailer behaviour were assumed to be independent of advertising support. The long-term trade effects, from which the brand previously benefited, were eroded.
— The short-term part of the return from advertising was uneconomic and was believed to be the whole story so advertising could safely be withdrawn.
— Price was treated as independent of advertising: value could be

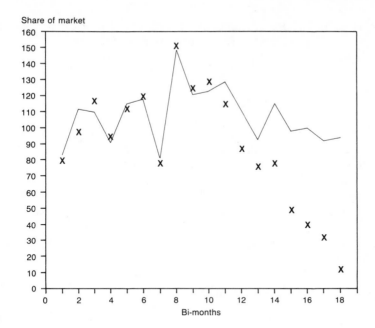

**Figure 2   The Prediction in Figure 1 Breaks Down: the Brand Dies in Year 3.
Previous average share of market = 100.**

Key: ——— = predicted; X = actual.

maintained without advertising and the cut price would work as well as before.

In similar vein, Nielsen (1) has reported on three well-established brands which stopped advertising and on one which halved its adspend. The sales falls that followed were less drastic than those in the case above, and little detail was published. Nevertheless, the examples are disturbing. They support the view that when advertising is cut, or much reduced, a steep sales decline is commonly observed.

Brand B had its share of market fall 15% in the first non-advertised year, and averaged a loss of 4.5% per year for the next six years. Brand D had its share of market fall 7% in the first non-advertised year, and averaged a loss of 3.5% per year for the next three years.

Brand C stopped its advertising several years before the period that was studied. Its share of market decline averaged 5.5% per year for ten years.

Brand E halved its adspend and its share of market fell 14% in the same year. This number happens to equal the fall predicted for a brand with very good advertising in Figure 1 in Chapter 2.

Ten Years of Franchise Building

This summarizes a case history published by Robert Prentice (2). The budget decision studied includes more than simply advertising. In consumer franchise building spend (or CFB), Prentice includes advertising, but also certain types of promotion: sampling, coupons, demonstrations, recipes, etc. The distinction is whether the activity registers with consumers unique and important selling ideas about the product, which help establish long-term brand preference. If not, as for example in a trade deal, the spend is counted as non-CFB. The total, CFB + non-CFB spend, equals the total advertising and promotion budget.

The case history studies two major brands in a grocery category. They were more or less equal in product quality and in the high proportion of revenue allocated in total to advertising and promotion. They were also generally equal in dollar sales for the first five years studied. To complete the similarities, both brands started to switch a significant proportion of total spend to promotions in Years 6 and 7.

Where the brand's policies differed significantly was in the proportion of spend which went to CFB activities. Brand A was always above Brand B and averaged 70% to Brand B's 57%. When the switch by both brands to non-CFB activities accelerated, Brand A maintained its actual CFB spend but Brand B cut this expenditure, presumably to pay for its non-CFB spend. See Figure 3 for details. The effect on sales can be seen in Figure 4. From having an equal share to Brand B, Brand A pulled ahead in Year 6, and then moved steadily up. Brand B went into slow decline.

The effect on profit was more dramatic, although directionally the same. Brand A started with profit as a proportion of revenue similar to Brand B's. In the last three years Brand A not only made three times as much profit as Brand B, but its profit as a proportion of revenue had risen from about 26% to 30% while Brand B's had fallen to 18%.

We can speculate that the major reason why Brand B suffered so badly was that it put its faith in trade deals. These ate into profit because they were, in effect, price reductions. Less money went into advertising, and the brand franchise declined.

As Prentice points out, 'Value isn't enough. Consumers must believe

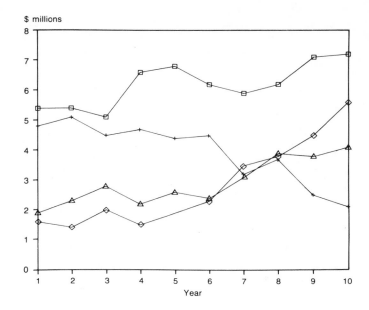

Figure 3 **Expenditure by Two Brands on Consumer Franchise Building and on Other Promotions (after Prentice, 1977).**

Key: □ = CFB, Brand A; + = CFB, Brand B; ◇ = non-CFB, A; △ = non-CFB, B.

the value is worth the price.' For Brand B, it is possible that value, in the consumers' mind, declined faster than the effect of any price reduction that the retailer decided to pass on.

A final lesson is the long length of time these results took to show but how overwhelming they were when they happened. Brand A's shift to heavy CFB spend started in Year 4, but sales and profit in Years 4 and 5 were no more than before. The debate in Year 4, and about its effects in Year 5, can be imagined. CFB spend did not increase in later years, but the growth in sales and profit continued.

Once the momentum of success starts, it may need no increase in effort to keep it going. In fact, the proportion of revenue going to Brand A's CFB spend (like an advertising-to-sales ratio) fell rather steadily in the last five years. We again see an example of a larger brand with higher actual spend, but one that is lower in proportion to actual sales.

Another ten-year case history has been published by Nielsen (1), but in less detail and using share of voice only as the explanation. Brand

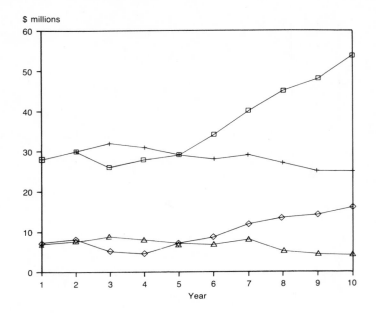

Figure 4   Sales and Profits for Two Brands (after Prentice, 1977).

Key: □ = sales, Brand A; ◇ = profit, A; + = sales, Brand B; △ = profit, B.

A let its share of voice fall to 50% of its initial level. Share of market fell 5%. Brand B, a very similar brand in the same category, increased its share of voice to 126% of its initial level. Share of market rose 38%.

An Agency Presentation

This case history is based on a real presentation, made by an American advertising agency to its client. The detail has been changed, for confidentiality, and the presentation has been abbreviated, but the spirit of the argument has been followed.

Background

You asked us whether you are spending the right amount on advertising. We are responding by suggesting to you a budgeting system, for your continued use. We have assumed that your business philosophy is permanent, that our advertising strategy and copy remain unchanged, and that the events we are supporting will continue.

Let's review the category we're competing in. We're still seeing growth, although at a declining rate. The reasons, we all know, are . . . In this category, our share has generally grown, and of course the product you offer is a big cause of that growth. We remember also that the variations you've introduced in the product played a big part and will continue to do so.

Our competitors have not been idle. In 1981 we tracked advertising for seven competitors, but we now face thirteen — and they advertise. Although the growth in our actual dollars on advertising has been large, they have kept pace. Our share of voice, in total, has stayed the same.

Our plans are to continue to grow. You are familiar with the growth target and the reasons for it. Here is what advertising should contribute in the short term:
— disseminate product news
— intensify product-led promotional events
— differentiate us from competition
— target broader sources of business.
In the longer term, we intend to:
— strengthen loyalty to our brand
— emphasize the proprietary aspects of our product.

Budget Determination Methods

Now we turn to the methods we have used to develop advertising budgets. These were selected after a review of textbook methods. Four seem to us particularly appropriate. Three of these suggest what to spend, then we determine how to spend it. In the last, we figure out what media job we must accomplish and then we determine how much it will cost to do the work.

Each of these ways has both strengths and weaknesses, but putting all four together guides our judgement more surely. And judgement *is* necessary because we are playing with intangible variables.

Many major advertisers use all of these budgeting methods. Packaged goods companies lean towards share of spending/share of market analyses. They have excellent data on sales share, through warehouse withdrawals, and at the retail level. Many have tracked relationships between share of spending and share of market. With other advertisers, the competitive data that are available and the financial needs of the distributors, bottlers, or franchisees lead them to emphasize advertising-to-sales ratios. Historical trends in advertising levels and sales results are looked at, in addition, by almost all advertisers.

1. Historical patterns: percent of sales
Historically, our actual advertising-to-sales ratios have been . . . The reported ratios, which we can compare with others, have been . . . Note, by the way, how these compare with promotional spends . . . Compared with competitors, we fall in the middle. We all know why X has been a heavy spender, while Y has relied less on advertising.

The numbers are not comparable, but it is useful to look at some reported advertising-to-sales ratios:

Advertising Dollars as a Percent of Sales (*Advertising Age*, 15 September, 1986)

Mail Order Houses	13.2
Perfumes/Cosmetics	13.1
Records	9.1
Malt Beverages	8.4
Soaps and Detergents	7.9
Service: Personal	7.5
Distilled Beverages	7.2
Soft Drinks	6.6
Candy	6.5
Canned Fruit/Vegetables	5.3
Jewelry Stores	6.2
Furniture Stores	5.8
Household Appliance Stores	5.7
Food	5.2
Dairy Products	5.1

Our recommendation, based on the success you enjoy at the current level, is that you would be comfortable with a ratio of . . . Because next year's plan calls for a turnover of . . . we have a budget of $. . .

2. Historical patterns: actual spends
Looking at annual changes in turnover, and in spending, we see some associations as well as trends. In 1983, you will remember, we saw our fastest growth, with correspondingly high spend. Recent slowing of growth is matched by reduced growth in spend. This is another way of looking at the advertising-to-sales ratio, because we can see the actual changes in each part of the ratio. The trend in spend which matches the plan for next year suggests an additional spend of $. . .

3. *Historical patterns: shares*

There is more life in quarterly data. Hence there is a positive relationship between our share of advertising dollars and our share of market in the following quarter. On average, the shares are associated in the following way . . . In recent years, the reaction to increases in share of spending has been more immediate. Possibly this is due to both promotions and advertising becoming more competitive.

Because we anticipate that the competition will spend next year, for the following reasons, $. . . the total advertising spend will be about $. . .

We are looking for an increased share in our category, aiming at . . . To continue the historical relationship between the two shares calls for $. . .

4. *Task method*

We have reviewed what research has suggested are the links between (a) putting our commercials on air and (b) message attention and learning, positive attitudes and preference, and brand switching/purchase behaviour. The task method sets objectives that the advertising must accomplish in these areas. We then develop a media plan that meets the objectives, we determine the cost of the media plan and that is the recommended budget.

How simple it sounds when I say it so quickly! In fact, this method is the most difficult. It requires an intimate knowledge of our customers and what motivates them. It requires an understanding of the strengths and weaknesses of the marketing plan. It demands that we think about the short- and long-term needs of our business. It incorporates as many variables as possible that can affect our sales. This method is designed to help us understand the most effective and efficient plan to drive purchase behaviour and build the business. Marketing judgement plays an important part in this process.

We have to understand our target customer. What does the customer have to learn? How tough will it be to make his or her attitude about the product or promotion positive? How difficult will it be to get the customer to make the purchase decision? This thought process can guide the development of our marketing events, of our product innovations, and of our media plan.

You are familiar with the outline media plan for next year. I would like to show you how it stems from your marketing plan, how each element of it is there for a specific purpose, how we can cost the effort we believe necessary to meet these objectives. Thus we are setting the ground rules for future media plan analysis and costing, again leading to a budgeting method.

We have always recognized the importance both of different marketing districts and of the demography of those of our customers who respond to different appeals. We therefore separate our plans by district and by the adult and youth targets. We have chosen to target mainly our heavy users, given their large contribution to our sales. We'd also like to see more of our medium to light users increase their purchase frequency and more of our competitors' users choose our product. We need to know our purchase cycles, both for adults and for youths, to use when examining the number of commercial exposures necessary to influence consumer behaviour.

When we apply our methodology in actual planning, special targets, daypart mixes and commercial allocations will be considered for each subject.

We will maintain local market flexibility by assuming that, where it makes sense, price point advertising and special promotions will be a local market obligation. Ethnic newspapers, outdoor, and other local media are assumed to be given and will be added to the final budget figures.

To start with, all reach and frequency curves used in developing the frequency computer model are based on average four-week data. Therefore, we will use a four-week period to generate our media plan. Then we determine the required message frequency. This is based on . . . [here follows a long section on purchase behaviour in this category, effective frequency for four-week periods for different targets and the way different dayparts in TV, and other media, are planned to reach such frequencies].

Now combine the different parts of the plan. Here are the marketing elements which each supports . . . the media units required, for each marketing district, customer target, and media type used . . .

Now for the finesse! We have a numerically grounded base plan to work with. Our next task is to put our heads together to mould this base plan into a plan that meets our strengths and weaknesses, a plan that talks directly to our customer. It's time to be even smarter.

We first address seasonality. Our goal is to deliver media in line with category usage. We want to be sure we are 'fishing when the fish are biting'. What this means is relatively more weight in November than, for example, January.

Then we have category spending. We want to ensure a competitive share of voice throughout the year, by taking into account industry spending.

Next, our philosophy is that we must place relatively more advertising behind a complex message, or concept, or to reach a difficult target group, than for a message that is easily understood.

Our final consideration is length of support. We want to be sure that shorter events and promotions are successful. Therefore, with any events lasting less than four weeks, higher weekly weight levels will be necessary, in order to build awareness faster.

Applying these ideas to the basic plan leads us to strengthen here . . . while we can relax here . . .

We now have a media plan we believe is appropriate to what we must achieve, and fine-tuned as well as we can. Next we are ready to consider buying the plan. Here we will follow this procedure . . . which we are confident will get you the exposure you need at the lowest achievable cost.

And this cost is $. . .

Conclusion

We were asked to determine the right amount of spending. We looked at four different methods, each of which generated a hypothetical budget. You have seen that these fall within a close dollar range.

We feel that basing future budgeting on the task method — whether used exactly in the manner that we did today or not — is the most appropriate way to address your spending decision. We started with a communication based goal. We added our best thinking and arrived at a plan tailored to address your objectives. You have seen how the task budget is in line with that suggested by other methods. It is the budget we recommend.

Managing Four Brands

This example is based on a real American case history, modified for confidentiality. It shows some learning about advertising's effects from recent history. There is a need to balance environmental changes, other marketing activity and product changes with company objectives. The example also indicates the complexity of portfolio management. In the real world, the situation is even more complicated than indicated here.

Memo to: Managing Director
From: Health Drinks Marketing Manager   September 1986

Re: Advertising Budget 1987

At last week's meeting we discussed the whole A&P programme. You asked for details of my recommended advertising budget and how it was determined. In particular, you wish to counter the objection to our advertising expenditure in view of our 'failure to increase gallonage'.

This memo supports the first item in the total advertising part of my budget:

	$MM
Working media, going brands	38.4
Advertising production and fees	5.9
Research, subscriptions, miscellaneous	1.7
Department overhead, salaries	3.6

2. Gallons are indeed steady, but our 1987 target is for growth of 7% above 1983–86 average:

	Millions of gallons
1983	316
1984	313
1985	320
1986 (estimated)	307
1987 (target)	337

3. Revenue and margin tell a different story, due to our rising prices (especially at the end of 1985 and in 1986) and cost reduction programmes. Raw material costs will rise in 1987, however, due to the new contracts, unfortunately pulling margin/revenue lower than in previous years:

$ millions	Revenue	Margin	Margin/revenue
1983	566	222	0.393
1984	593	230	0.388
1985	639	263	0.411
1986 (estimated)	685	300	0.438
1987 (target)	780	294	0.377

4. Our price increase has been nearly 8% a year and this more than cost reduction has helped us to improve margin by nearly 35% (1986 estimate over 1983).

Brand audit surveys explain why: we have had regular increases in the perceived value of our brands, and image measures show that advertised brand claims are the major reason. Advertising has communicated to people — especially to our key target purchasers — the reasons for consumption of our brands. We do not refer to price in our advertising, but focus groups leave us in no doubt that the purchaser is aware of the rising price but considers it worthwhile for the reasons given in the advertising.

Sales reports show that pricing our brands higher than competitors is acceptable, due to our good turnover per foot of shelf space. The trade discounts we give are comparable to, or lower than, competitors'. Promotional spend/revenue has decreased slightly.

It might have been possible to increase volume if we had held price or reduced it. Production limitations, and pressure for contribution, made increased margin the preferred route.

The margin *increase* of $78 million a year (1986 est. on 1983) is well above our current *total* rate of adspend.

I suggest that these facts be used to explain 'failure to increase gallonage despite heavy advertising'.

5. Working media spend rose sharply mid-1985 and in 1986, as the planned price increases took effect:

| | $/Gallon | Working media | | |
		$ millions	as % of revenue	as % of margin
1983	1.79	27.9	4.9	12.6
1984	1.90	27.3	4.6	11.8
1985	1.99	41.2	6.4	15.7
1986 (estimated)	2.24	42.0	6.1	14.0
1987 (target)	2.31			

Our average media spend as a percent of margin has been 13.6%.

6. My recommendation for 1987 is to base the budget on this ratio, but checking first on the individual brands' allocation, and second on their volume and margin targets. Thus $40 million is the provisional media spend which has to be allocated and checked for feasibility.

7. Overall, we look for only 3% increase in price, but 10% in volume. Our experience of comparable changes is as follows:

	Price increase (%)	Volume change (%)
1984	6	−1
1985	5	2
1986 (estimated)	13	−4

The GRPs we expect in 1987 will be about 10% below 1985–86 but 20% above 1984.

Obviously, the high volume increase at a low price increase, with advertising support at a comparable level, is outside previous experience. In my view, it is not impossible. Creative strategy changes are in hand, aimed at widening the drinking occasions portrayed.

8. A summary follows for each brand's recent history, market situation and 1987 objectives:

Health Drink Division, Sales and Advertising 1983–86

	Apple MM Gallon	MM$	Orange MM Gallon	MM$	Grape MM Gallon	MM$	Lime MM Gallon	MM$	Four-brand Total MM Gallon	MM$	$/ Gallon
1983	137.0	266.7	105.0	181.2	37.3	62.0	36.2	56.2	315.5	566.0	1.79
1984	143.5	282.8	95.7	182.8	40.6	73.2	33.2	54.4	313.0	593.2	1.90
1985	142.5	306.2	104.9	192.9	44.2	82.1	28.8	57.9	320.4	639.1	1.99
1986	142.2	317.2	97.5	223.4	39.4	87.5	27.5	57.1	306.6	685.2	2.24
Avg 83–86	141.3	293.2	100.8	195.1	40.4	76.2	31.4	56.4	313.9	620.9	1.98

	Apple Margin	Ad-spend	Orange Margin	Ad-spend	Grape Margin	Ad-spend	Lime Margin	Ad-spend	Four-brand Total Margin	Ad-spend	Ads/ rev.	Ads/ marg.
1983	110.2	8.1	67.3	11.8	20.0	6.6	24.9	1.5	222.4	27.9	0.049	0.13
1984	113.8	8.2	69.6	10.1	21.8	6.3	25.2	2.6	230.3	27.3	0.046	0.12
1985	124.6	14.1	82.9	14.6	29.7	9.0	25.6	3.5	262.8	41.2	0.064	0.16
1986	138.8	13.2	97.9	16.1	37.2	10.1	26.1	2.7	300.0	42.0	0.061	0.14
Avg 83–86	121.8	10.9	79.4	13.1	27.2	8.0	25.4	2.6	253.9	34.6	0.055	0.14

Apple
Apple represents 45% of our gallonage and 47% of revenue. Our trade relations are excellent, due to this brand's history. Apple's image among consumers is also our best. The evidence is that the current level of advertising support has been adequate. We plan the highest price change here but see no reason to increase adspend.

Orange
Orange volume has fluctuated recently with competitive pressure. The new packaging is doing well where it has been introduced. We plan to roll it out nationally next year. This will enable us actually to reduce price, a different strategy from the other brands. The very high level of ad support has not been successful and will be reduced.

Grape
Grape is also in a very competitive sector. The advertising share of our budget is certainly high, given the low margin on this product. Grape's image is below Apple's but seems to respond to advertising weight so it makes sense to maintain the high share of spend.

Lime
Lime is our problem child. Sales are declining. The media budget has been at a maintenance level. However, the low production cost and high margin argue for an increase in media spend. We plan an average price rise. The real choices are whether we allow the brand to die, or continue to milk it, or at least arrest the decline. My recommendation is the last of these.

9. The provisional brand data show:

	Apple	Orange	Grape	Lime	Total
Working media ($ millions)					
1986 (estimated)	13.2	16.1	10.1	2.7	42.0
1987 (proposed)	13.2	13.3	9.6	3.9	40.0
Percent change	0	−17%	−5%	+44%	−5%
Price change	+10%	−9%	+9%	+4%	+3%
Gallons (millions)					
1986 (estimated)	142.2	97.5	39.4	27.5	306.6
1987 (target)	155.0	109.3	45.6	27.5	337.5
Percent change	+9%	+12%	+16%	0	+10%

10. When checking the individual brand budgets for feasibility, the only problem is with Grape. The volume target is very ambitious, and with a high production cost, it would be expensive to restore the 1986 working media budget. In fact, we should improve contribution at a smaller gallonage target and a reduced working media budget.

I recommend Plan B below as a realistic alternative to the current Plan A.

| | Grape, 1987 | |
	Plan A	Plan B
Working media ($ millions)	8.0	9.0
Gallons (millions)	43.5	45.0
Contribution ($ millions) (margin less overheads and A&P)	16.4	15.9

The Quarterly Budget Review

At one time I regularly attended the quarterly review meetings which directed a particular brand's budget — not just for advertising but for the other marketing investments as well.

The order of the agenda says a lot about the pressures which brand management work under. The summary which follows gives a feel for the subjects and priorities which impinged most on this advertising budget. I do not put forward the practice in this company as an ideal, though this was one of the best marketing companies I have worked with. Rather, it is meant to add a flavour of realism to what can seem otherwise academic.

First on the agenda were always the most up-to-date volume sales figures. Ex-factory, or deliveries to retailers, were the most important. It was these which brought in the revenue on which everything else depended. They were real in a sense which was lacking in the retail audit data — the result of a survey, subject to error, not covering all outlets, and less timely. However, merely filling the pipeline was never enough, especially since for this brand the consumer marketing effort was a major expense. Were the sales being pulled through by this effort? Was it earning its keep?

Often the two sorts of figures pointed in opposite directions. Ex-factory looked good, but the audit data had not moved correspond-ingly. Or the audit demonstrated a reaction to marketing activity not yet reflected in deliveries. The audit itself might show volume moving in a different direction from share, which brought in questions of category movement, seasonality, competitors . . .

I often saw these discussions as very short term, and dishonest in the sense that when one of the indicators gave cause for optimism then that was the one concentrated on. Next quarter, another indicator which happened to move well was prominent.

Naturally, a lot of the work was very detailed. Individual retail chains, sales districts, pack sizes — variations at this level tested the memory or at least the data systems of the brand manager.

Year-end profit forecast was always second on the agenda. The volume sales trends were used, with other numbers, to defend, or occasionally to change, this prediction. Obviously this was the stage at which price to the trade mattered.

There was often a division here between marketing and sales management. On the whole the marketing people, responsible ulti-mately for profit but not in this case responsible for the detail of trade negotiation, fought to keep price up. Money going on trade deals was seen as coming straight from the bottom line. Salesmen saw trade deals as part of the cost of doing business, and resented the office-staff knowing too little of the atmosphere in a buyer's office.

When a compromise had been reached on the volume, price and profit figures, or often before, there was usually an interruption by the Marketing Director. This was about pressure on the brand's budget from other parts of the company, rarely under the control of anyone in the room. The usual sources were the finance people and the needs expressed by other brands, which we heard about, it seemed, only when they were doing badly. Financial demands could be aimed at the year-end or a quarter's results; they could be from other divisions or overseas; they could be expressed as requests or edicts: 'Can we reduce . . .?' or 'No more spend on . . . ' The results of both sorts of pressure were the same: money for advertising was withdrawn. The circum-stances for our brand had to be very special — during a re-launch for example — for any activity other than advertising to be the first choice for cuts.

Useful summaries at this stage were provided by two sorts of plot:
- the brand's recent sales history against time, for volume, for sterling, as share of category, against last year and so on
- the brand's relative price and advertising support (TVRs), shown

on a scatter plot as a line connecting its recent annual positions; when price was low and TVRs were high we expected, and often got, good sales shares; as the position moved towards the corner of high price and low TVRs, we all saw the threat.

When the demands for money were compared with this threat to the next year, or to the longer term, then the decision was never a purely logical one. To call it emotional may be stretching the facts, but it certainly drew more on instinct than on accountancy. There were occasions — though rare — on which the demands were resisted and the brand won.

There were actually mathematical models available, quantifying the effects of our marketing activities and 'explaining' the sales movements. They were used in the meetings much less than the simple descriptive plots outlined above. The latter were interpreted naively perhaps, but always vividly.

There were also what-if models, forecasting the financial effects of marketing decisions. These were used even less, and more to build up a case outside the room, which was then presented to the meeting in simpler terms. The reason was that the models were so restricted in the decision-making and criteria represented. Balancing opposing and often unquantified pressures was the main job of the meeting.

Timing was a major subject. When would commercials be ready, money released, product improvements or trade events scheduled? Were the gaps between bursts too long? Was the coordination correct between advertising and the development of other marketing tools?

The actual media schedule itself was always important. It was understood that to talk about money alone was not enough; TVRs laid down over time were a translation of the budget decisions into another, and, in its way, more practical language. Thus a budget change was always accompanied by a discussion on the resulting changes in the size of the advertising bursts.

On the few occasions when completely fresh creative was to be shown, the schedule became even more important. Were the TVRs heavy enough to give a fair chance to the new (code for 'better') advertisements? After the new work had appeared, was the higher spend seen to be justified?

Occasionally, the reviews turned into crisis meetings. Sometimes it was the creative work, sometimes a packaging or other product breakthrough, sometimes a competitive initiative, which demanded a re-think. Because the team was used to meeting under normal circumstances, these more fundamental reviews seemed to me to be better run than in some companies. They were absorbed into the flow of normal brand management.

Competitive activity was always on the agenda. Should their efforts cause us real anxiety? What could be learned from their way of working? What did their results teach us?

To sum up, for this advertiser, advertising decisions were reached by a continual compromise. Three forces were the main supports for the advertising budget: evidence of its effectiveness, the threat presented by competitors, and a natural inbred belief in branding and in the benefits of added value. The main opposition was simply other needs for the cash; sometimes these were opposing marketing activities, a trade deal, for example, or a consumer promotion, but, much more often, the money was called for by other parts of the company.

The following is not a real agenda, but summarizes an order which often occurred:

1 (a) Ex-factory sales: report.
  (b) Audit sales data: report and reconciliation with item 1 (a).
2.　　Year-end forecasts, including profit: discussion.
3.　　Budget trends, especially relative price to consumers and advertising support: long-term goals.
4　　Timing plans over next six months: review.
5.　　Competitors' activity: report and implications on items 2, 3 and 4.
6.　　Advertising budget and other decisions.

Determining the A/S and Other Ratios

In Chapter 3, one of the ratios which we examined was that of media spend to sales revenue. For many reasons, this is an extremely important figure. It is now looked at in more detail, particularly as a method of suggesting or evaluating a budget, as was discussed in Chapter 5. One way of doing this is to make our advertising-to-sales or some other ratio equal to some average. But while it is easy to calculate our own ratios from the budget, it is much harder to do this for other brands or for the total category. In addition, we have to decide what is average or typical.

There are five parts to the work we have to do, each discussed below:

1. Define the category.
2. Decide whether to look at individual brands or at only the category total.
3. Settle on the period of time covered.

4. Find the advertising number to use.
5. Find the sales number to use.

Note that many of the comments which follow apply more generally. For example, every time we talk about the category, it is assumed that it has been defined. Any application of advertising or sales data needs the same attention. In particular, share of voice and share of market definitions require exactly the same data; indeed, a brand's advertising-to-sales ratio differs only by a constant from its share of voice divided by its share of market (the constant is the advertising-to-sales ratio for the whole category, and Example 3 goes into this in detail).

Category

The decision on how to define the category depends, like many other choices, on what data sources are available, which often limits us severely. Out of the brands and sectors which we may use as a definition, do we take the largest possible group, or do we include only what we regard as direct competition? Usually there are some brands which are obvious candidates, but, for example, do we include unadvertised brands? These may market themselves in quite a different way from us, and their inclusion pulls down the A/S ratio, perhaps misleadingly. Do we include store brands or own-label, which may benefit from advertising which the store runs across all categories? Do we count brands in their first year, which may have A/S which are untypically high?

Total or Individual Brands

It is recommended that individual brands are studied. Sometimes only category totals are available, but then the data will suffer in other ways explained below, and the average will turn out to be a very poor guide. The first reason for looking at individual brands is that it is then possible to limit the choice to those brands that consumers use as substitutes for ours. There is no need to include products which are non-competitive. The second and more important reason is that the variety we then see makes the choice of our own ratio more relevant to our own brand situation, since we see the way other brands' ratios relate to their situations. The brands which we can choose as typical may be those in a very roughly similar situation to our own. That is, they are not too different in size, and do not undertake markedly different marketing activities.

When a total is used there is only one way to define an average ratio, but when brands are studied there are several ways of choosing a typical ratio. Averaging the ratios for brands, even when they have very different market shares, is one way of proceeding. It is reasonable when our brand is not extreme in size, but a more careful selection of typical brands is usually possible, as we see in the examples later.

Period

Less than a year can be very misleading, since we may easily hit on a time when spend or sales were untypical. Looking at the most recent year is common, but looking at two years separately is best.

Advertising

This is the easier half of the ratio. Figures for all brands and for most media can be got from MEAL (Media Expenditure Analysis Limited) or the Media Register. Though the actual amounts paid for each unit are confidential, a sufficiently accurate overall figure for each brand's real spend can be provided, as was explained in Chapter 3. We usually look at competitors' spend in order to compare it with our own, so the discounts applied must be carefully considered and all the figures must be on the same basis. Do not, for example, compare our actual budget with competitors' at full ratecard.

Alternatively, we sometimes use the data on exposures of advertising to the target, in order to look for associations between advertising exposure and its results. In this case, the representation of media weight which unadjusted ratecard figures give, or actual media exposure data like TVRs, is what we want. In the latter case, ratings should be adjusted for spot length and 30-second equivalents are often used. In many ways, A/S and 30-second equivalent TVRs per tonne (or whatever) may be used similarly. Which is best? The answer depends on two things: first, the purpose of the investigation, and second, whichever gives the most meaningful regularities in analysis.

The absence of some media group (for example, outdoor in MEAL) often does not matter, but ensure that every group is included which is seriously used in the category.

Expenditure on the media advertising covered by MEAL (after adjustment for estimated discounts) more than doubled between 1981 and 1987, as shown in Table 1. This increase is in current money. When inflation is allowed for, by the rise in the Retail Price Index, the increase was just over 50%. Between the same years, the Gross Domestic Product increased in real terms by 17%. Thus the fact there were more goods available accounted for part of the advertising increase. After these two factors were allowed for, the increase in advertising was 30%. A lot of this was due to whole categories deciding to spend more on advertising, or indeed advertising for the first time. The same 1981 and 1987 totals are shown in Table 2, but this time in seven broad categories. These are listed in increasing order of growth. It is clear that the Financial and Industrial sectors, and to a lesser extent, Government, grew at a faster rate than average.

Table 1   Summary of MEAL Adjusted Advertising Expenditure, 1981 and 1987

	£ millions (current)	Retail Price Index (1974=100)	£ millions (at 1987 prices)	Gross Domestic Product (£000 million) (current)	(at 1987 prices)
1981	1386	295	1888	255	347
1987	2873	402	2873	407	407
Percentage change	+107	+36	+52	+60	+17

Table 2   MEAL Adjusted Advertising Expenditure, Current £ Million

	1981	1987	Percentage change	Percentage share in 1987
Retail	242	380	+57	13
Services	133	249	+87	9
Durables	304	579	+90	20
Consumables	496	1018	+105	35
Government	44	94	+114	3
Financial	104	317	+205	11
Industrial	64	235	+207	8
Total	1386	2873	+107	100

Sales

You may be fortunate enough to work in a category where a Trade Association or Government or some similar body publishes figures based on each manufacturer's declared sales. You will know that even these numbers have flaws, but they are superior to the data which most manufacturers have. Good sales data about competitors are expensive and difficult — sometimes impossible — to collect. Remember to allow for the under-reporting or low cover which may affect the totals, and distinguish between sterling sales at the prices paid by consumers and at the prices at the factory gate, before retailers and other middlemen have added their margins.

These difficulties have in some years prevented the Advertising Association from publishing advertising-to-sales (A/S) ratios for more than a few categories, and the Association gives clear warnings about the interpretation of these statistics. However, in the 1988 *Yearbook* (1986 data), such ratios are given for many categories, as well as very sensible comments on sales data. We see, for example, a ratio of 0.3% for gin, and 17.4% for toothpaste (these are not extremes: the lowest shown is 0.01% and the largest is over 34%).

Remember that the *Yearbook* cannot give the detail for individual brands, nor explicitly distinguish between categories where there are many or few unadvertised products, or where the manufacturer receives a high or a low proportion of what the consumer pays (in the case of gin, duty obviously affects this). Therefore the A/S ratio published for your category is not intended as a recommendation for the ratio of your own advertising spend to your actual revenue.

Example 1
In this simple case, suppose you manage Brand B, with a 10% share of market. You compete with a much larger Brand A, which has 40%. The rest of the products in the category do not advertise. Brand A spends half a million pounds, correctly reported by MEAL. You spend the same, since your intention is to grow, and part of your strategy is to look as big as Brand A. Turnover of the category at the consumer level is £100 million, but trade margins take 20% of this.

The apparent advertising-to-sales ratio for the category is 1%, from £1 million on £100 million. However, you are spending £500 000 on a revenue of £8 million, and have a ratio of 6.25%.

Your ratio looks seriously out of line with the category, but may still be reasonable. Indeed, I have picked these figures as fairly typical for an ambitious brand some way behind the leader, in a category with substantial own-label or commodity presence. The ratio is in many actual cases justified by a combination of volume growth and the price per unit which the advertiser is able to charge.

One way of overcoming the problems of under-reporting and other biases is to work with a different ratio. If all brands suffer from the same bias, share of voice/share of market is a good replacement for A/S. Share of voice is simply the advertising figure for the brand (spend, ratings, or whatever) divided by a similar figure for the category. Share of market is sales for the brand divided by sales for the category. These shares may be more precise than the raw numbers. Their ratio may be used in much the same way as the A/S ratio, as Example 3 shows.

Note that share of voice (or share of advertising) is a sensible way to summarize our adspend compared with competition only when we are using long periods of time (a year, or at longest a quarter). It can fail, when a short period is used (a week, for example), to provide a reasonable measure of advertising pressure. This is because our own and competitive TVRs can then fluctuate so much that share of voice changes become an almost meaningless statistic.

Example 2
Over a year, our 1000 TVRs is 10% of the category's 10 000. Next year, we expect the category to buy 12 000 TVRs. If we stay at 1000, then our share of voice drops to 8.3%. This is a sensible description.

Over a week, the category buys 200 TVRs on average and we buy 20. If the category figure varies from 100 to 300, then our share of voice swings between 20% and 7% (3 to 1), even when our actual TVRs are unchanged. This is not likely to lead to sensible results in an analysis.

Sometimes there is debate on whether it is share of voice or actual TVRs (or the equivalent) which drives sales. In most applications there is little difference between the way these two figures move. There is no general answer: the question is resolved by determining which number gives better explanations in the analysis of history. Note again that for low advertising expenditures (over a short period, for example), a brand's share of voice can be extremely variable and so is unlikely to relate closely to sales effects.

You have also to decide whether sales should be in sterling or in volume (kilograms, gallons, or whatever). When brands differ in price, so will the results. An expensive brand obviously has a higher sterling share than its share by volume. It can also afford to spend more and often does. Sterling is therefore preferred, and this is also the way we look at the ratio in our own budget. But adspend per case, or ratings per tonne, or similar figures, do much the same job.

The most usual sources of sales data are retail audits (example, Nielsen) and consumer panels (example, TCA). These give both value and volume. Consumer surveys can also provide estimates, but of course unchecked claims to buy, or claims to buy most often, are subject to greater error. Again, in your own category you will be aware of the biases. It is in fast-moving categories that claimed shares are closest to reality, and the *Food Forecast* and *Drink Forecast* (published by Industry Forecasts Limited) use Target Group Index data for shares. These also publish MEAL advertising numbers for recent years.

Example 3. What A/S ratios for three brands?
This American manufacturer marketed three brands in a crowded category of fast-moving packaged foods. In 1987 there were 16 advertised brands. These spent in total $120 million on advertising. Sales in the category totalled $1600 million. Both these are as recorded by syndicated sources, which are used throughout this example. The overall average advertising-to-sales ratio for the category was 7.5%. The manufacturer's brands, however, had very different ratios:

Brand	Sales ($MM)	Share of market (%)	Adspend ($MM)	Share of voice (%)	A/S (%)
X	202	12.6	15.9	13.2	7.9
Y	76	4.7	6.6	5.4	8.7
Z	32	2.0	6.8	5.6	21.3

Note that for some purposes it is the same to compare brands by share of voice/share of market as to use the advertising-to-sales ratios. The first has the advantage that we do not need to know the adjustments to convert reported adspend and sales to actuals. The second is simply the brand's share of voice/share of market times the advertising-to-sales ratio for the category.

Thus A/S for Brand X can be calculated from

$(13.2/12.6) \times 7.5\% = 7.9\%$

which is the same as

$100 \times 15.9/202 = 7.9\%$.

Thus we can say that Brand Y has A/S 10% higher than Brand X, simply because $5.4/4.7 = 1.15$ is 10% above $13.2/12.6 = 1.05$.

Data on the category were to be used to decide whether ours were appropriate A/S ratios, that is, whether they were normal.

Two scatter plots summarize how these three brands compared with others in the category. On these plots, other brands are shown by their sales rank order: '1' stands for the brand with the largest sales, '16' for the brand with the smallest sales. Both plots were against share of market. Figure 5 shows the advertising-to-sales ratios. Figure 6 shows share of voice which is proportional to actual adspend.

The first finding is that there is large variation in the A/S ratios: for the smaller brands these lie between nearly zero and 24%. The unweighted average of all 16 brands is 11.8% (here a small brand counts as much as a large one and only advertised brands are counted, which is why this average is larger than the 7.5% above).

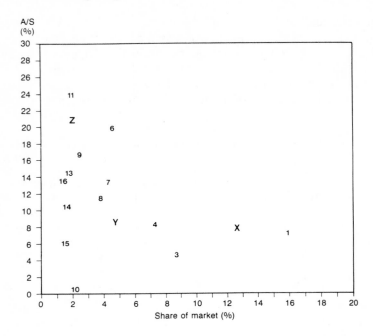

Figure 5   Advertising-to-Sales Ratios for 16 Brands: Large Brands Have Low A/S Ratios.

The five larger brands have A/S ratios that are closer together and average 7.4%. This is lower than the general average, as is normal, and was commented on in Chapter 5. The 11 smaller brands have on the average A/S ratios nearly twice as high at 13.8%.

Figure 6 tells us that the larger brands with larger sales also have larger shares of voice, so larger actual adspends. This is again usual. These brands can afford to spend more because they have a larger revenue than the others. But they have chosen to do so at a lower A/S ratio.

The manufacturer, of course, knew the strategies for his own brands. It was not difficult to infer what his competitors' general strategies were. There were clues in their trade activities, product formulation changes or lack of change, positioning in advertising as well as adspend, pricing and so on. It was largely these different strategies that seemed to determine the brands' A/S ratios.

Of the medium-sized brands, the main contrast was between Brand 6 (aggressive, just re-launched and very active in the trade) and Brand 3 (old-fashioned and low-priced). The big difference among the small brands was whether they were relatively new and still growing (Brand 11 was in only its second year) or whether they were mature, stable and probably relatively profitable (especially Brands 10 and 15).

Our own Brand Z was in its third year and seemed in this comparison to have

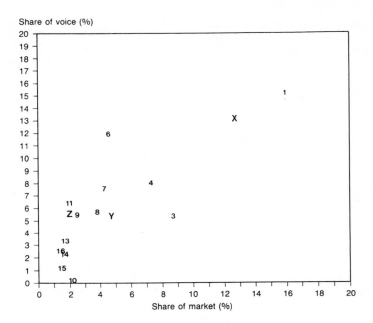

Figure 6   Share of Voice for 16 Brands: Large Brands Have Large Adspends.

too high an A/S ratio to be continued to the next year. Brand Y's ratio was, however, comparable with other brands with a similar share.

The recommendation was as follows. It reduced total spend in 1987 by about $750 000.

Brand	A/S (%)
X	7
Y	12
Z	15

Note that this recommendation does not itself determine the budget: the process of Chapter 4 still has to be applied. All that has been done is a comparison with competitors, in order to demonstrate reasons why advertising-to-sales ratios may vary, and to suggest likely ratios for our brands.

Example 4. Car sales and advertising
Data on advertising by car manufacturers, from MEAL, covers TV, newspaper and magazine advertising, and most radio, but not posters (though these are an important medium in this category). The numbers below include advertising expenditure on dealer support. They are all unadjusted figures, without any allowance for buying discounts; these are not very important for the present purpose, which is to work with the shares of the different manufacturers.

Total advertising expenditure has been climbing sharply: from £142 million in 1984 to £237 million in 1987; an increase of 67%. Some of this growth is due to more new cars being sold; these rose from 1.75 million to 2 million a year. Some is due to these cars being sold at higher average prices. But mostly it is because the high level of competition within the industry has made higher advertising costs worth paying, so that the pounds spent per car sold rose from £81 in 1984 to £118 in 1987. Pounds per car can be treated as the equivalent of an advertising-to-sales ratio.

The Society of Motor Manufacturers and Traders publish the number of cars of each make sold each year. Ideally, we should allow for their average prices, since the revenue and margin are very different if a Bentley is sold to an individual rather than a Mini to a fleet manager. Note that the three largest manufacturers sell the highest proportion to fleets, and can also claim to be 'British'.

The 12 largest manufacturers took 89% of the sales volume in 1987, leaving 11% for the others, who accounted for 19% of all expenditure on advertising. A Jones diagram has been drawn in Figure 7 for the 12 makes, and with one point for all others. To simplify the diagram, the nine smaller manufacturers are not shown separately. Both 1984 and 1987 values were used; movements from 1984 to 1987 are indicated by arrows.

It was pointed out in Chapter 5 that when share of voice is greater than share of market, the brand has an A/S ratio above the category average. In this case a point above the horizontal line at zero for SoV − SoM means that the manufacturer spent more per car sold than average. A move upwards between 1984 and 1987 means that the manufacturer increased his spend per car faster than the +46% for the category.

The first conclusion from Figure 7 is that it follows closely the general shape of Figure 3 in Chapter 5. The group of 'others' would, as individual manufacturers, make a scatter of points in the top left corner. Perhaps our line slopes down a little more steeply than average, indicating great competitiveness among the smaller manufacturers and importers. In packaged goods, a manufacturer at 28% market share would normally expect his share of voice to be about 23%, not the 13% which Ford spend. The omissions of unit price in our share calculation, and of outdoor advertising expenditure, account for some of this difference.

Second, the changes between 1984 and 1987 are relatively small for most makes: there is high consistency from year to year. The exceptions to this pattern are worth notice, and the largest of them are not in the direction we normally expect, showing that there are reasons other than volume change for the advertising spend decisions made. Ford hardly altered its pounds spent per unit, so has dropped its share of voice, but has had a small gain in share of market. Both Austin Rover and Vauxhall put up their advertising spend faster than average, but lost share of market.

Not visible in the figure, but worthy of comment, is Peugot's sales success. This is partly due to the phenomenal growth of the 205, with the rounding out of their

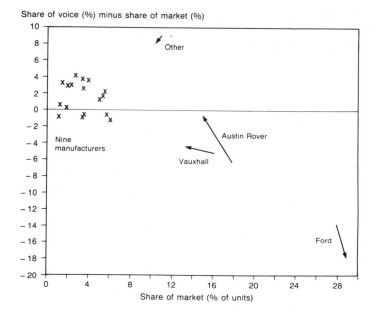

Share of voice (%) minus share of market (%)

Figure 7   Car Sales and Advertising: Jones Diagram for 1984 and 1987.

aggressive new model programme. There are two other manufacturers who have grown significantly: Fiat and Citroen. All three of these manufacturers have advertised consistently at a rate well above their market share. They may be reaping the benefits of this policy. High spend and consistently good image advertising can pay off.

Then there are four manufacturers who seem to have decided to keep their share of voice about equal to their share of market. Volvo is one of these, then there are three who have been affected by quotas: Nissan, Toyota and Honda (though the last has started to increase its spend, and building in the UK may of course make a difference over the next few years).

None of these has seen much share change in 1984–87. Why should a manufacturer, whose unit sales are limited by quota, advertise even as heavily as this? One reason may be to move purchasers up the line, in order to sell a fixed number of units at a higher price. Mazda has certainly achieved this (3).

Another objective may be to motivate dealers and salesmen. Finally, above average spending may pave the way for a future advance.

It is, however, not enough to spend above your share of market to get growth. Volkswagen/Audi and Renault have both been heavy spenders, but have seen little change in their shares of market. Of course many other factors are important in determining sales changes. Product, distribution and pricing are obviously vital. It is also critical that the advertising money is put behind an effective campaign.

The purpose of this example is to demonstrate that the effort needed to produce and explain such a diagram can pay off in the questions raised and the increased insight given into your category.

Example 5. Confectionery sales and advertising
The data which follow report sales at the manufacturer's level, that is, after the retailer's margin has been allowed for. Advertising expenditure allows for the discounts given by media owners, and includes outdoor. Hence the advertising-to-sales ratios which can be calculated are as they appear in a brand's actual budget.

The confectionery brands included have all been advertised in 1982 or 1987 or both, and spent at least £100 000 in one year; they were on sale in both these years, so that small brands, launches and deaths during these five years are omitted. The confectionery category is a very crowded one, and within these definitions there are 60 brands; 45 are in the chocolate sector and 15 in sugar. The following table summarizes the totals for the two years 1982 and 1987:

	Sales (£ million)		Adspend (£ million)		A/S (%)	
	1982	1987	1982	1987	1982	1987
Chocolate	672	901	44.8	39.8	6.7	4.4
Sugar	100	136	7.7	10.2	7.7	7.5
Total	772	1037	52.5	50.0	6.7	4.8

There are clearly big changes in these advertising-to-sales ratios, between years and between sectors. The differences between brands are even larger, ranging from 0.2% for the least advertised brand, and 33% for the most heavily advertised. The purpose of this section is to discuss this variety of ratios.

Several preliminary comments are necessary. Because launches have been omitted, but come from the same manufacturers already represented, the fall in the average chocolate A/S between 1982 and 1987 is understandable: existing brands have sometimes had their advertising reduced to pay for the new brands. Launches in sugar are more rare. Further, 16 of these brands had no advertising at all in 1987, either for the same reason or because they were being milked for some other purpose. Next, the average sugar brand is smaller than the average chocolate brand, because of a few chocolate giants. Sugar advertising spend is expected to be larger in proportion, for the reasons explained in Chapter 5. So the differences in the A/S ratios between years and sectors are quite normal.

It would be unreasonable to take the averages of 4.4% or 7.5% in the table, and expect these to apply to any particular one of these confectionery brands in 1987. We can investigate, as possible reasons for differences:

— The actual sales of these brands, since we expect larger brands to spend less in proportion.
— Changes in these sales (both sectors grew by about 35% between 1982 and 1987, but individual brands changed very differently).
— What can be assumed about the policies being followed.

The first step is to calculate shares of market and of voice within this group of

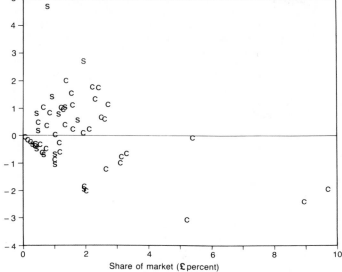

Share of voice (%) minus share of market (%)

Figure 8   Sixty Confectionery Brands: Jones Diagram for 1987.

Key: C = chocolate; S = sugar.

brands, and to plot a Jones diagram for 1987; this is given as Figure 8, where chocolate brands and sugar brands are distinguished, but brand names are not given. This clearly follows the general pattern indicated in Figure 4 in Chapter 5. We can see:

— The diagonal line of unadvertised brands.
— The line of brands just above the diagonal, for brands with token advertising.
— The single sugar brand in the position we usually see launches; this is *Wrigley's Spearmint Gum*, actually a mature product.
— Two groups of large brands, most of which have share of voice one or two points below share of market. The first group includes the very largest: *KitKat*, *Mars Bar*, *Cadbury's Dairy Milk* and *Twix*, while the brands in the second group are not quite as big: *Quality Street* and *Roses*, *Maltesers* and *Milky Way*.

There is then a fairly close group of highly competitive brands. The most interesting are those which are substantial in size, say over £25 million in sales, but which still advertise above their share of market; these are brands such as *Flake*, *Aero*, and *Marathon*. They should be compared with those which are also large, over £20 million, but which did not advertise in 1987, for example *Fruit & Nut* and *Whole Nut*.

In order to understand these 14 brands better, the way their share of market has changed can be inspected. This is shown in Figure 9, where the increase or decrease in share since 1982 is plotted against average share of voice minus share of market for both 1982 and 1987. This is similar to the dynamic difference plot discussed in Chapter 5, but adapted to the data available. Here is an example of trying out different ways of looking at data, as recommended also in Chapter 5. We expect to see an association between spend above share of market and sales growth. The direction of causation is not implied: it may well be that growing brands get more support, rather than that more advertising causes growth in a simple way. We also expect the exceptions to indicate particular brand strengths, weaknesses or other factors at work.

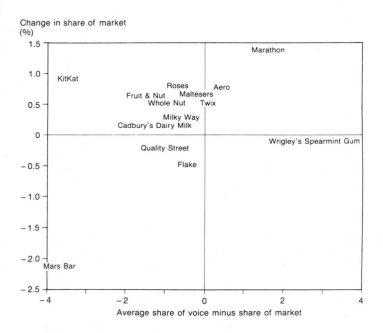

Figure 9   Fourteen Selected Confectionery Brands: Sales Changes 1982 to 1987 Against Share of Voice Minus Share of Market.

The first point to make about Figure 9 is that most of these brands grew in share: we are dealing with the successes in this category. The second point is that, if we draw a line between *Mars Bar* and *Marathon*, many of the brands lie close to it. This is, in fact, suggested as the sort of relationship that exists between adspend and sales change. *Mars Bar* has had advertising well below its share of market, and has declined; *Marathon* is the reverse.

The two major exceptions are in different directions. *KitKat* is clearly a success, with substantial growth but spending less for its size than nearly every brand. Other reasons for growth are to be looked for, perhaps in pricing, or in the quality of its creative work. The same comments could be made about *Roses*. *Wrigley's Spearmint Gum* is a heavy spender, but its sales are static. Perhaps its cost structure, or the different nature of the chewing gum sector, allows it to maintain sales in this way.

Cadbury's Dairy Milk has also seen little growth, but its stable mates *Fruit & Nut* and *Whole Nut* have between them gained a whole share point though unadvertised in 1987. A manufacturer decides simultaneously about all his brands, both on their advertising support and on the copy to be run, if they are advertised. It is the best combination he is searching for, not the best for each brand on its own. This is particularly true when the brands have a family feel (both *Fruit & Nut* and *Whole Nut* bars are made with the same chocolate as *Cadbury's Dairy Milk*).

In conclusion, this short analysis has indicated that what at first may have seemed a chaotic mixture of A/S ratios, and hence advertising budget decisions, can be reduced to a few simple patterns and some understandable exceptions. A real analysis would of course be done in greater depth and with more insights.

9　Postscript

The last few chapters have covered a variety of subjects. While reviewing these special applications, and immersing yourself in detail, you may have lost sight of the main recommendations. I therefore conclude by reminding you of what was said in Chapters 2 and 3, and especially in Chapter 4, which suggested a methodical way of determining the advertising budget.

Every investment decision is difficult. The reasons are now clear: more than one criterion has to be met, we all suffer from our ignorance about the effects of advertising, and in any case we are uncertain about the future. None of these need prevent you from using the information that you do have to your best advantage. You are unlikely to get the amount absolutely right, but you can set a sensible and defensible budget.

In your own case, the information available may cover only some of the areas I have described. It is, however, likely that, after a thorough review, you will be surprised at how much you do have. In addition, much of what you have read here may be inapplicable; certainly no one will need everything. Make the best use you can of what data you do have, and pick and choose what is relevant from the material provided here.

Budgeting is part of normal brand management. The advertising budget is only one of several marketing budgets (and only the media spending part of it is studied in this book). All your expenditures should be subject to similar disciplines.

Match the Brand Strategy

Do not start with the advertising, or even with the current budget. Begin further back than this, with what the company wants to get from the brand (or service, or whatever is being advertised).

The budget is not plucked out of thin air. It can be set only after thorough preparation. Most of this work follows normal management procedures.

It is vital to distinguish among a maintenance strategy, and one that goes for growth, and another that milks the brand, and so on. It is out of these differences that very different spending policies are derived. You should state these objectives both in the long term (for example, the next five years) and over the period for which you are setting a budget (say, a year).

It will help to complete the four boxes in this simple table:

We want the brand to achieve these objectives:

	in the long term . . .	in the short term . . .
Volume		
Profit		

At first, such targets may be a wish-list, the reality of which has not been checked. It is an essential discipline to subject such objectives to the test of feasibility, given what you know about the outside world. You will also find that you have to put the objectives in order of priority; it may, for example, be impossible to maximize profit while also growing or even maintaining volume.

Budgeting is always done on the move. It is a balancing act, under pressure from various directions. It is never a one-dimensional optimization. With one hand, you are adding value; with the other, you are taking profit.

Except in real emergencies, leave the brand in at least as good a shape as you found it. Feel for the brand in much the same way as a farmer does about his land. It can feed you for a good time to come, if you take the proper care.

Planning what our advertising is to achieve is clearly central in deciding how much to spend on it. If we under-estimate what advertising can do, then we will certainly under-spend. If we do not spend enough, we cannot expect satisfactory sales results. But if our ideas of what advertising can achieve are too grand, then we may over-spend and financial disappointment will follow.

Make Use of History

Study the marketing records of the brand and of its competitors. What evidence do we have that the marketing effort planned can actually have the effects required? Usually this means that the category itself, the group of brands of which we are part, is examined first, and forecasts are made about it.

Organizing history so that its lessons emerge clearly is a definite skill. Remember to look at averages, as well as at movements round them. Experiment with different calculations of shares, indices and ratios. Graph the data. Make comparisons with other brands as well as studying your own brand. The first purpose is to make the important similarities and differences stand out, and the second is to show the connections between marketing input, sales, and the bottom line.

Once you have set up a procedure that turns the raw data into a meaningful pattern, it is comparatively easy to get it regularly updated. This can save a great deal of time when the latest period's figures arrive. You have to answer this question regularly: Are my marketing activities having the effects which I expected?

Very few people know accurately what their advertising has achieved in the past, but this is partly because few people try. When we study advertising, we want more than its short-term effects; we need also to understand what it has done over years. We want more than its effects on consumers, we need to see what it has done over the whole chain between management and users. Another reason why the problem is hard, and why advertising's effects are difficult to measure, is that all our marketing activities are inter-related. What we do with our advertising has effects on how our promotions work and on what price we can charge. And, of course, the opposite is true. When we come to decide what we should do in the future, we should be taking these indirect effects into account.

One of the conclusions you may reach after going through such questions is that it is worth your while to find out more about the process. You should plan advertising and budget evaluation at the same time as you plan the campaign. At the very least, set out clearly, for everyone on the team, how you expect your activities to work. Research may be able to refine, to quantify or perhaps to modify, some of these assumptions.

The Budget Decison

Now return to the objectives table you completed above. You have various activities in which you may invest. It is not only advertising that should be evaluated at this stage: each item in the marketing budget should be examined, in order to see how it matches these targets. You are not restricted to using each activity one at a time, and, as has already been pointed out, each will impact the efficiency of the others, as well as volume, costs and revenue.

Various methods have been explained that will have given you suggested amounts to spend on advertising. These will bracket the sum you are likely to spend.

Affordability is the one check on the advertising budget that you may be sure someone else will make. You need also to understand at this stage the importance of other lines in the brand's budget. The various ratios of these entries that bear on the advertising decision have been explained, and you should have them ready to apply in your case.

Of course, you have in mind also the copy that the budget is to support. And you are able to turn sterling into media exposure numbers in your target audience.

The actual determination of the budget uses all these pieces of information. It is a decision made by a marketing person, essentially by an entrepreneur, not by a formula. You are now in as good a position as anyone to make the choice.

Epigraphs

Where a quotation given at the heading of a chapter or section is not already referenced, its source will be found below:

Association of National Advertisers (1967) As Chapter 4, Ref. (1).
Braine, J. (1985) *These Golden Days*. Methuen.
Burnett, L. (1961) *Communications of an Advertising Man*. Charles P. Young: Leo Burnett Co. Note that this book collects talks given in different years.
Hopkins, C. (1923) As Chapter 1, Ref. (3).
Piercy, N. (1985) As Chapter 1, Ref. (10).
Trollope, A. (1864) *Can You Forgive Her?* Chapman and Hall.
McArtor, T.A. (1987) *Chicago Tribune*, 19 August.

References and Notes

Chapter 1

(1) Broadbent, S. & Jacobs, B. (1984) *Spending Advertising Money*. Fourth edition. Business Books.

See Chapters 4 to 7 in this reference; these are about the main media, and definitions of media exposure terms are given there. Questions about targeting are discussed in Chapter 16 there.

(2) Cost per thousand (C/000 or CPT) is one way to translate pounds into average advertisement exposures and will be estimated for you by your advertising agency; it depends, of course, on who the target is, the length of your commercials, and much else. C/000 is the cost of having one thousand people in the target see your advertisement. It is the media cost of showing the advertisement, divided by its audience in thousands. Cost per hundred points (C/00 or CPH) is also used. This is the media cost of showing the advertisement divided by the number of rating points it achieves. These two numbers are connected by the number of people there are in the target.

Example 1
Cost per thousand is £9 for housewives, of whom there are 21 million. Since 9 × 21 000 000/1000 is 189 000, the cost of each of these women seeing our advertisement once on average is £189 000, and this is the cost per hundred.

When we know the adspend (working media budget), and one of these costs, we can convert from pounds to the number of rating points or of opportunities to see.

Example 2
Adspend is £1 million and costs are as above. We buy 529 rating points, since 100 × 1 000 000/189 000 = 529. This is 5.29 opportunities to see.

In words, cost per hundred (rating points) is the population in thousands times the cost per thousand (people). The media budget is the number of opportunities to see times the cost per hundred.

(3) Hopkins, C. (1923) *Scientific Advertising*. Lord and Thomas. See also Hopkins, C.

(1927) *My Life in Advertising*. Harper.
Both books were republished in one cover in 1966 by Advertising Publications, and in 1987 by NTC Business Books.
(4) Association of National Advertisers (1961) *Defining Advertising Goals for Measured Advertising Results*.
(5) Institute of Practitioners in Advertising (1981, 1983, 1985 & 1987). *Advertising Works 1, 2, 3* and *4* (Eds. S. Broadbent 1981, 1983; C. Channon, 1985, 1987). Holt, Rinehart & Winston (1981, 1983, 1985); Cassell (1987).
These books contain selected papers from the Institute of Practitioners in Advertising's Advertising Effectiveness Awards, plus comments by the editors.
(6) Stiansen, S. (1987) More clients ask: does advertising work? *Adweek*, 11 May, 12.
(7) Simon, P. (1987) Custodians of the brand. *Campaign*, 25 September, 53–54.
This suggests that the involvement of senior management, who will ultimately make the decision, should start early. Otherwise there is much frustration and waste of time in double-guessing what they will say. A similar point is made in Michell, P. (1988) Where advertising decisions are really made. *European Journal of Marketing*, **22**(7), 5–18.
(8) *The Times* (1988) 28 April, 15. © Times Newspapers Ltd, 1988.
(9) Isham, R.C. (1984) Winning budget okays by the new rules. *Business Marketing*, June, 142–44.
Isham, R.C. (1982) How to sell top management on your ad budget. *Industrial Marketing*, April, 56–59.
(10) Piercy, N. (1985) What really determines advertising and marketing budgets? *Admap*, December, 612–618.
A fuller analysis of the framework in which budgeting decisions are made is in Piercy, N. (1986) The politics of setting an advertising budget. *International Journal of Advertising*, 5(4), 281–305; and in Piercy, N. (1987). The marketing budgeting process: marketing management implications. *Journal of Marketing*, **51**, October, 45–59.
On the first of these three papers, IPA Appraisal 255 commented (in part):

'*Summary*: Piercy, noting a gap between what the text books recommend and what marketing people actually do, has . . . made a study of 300 medium-sized UK manufacturing firms, investigating not only the techniques but also the budgeting process (bottom-up, top-down, etc.) and the status and politics of the marketing function within the firm. From his study Piercy concludes that the power of the marketing department and the politics of budget making are a key factor in determining the size of advertising and marketing budgets.

'*Comment*: We should not be too surprised by the findings . . . In the absence of absolutely conclusive evidence relating sales to budget size, it is inevitable that "political" argument will tend to hold sway and that this argument will be supported by a range of techniques ranging from rules of thumb to sophisticated models. In many cases, economic analysis tends to show that the profit response function (relating profit and advertising expenditure) has a shallow, "dome" shape around the optimum.

'In other words one can move quite some way up or down from the theoretically profit-maximising budget before profits suffer in any significantly noticeable fashion. Such situations, coupled with uncertainty about the advertising sales relationship, serve to strengthen the role of company politics.

'Something which often seems to escape practitioner and commentator alike is how many of the techniques used merely beg the question. For example, how does one decide what is affordable? How does one put a value or, for that matter, a cost, on achievement of the objectives and tasks? How does one decide what percentage of sales should be allocated to advertising when the range of percentages used by different industries and different companies within an industry is enormous?

'Part of the answer lies in the fact that advertising is a competitive activity and what constitutes a reasonable budget is determined to a degree by what your competitors spend.

'Perhaps the most important unanswered question is how much should be spent on advertising to achieve long-term goals, as opposed to short-term profit maximisation. Long-term goals include warding off new entrants to the market, building dominant market share, increasing profit not just by increasing sales but by reducing the price elasticity of one's brands and increasing their resistance to competitors' promotional activity. These are issues not properly addressed by the supposedly sophisticated techniques like experimentation or econometrics, which inevitably tend to fix on the short to medium term and which could, as a consequence, underestimate what it would be wise to spend on advertising.'

On the second paper, IPA Appraisal 280 said:

'*Summary*: Recent research (see appraisals 255, 263, 267) has shown the techniques used by companies for setting advertising budgets can be classified under three headings:

(a) *Rules of thumb*, e.g. fixed advertising/sales ratios, matching competition
(b) *Pragmatic*, e.g residuals, 'what we can afford', bargaining between marketing and finance departments
(c) *Analytic*, e.g. market modelling, test marketing.

'This paper concludes from a survey that the third category is gaining in importance in medium-sized companies, although many larger ones (surprisingly) appear still addicted to the archaic first category.

'It goes on to explore the second category, particularly the mechanism by which different departments make inputs to this decision. It compares the "bottom-up" budgeting process where marketing managers first determine how much is needed to carry out their tasks, for the approval of top management; versus "top-down", where senior management allocate a total sum for marketing, which is then divided among the marketing managers, who finally allocate money to functions.

'It concludes that unless a marketing department has considerable political power in an organisation (compared with other departments, particularly production, finance and corporate planning), the results of the bargaining process are likely to make nonsense of any rational or analytic methods of budgeting.

'*Comment*: This article is particularly important because it is the first example of academic research focussing upon the process of marketing decision taking rather than its end result.

'The case is very strong for setting marketing and advertising budgets at levels appropriate to achieve specific tasks, justified by evaluative research such as econometric modelling.

'The fact that this does not happen very often is partly because some marketing departments do not invest in the acquisition of sufficient market data to make their efforts fully accountable. It is also due to the fact that other departments have equally valid claims on corporate funds, and may have manoeuvred themselves into positions of greater power within the organisation.

'This makes it particularly important for those who have to allocate budgets to tasks, that their budgetary needs and their justification are stated cogently, in terms likely to be accepted by others, particularly financial controllers.'

(11) Hodges, A. (1983) *Alan Turing: The Enigma of Intelligence.* Burnett Books (Hutchinson).
(12) Cowley, D. (1987) *How to Plan Advertising.* Cassell Educational Limited.
   It may surprise the reader that both this book, and the work of account planners in agencies, are little concerned with budgeting, since this seems central to the advertiser. Hardly any of the *Advertising Works* papers cover budget-setting. The reason is that account planning is almost totally concerned with the advertisements themselves. Indeed, the words 'budget' and 'cost' do not appear in the index to the book above. It is, however, essential reading on the subject of branding, since the account planner concentrates on how advertisements are to achieve the desired results, and the way that the advertisements work is essential information. Note particularly the chapters on the roles of advertising (Sev D'Souza), brand positioning (John Ward) and campaign evaluation (Jeremy Elliott).
(13) Lodish, L.M. (1982) Advertising budgets don't leave well enough alone. *The Wharton Magazine,* Summer.
(14) Eva, G. (1978) *Setting Advertising Appropriations.* IPA.

Chapter 2

(1) Elliott, J. (1987) *Acorn to Zapping.* J. Walter Thompson Co. Ltd, London.
(2) Jones, J. P. (1986) *What's in a Name? Advertising and the Concept of Brands.* D. C. Heath, Lexington Books.
   As the title implies, this perceptive book is mostly about branding.
(3) The following quotations and their sources indicate the lack of agreement in published work on long- and short-term effects. My own sympathies are with King, Corlett and Baker, quoted last here. First, Bloom:
Bloom, D. (1976) Consumer behaviour and the timing of advertising effects, *Admap,* September, 430–438.

   'On the whole, one has to be agnostic about whether there are long-run *sales* effects from advertising, since it is not necessary to assume them to explain what goes on in the market place.

'Certainly it is difficult to accept a "time-bomb" effect in which an advertisement now — barely noticed by the television viewer or magazine reader, probably forgotten in any conscious sense within a very short time even if it is noticed, and supposedly having no effect on her propensity to purchase on the next occasion that she buys in that product group — can nevertheless 'explode' 18 months or three years from now so as to induce a sale that otherwise would not have taken place.'

Ramond, C. (1976) *Advertising Research: The State of the Art.* Association of National Advertisers, p. 105.

'Some media produce quicker effects than others. In the "quick-effect" media, the results can be reliably detected after one to three months. In the delayed-effect media, it may take three to eight months. No study of which I have first-hand knowledge shows effects beyond a year.'

OHerlihy, C. (1976) How marketing must become a profit centre. *Admap*, August, 361–369.

'Sales increase immediately and build up to a peak at the end of the burst so that there is a cumulative effect on sales from the advertising. However this incremental sales gain from the advertising then declines or decays in the following few months. This effect is often called the carry-over effect of advertising.
'This particular law has been empirically measured on sales by isolating the effects of a very large number of other factors. Its existence has been determined by the data we used and not by any assumption imposed on the data. Our methods or measurements are such that if the law did not hold, we would have been unable to measure its existence. We define the sales life of advertising as the period in which 95% of the incremental sales gain due to advertising arises. Our measurements are centred about four months. The bulk of the sales gain arises in the ten weeks from the start of the campaign burst.'

Treasure, J. (1973) *How Advertising Works.* University of Chicago, November.

'The short-term effect of advertising on sales is, no doubt, tiny and unimportant whereas, in the long run, its effects on brands and companies may be of great importance.'

Cowan, D. (1977) Long term advertising effects — an agency view. *Admap*, April, 180–181.

'It is our belief that for established brands the major role of advertising is usually to strengthen the base or to build *allegiance* to the brand.'

Dhalla, N. (1978). Reprinted by permission of the *Harvard Business Review.* Excerpt from 'Assessing the long-term value of advertising' by N. Dhalla (January–February 1978). Copyright © 1978 by the President and Fellows of Harvard College; all rights reserved. pp. 87–95.

'When only the immediate effects are considered, the marginal advertising dollar does not always contribute to profit . . . In other words, in many cases, the last dollar of advertising is likely to cost more than the return it yields. However, it would be a mistake to stop here. To assess properly the real economic worth of expenditures in mass media, the entire cumulative effect has to be included.'

Bogart, L. et al (1970) What one little ad can do. *Journal of Advertising Research* **10**(4), August, 3–13.

'Advertising works for national brands, the evidence seems to say, not merely by creating or reinforcing a brand's reputation among the general public, but by directly and rather quickly motivating or activating the very small number of people who may already be potential customers . . . the consumer is continually pushed, pressured and battered from every direction, though she is so inured to it all that she scarcely notices.

'Advertising men generally assume that even those messages which leave virtually no discernible memory trace at all may, through the force of repetition, turn out to have a residual effect [but] an advertisement's duty may *not* merely be to add its trivial mite to the pile of previous trivial exposures, but also to produce an *immediate* effect on the very few people who were already (whether they knew it or not) "ready to buy" and predisposed to attend to the message with more than casual interest.'

King, S. (1976) MRS Seminar, The Proof of Advertising Value, 18 November.

'No-one has suggested that advertising doesn't have both short-term and long-term effects. Certain measures of effect can measure the short-term *only*; and therefore must be seen as only *partial* measures.

'It's possible by confining ourselves to short-term measures to over-estimate the importance of something affecting the variations from a norm or base, and under-estimate the importance of what has affected the size of the base.'

Corlett, T. (1976) How should we measure the longer-term effects of advertising on purchasing? *Admap*, September, 420–428.

'It is generally accepted that the effects of advertising on the sales of a brand are of at least two distinct kinds — a *long-term* effect which contributes to and helps to sustain the "saleability" of the brand (its image and priceworthiness in the eyes of consumers) and a *short-term* effect which exploits this "saleability" by stimulating additional sales in the short term.

'But the nature of the evidence about the size of these two separate kinds of effect is so different that it is very difficult to take them equally into account when planning marketing budgets. The evidence for the existence of *long-term* effects is derived mainly from "case studies" in particular markets in which brand attitude, brand use and advertising data are monitored over a long period and their relationships examined; but the evidence from such studies, however convincing, is usually general rather than specific and is often difficult to translate into the quantified terms ideally required for budget-setting. On the other hand, the *short-term* effect of advertising can be estimated with apparent precision.

'The danger is that, in a situation where one of these effects (the short-term one) can be quantified with apparent precision while the other (the long-term one) cannot, an advertiser may be led to take only the more quantifiable short-term effect of advertising into account when planning a marketing budget, and so place the future of the brand at risk.'

Baker, C. (1984) The evaluation of advertising effects: philosophy, planning and practice. *Admap*, April, 192–199.

'I believe that it is *impossible to quantify* longer-term effects of advertising with any confidence. Because of this, *wrongly*, longer-term effects are often completely ignored in an evaluation, being assumed to be some sort of "invisible bonus" which automatically accrues whatever the advertising.

'The fact that we generally cannot quantify the long-term business effects of advertising should not be used as an excuse not to evaluate them in any way at all.

'What we can do is monitor brand standing — in general terms, and ideally against specific (long-term) objectives that have been set.'

(4) Steiner, R.L. (1987) The paradox of increasing returns to advertising. *Journal of Advertising Research*, February–March, 45–53.

This quotes findings from Bliemel, F.W.A. (1982) The goal structure of consumer advertising for branded products. Working paper No. 82–3–R. Kingston, Ont: Queen's University School of Business.

(5) The original formulation is in Nerlove, M. & Arrow, K.J. (1962) Optimal advertising policy under dynamic conditions. *Economica*, 39, 129–142.

This model, and the Vidal and Wolfe model, have been studied by operational researchers but I am not aware of practical applications today. See Sethi, S.P. (1977) Optimal advertising for the Nerlove–Arrow model under a budget constraint. *Operational Research Quarterly*, 28(3), ii.

(6) Adstock has been used both in fitting observed advertising effects and in budgeting models: Broadbent, S. (1984) Modelling with adstock. *Journal of the Market Research Society*, 26(4), 295–312.

(7) Falk, H. & Miller, J.C. (1977) Amortization of advertising expenditures. *Journal of Accounting Research*, Spring.

This showed associations, based on quarterly data in the auto business, between sales revenue and advertising expenditures for manufacturers.

Note that start-up costs, including advertising, for a new product are in effect carried forward when a loss is reported. Occasionally, advertising production costs may be spread over two years, as when a commercial, made towards the end of the financial year, is mainly used in the following year. But these are exceptions in traditional advertising. In direct marketing it has been recommended that 'if showing earnings is your objective, as with a publicly held company, it appears reasonable to capitalize advertising costs, making them a current-year asset in the year they are paid for, and then write off the expense during the years when the income is produced. This would be most applicable to programs with long-term customer relationships.' This is from Nash, E.L. (1982) *Direct Marketing*. McGraw-Hill.

Falk and Miller suggested that a previous analysis of annual data failed to find an association probably because of the time interval. There is more on this in Clarke, D. (1976) Econometric measurements of the duration of advertising effect on sales. *Journal of Marketing Research*, **13**, November, 345–357.

Falk and Miller also concluded that each firm should have different amortization rates, because they fitted different rates of decay. Since no other explainers were used (prices, model quality, launches, distribution, etc.), this variety is hardly surprising. We are now in the battlefield when econometricians do their stuff.

(8) Henry, H. (1984) Does advertising affect total market size? *Admap*, November, 524–532.

(9) Robb, D. (1987) The GLC's anti-paving bill: advancing the science of political issue advertising. *Advertising Works 4* (Ed. C. Channon), Cassell, pp. 25–38.

(10) Mintel (1987) *Special Report — Marketing Services*, pp. 97–106.

This comments that 'sales promotion' is a highly elastic term. It reports estimates of the size and trends of its main constituents: special tailor-made offers, reduced price, coupons and premiums.

(11) Institute of Sales Promotion News (1987) November, 10–11.

(12) Special Report (1988) *Marketing Week*, 22 April, 47–68.

(13) Adams, J.R. (1987) The uses and abuses of sales promotion. *Admap*, January, 36–39.

(14) Haselhurst, L. (1988) How Pedigree Petfoods evaluate their advertising spend. *Admap*, June, 29–31.

(15) Nielsen (1984) Life beyond the life cycle. *Nielsen Researcher*, No. 1, pp. 2–12.

(16) Farris, P.W. & Reibstein, D. (1979) How prices, ad expenditures, and profits are linked. *Harvard Business Review*, November–December.

Farris, P.W. & Albion, M.S. (1980) The impact of advertising on the price of consumer products. *Journal of Marketing*, **44**, Summer, 17–35.

(17) Ehrenberg, A.S.C. (1986) Pricing and brand differentiation. *Singapore Marketing Review*, **1**, 5–15.

(18) Bass, F.M. (1969) A simultaneous equation regression study of advertising and sales of cigarettes. *Journal of Marketing Research*, **6**(3), August 291–300.

(19) There are reviews with very promising titles. For example: Corkindale, D. (1983) A manager's guide to measuring the effects of advertising. *Marketing Intelligence and Planning*, **1**(2), 3–30.

On this paper, IPA Appraisal No. 224 commented:

'*Summary*: This detailed article takes the reader through all the thinking processes related to assessing the effects of an advertising programme.

'The principal sections review the need for measurement; the essentials of measurement; measuring the advertising process; and pre-testing advertisements. Each issue is covered in depth and combines both theory and case history examples.

'As a comprehensive review and checklist of the elements of decision making, the article does not lead to a specific conclusion. Nevertheless, the article stresses the need for clear thinking about what the advertising is expected to achieve *before* embarking on advertising development and measurement, and the need for very careful design and construction of the evaluatory technique.

'*Comments*: The article will not only be of use to intermediate marketing management but will draw valuable attention on the part of senior management to the real dangers of superficial measurement. Inexpertly designed advertising measurement will produce not just inaccurate results, but possibly highly misleading results.'

The Corkindale paper actually updates and summarizes a book: Corkindale, D.R. & Kennedy, S.H. (1975) *Measuring the Effects of Advertising.* Saxon House (UK) and Lexington Books (USA).

This contains much that is helpful, but is not easy to use. Indeed, a comment (which itself is worth looking up) encouraged 'anyone who has any serious interest in this business . . . [to] fight his way through' Adams, J.R. (1976) Managing advertising. *Admap*, August, 358–360.

Law, I. (1987) *Is Your Advertising Budget Wasted? How to Measure Advertising Effectiveness.* Economist Intelligence Unit Special Report No. 232.

IPA Appraisal No. 282 was not enthusiastic about this:

'*Summary:* This report has 112 pages, 9 chapters, 4 appendices, references, 27 figures and 12 tables and costs £75.

'The subtitle of this report together with the stated objective — "to enable managers in firms which advertise to take advantage of the information technology revolution to carry out their own monitoring, the way they should go about the task, points to look for and pitfalls to avoid, and the use to which the results may be put" — claims much for its subject matter and contents.

'Chapters 1–4 discuss some of the theories of advertising, key data sources and collection methods with respect to advertising and sales activity.

'The material covered in these chapters will be familiar to anyone involved in advertising and marketing. The author missed an opportunity to include some of the more up-to-date theories of advertising and there is a clear omission in failing to discuss some of the limitations and difficulties concerning the data sources which are quoted.

'In particular much of the material in this report is concerned with the theories of advertising developed in the 1930s and 1960s which current knowledge shows to be inappropriate and which cannot, in any case, be used for the purpose for which this report intends them.

'Chapters 5–6 examine, with the aid of a case study, the way in which econometric methods can be used to examine the influence of advertising on sales. These chapters are potentially the most useful of the report. However, while a great deal of emphasis is placed on "choosing the correct model" and testing alternative hypotheses — which of course is the essential part of any econometric modelling exercise — the discussion falls between two stools. On the one hand technical devices are discussed in such a way that the practitioner/technician would find the treatment superficial, while on the other hand there is nothing to tell the non-technician how to go about model derivation, selection and converting hypotheses into testable models. Similar criticism can be levelled at the discussion of the interpretation of results.

'The remainder of this report, Chapters 7–9, draw together the use of econometric results for assessment, scenario evaluation and forecasting and provides a number of caveats and potential problems for the use of econometric methods.

'*Comments*: Given the current interest in econometric analysis with respect to advertising issues, there is clearly a need for a "cook book" that provides the practitioner/technician with some of the "tricks of the trade" but which also provides the non-technician with an overview of what is practical and feasible. This report is not considered to be a valuable contribution to the state of the art.'

McDonald, C. (1986) Advertising effectiveness revisited. *Admap*, April, 191–195. A full summary of this thoughtful paper was given in IPA Appraisal No. 262:

'*Summary*: Taking as its starting point some issues and techniques raised at a *Campaign/Admap* seminar on tracking studies in March of this year, this article reviews the current state of the art of research into the effects of advertising and makes some suggestions as to how that research and the thinking behind it might be improved.

'The author begins by noting what he calls "The Lure of the Simple Relationship" and the traps of simplistic assumptions and simplistic analysis which this kind of unconscious wishful thinking can lead one into.

'The author concludes that simplistic mechanistic models of causality need to be replaced by analogies which do more justice to the complex interactive environment of advertising and make explicit allowance for the way the advertising task varies with the different user relationships to a brand.

'Colin McDonald then goes on to examine the importance of single source behavioural tracking (as supplied, for example, by *BehaviourScan* and by Nielsen's *ERIM*) and its limitations. He also tentatively reports on some new US experimental data which appear to confirm the findings of his earlier work on diminishing returns in direct effect after two OTS, especially within short time periods before purchase. Competitive share of OTS (reassuringly) seems also to be a factor and he emphasises the importance of the maintenance task among committed users as well as advertising's more conversionary role among the less committed. The author makes a good point here about the constraints on what competitive advertising can achieve in what one might call "zero sum" product fields.

'The later part of the article is concerned with diagnostic tracking of awareness and image, starting with the concept of salience and the relative claims on our attention of salience of the brand's advertising, salience of the brand name and salience of "the configuration of ideas and feelings around the brand". Colin McDonald stresses that there is no single right answer as to which is the key measure in a given case though he does support the view that advertising which concentrates on enhancing the response to the *brand* tends to be the most successful.

'The author ends with a reconsideration of the relationship between usage and image and the importance of tracking changes of image *within* user groups (e.g. committed users, uncommitted users and non-users). He also has some useful things to say about classifying image variables in terms of their possible role as "thresholds" or "triggers" for purchase (i.e. characteristics you must have even to be considered, and characteristics you may need to close the sale).

'*Comment*: This article is wide ranging, thought provoking and helpful, as one would expect from one of the few British pundits to have made a reputation for himself in this area on both sides of the Atlantic. The stress that is laid on the importance of the brand user relationship and commitment in determining both the changing task of advertising across the spectrum of its target audience and the proper interpretation of both behavioural and diagnostic tracking data is particularly to be welcomed — as, too, is the consistent avoidance of over-simplification and misleading half-truths. This is one of those articles that can help both the knowledgeable and the less knowledgeable further up their respective learning curves — though not all of the former will completely share its optimism about the power of correct methodology to solve all the problems.'

The trade press, particularly *Admap*, carries many articles on the subject. See, for example, the issue of March 1986, where monitoring advertising performance was the central theme. Note especially Brown, G., The link between ad content and sales effects, 151–153; and Elliott, J., Never mind the data — what we want is information, 160–163.

It is also worth reading Brown, G. (1988) Facts from tracking studies — and old advertising chestnuts. *Admap*, June, 20–25.

The *Advertising Works* series (see Chapter 1, Reference (5)) is a collection of practical examples of how campaign evaluation can be done. Of course, only successes are reported. Be prepared for disappointments. In your case the right measurements may not be affordable, or the conditions for observing effectiveness may not be favourable. For example, if advertising is nearly continuous, or is used only simultaneously with other marketing tools, it may not be possible to see its separate effects.

Note also the ideal campaign evaluation in Chapter 6.

(20) Telser, L.G. (1961) How much does it pay whom to advertise? *American Economic Review*, **51**, 194–205.
(21) Elliott, J. (1981) Kellogg's Rice Krispies: the effect of a new creative execution. *Advertising Works* (Ed. S. Broadbent), Holt, Rinehart & Winston, pp. 78–88.

For a considerably wider discussion of price research, see Gabor, A. (1988) *Pricing, Concepts and Methods for Effective Marketing* (2nd Edn), Gower Publishing Company Ltd.
(22) Rubinson, J.R. (1978) Analysis of market response elasticities from telephone tracking data. Advertising Research Foundation Annual Conference, New York.

This gives key findings: a more mathematical explanation of the loyalty segmentation is in Starr, M.K. & Rubinson, J.R. (1978). A loyalty group segmentation model for brand purchasing simulation. *Journal of Marketing Research*, **15**, August, 378–383.
(23) Fudenberg, D. & Tirole, J. (1984) The fat-cat effect, the puppy-dog ploy, and the lean and hungry look. *American Economic Review*, **74**, May, 361–366.
(24) Brown, G. (1985) Tracking studies and sales effects: a UK perspective. *Journal of Advertising Research*, February–March, 52–64.

Note that this issue contains several relevant papers on answering the 'what happened' question.

Chapter 3

(1) In 1960, *Printers Ink* surveyed advertiser practice in budgeting. This made a neat distinction between the person who *works out* the advertising budget and the person who *approves* it (both are decision-makers). The survey is most noteworthy for setting a precedent in researching what is actually included in the budget. This has been updated in mailed surveys of 54 of the '100 leading advertisers' and 64 of the 'top 100 industrial advertisers'.

Patti, C.H. & Blasko, V. (1981) Budgeting practices of big advertisers. *Journal of Advertising Research*, **21**(6), 23–29.
(2) Hardy, K.G. (1984) Factors associated with successful manufacturer sales promotions in Canadian food and drug business. Research on sales promotion: Collected papers. Marketing Science Institute, July, 63–82.
(3) Fulop, C. (1988) The role of advertising in the retail marketing mix. *International Journal of Advertising*, **7**(2), 99–117.
(4) Roberts, A. (1980) The decision between above and below the line. *Admap*, December, 402–404.

(5) The business and trade press carry many articles on the economic effects of price-cutting promotions.

'The costly coupon craze . . . even companies feeling the boom say it has got out of hand, but they're afraid to stop', said Felix Kessler in *Fortune*, 9 June 1986, p. 83.

'I think we have all seen categories, like coffee — an intense brand-loyal category — disintegrate,' said Carl Spielvogel, in *Adweek*, 5 January 1987, p. 39. He cites heated price-cutting and adds that consumers, once trained to shop on coupons and other special promotions, are not easily won back.

The subject also concerns academics. See, among many examples: Dickson, P.R. (1985) Can manufacturers de-escalate sales promotions? Marketing Science Institute, Sales Promotion Conference, October. See also an early but still relevant review: Quelch, J.A. (1982) Trade promotion by grocery products manufacturers: a managerial perspective. Marketing Science Institute, Report 82–106. See also Ref. (2) in Chapter 2, pp. 76–83.
(6) See Ref. (1) in Chapter 1.
(7) John Johnson, Chairman of Kellogg (Japan) KK, kindly got this quotation for me from the unpublished *History of Kellogg Company*, Horton and Henry Inc. Industrial Historians, 1948. Reprinted with the permission of Kellogg Company.
(8) Mintel (1987) *Special Report, The Marketing Series Business*. Mintel Publications Ltd.

Note that a later estimate reduced the consumer promotions figure, but raised trade price promotion, in 1987 estimates:

Advertising	:	£6 billion
Consumer sales promotion	:	£2 billion
Trade price promotion	:	£4 billion

Euromonitor (1988) *Sales Promotion and Merchandising in the UK 1988*, Euromonitor Publications Ltd.

Both sources report that the Institute of Sales Promotion is researching this subject.

(9) Rowney, P. (1988) Direct marketing — £1 billion and growing. *Direct Response*, March, 80–88.

This review article gives many short case histories, showing various ways in which direct advertising may be used.

(10) Schultz, D.E. (1987) Above or below the line? Growth of sales promotion in the United States. *International Journal of Advertising*, **6**, 17–27.

The IPA appraisal of this paper follows:

'*Summary*: The article quotes figures for the period 1975–1985, showing that not only have manufacturers in the United States spent more on sales promotion than on advertising throughout this period, but also that spending on sales promotion has been rising at a higher rate than advertising in almost every year.

'The author offers three main reasons for this shift of marketing spending "below-the-line". First the increasing power of the retail trade to demand discounts. Second, that in an increasingly competitive environment, marketing management have shifted their focus to the short term and spend more of their budget on activities which affect sales in the current year, even at the expense of future sales. Third, the increasing tendency for top management to demand accountability for all activity. Advertising, whose effects tend to be strategic and indirect, is at a disadvantage to sales promotion which can more easily be demonstrated to have "shifted product" within the financial year. The author forecasts that all three pressures will continue, or even intensify in future.

'*Comment*: These data and their analysis show a number of parallels with the UK, in both causes and effects. It therefore seems likely that the trend will continue against traditional media advertising and in favour of various types of tactical below-the-line activities, particularly sales promotion and direct marketing.

'However, an obsession with tactical "pipeline-filling", particularly by price-cutting, is already showing unfortunate strategic effects. Namely, weakening brand images, the undermining of brand loyalty, the growth of retailers' brands and the squeezing of manufacturers' margins. In terminal cases branded markets have degraded into commodity markets.

'The solution to this will probably begin with a proper evaluation of all marketing activity for cost-effectiveness in short and long term. This will be facilitated in the case of packaged goods by accurate collection of sales data by scanners followed by econometric modelling. This is *likely to demonstrate* in a number of cases that advertising is a more cost-effective activity than price-cutting, leading to the development of new well-advertised "value-added" brands.'

Chapter 4

(1) The US Association of National Advertisers recommended in 1967 three rather similar steps, and added two more. 'Understanding corporate objectives' and

'Defining objectives and strategy' were followed by 'Determining how much to spend' which was 'in proportion to the tasks the advertising is expected to perform'.

The last two were 'Regular review', since 'advertising budgets are not blank checks but management control devices', and 'Discipline in applying a profit viewpoint'.

Kelly, R.J. (1967) *The Advertising Budget — Preparation, Administration and Control.* Association of National Advertisers.

Note that this publication was rapidly followed by one more specifically about *methods* to determine the advertising budget.

McNiven, M.A. (1969) *How Much to Spend for Advertising?* Association of National Advertisers.

In his introduction, Mal McNiven distinguishes three approaches:

— guidelines:	advertising-to-sales ratio
	percentage change on last year
	task and share of voice.
— theoretical models:	including the analysis of historical data and the Hendry method.
— empirical models:	including feed-back from the marketplace through occasional experiments or continuous experiment.

The book consists of individual papers. Some, by Hurwood, Peckham, Butler, Banks and Little, are still relevant. They summarize views held at that time, which are similar to the authors' other papers or books referred to elsewhere.

Even in 1968, and more so today, there was agreement that you should not look for 'a method' to set the budget. It is reported below that several factors were usually taken into account. It was more common then than is probably the case now that contingency funds were built in: the budget was flexible.

Hurwood, D. (1968) *How Companies Set Advertising Budgets.* Conference Board Record 5, pp. 34–41.

(2) An alternative to evaluating several different methods by judgement is to combine their results in a formal way. This has been used in a technique which has another point of interest: a large database. The PIMS Program (Profit Impact of Market Strategy) is run by the Strategic Planning Institute, Cambridge, MA. This combines data provided by a number of businesses.

Based on the analysis of these budgets, 11 'rules' emerge, those which successful businesses follow:

1. Budgets are proportional to the value in dollars of the sales (at manufacturer revenue level) of all manufacturers in the category.
2. They are also modified by your share of this market. Thus the advertising-to-sales ratio method is used, the ratio being the average of those determined by sales share and by the following factors.
3. New product activity.
4. Category growth rate.
5. Plant capacity utilization.
6. Unit sales price.
7. Proportion of customers' purchases you account for.
8. Price relative to category.
9. Product quality.

10. Breadth of product line.
11. Standarization vs custom products.

Details are in Kijewski, V. (1984) *How Much to Spend on Advertising*. The Strategic Planning Institute.
For examples of the application of these ideas to advertising in a particular category, with a very practical discussion, see McCarthy, E.J. (1987) How much should hospitals spend on advertising? *Health Care Management Review*, **12**, 47–54.
Another flowchart is in Lake, J. (1979) Setting the company advertising budget using a sequential approach. *Advertising and Marketing*, Autumn, 47–50.

Chapter 5

(1) Henry, H. (1979) *Deciding How Much to Spend on Advertising*. Cranfield Broadsheet No. 2, Cranfield School of Management.
(2) Rohloff, A.C. (1985) *Using Weight Tests Results Market by Market*. Advertising Research Foundation Advertising heavy spending tests workshop, 19 April.
(3) For some general comments, see Gale, B.T. (1987) *How Advertising Affects Profitability and Growth for Consumer Businesses*. The Strategic Planning Institute.
Buzzell, R. & Gale, B.T. (1987) *The PIMS Principles: Linking Strategy to Performance*. The Free Press.
Hagerty, M.R., Carman, J.M. & Russell, G.J. (1988) Estimating elasticities with PIMS data: methodological issues and substantive implications. *Journal of Marketing Research*, **25**, 1–9.
Other data bases have been used. For example, Nielsen case histories are the subject of Whitaker, J. (1984) Advertising share and brand share: the relationship re-examined. *Admap*, November, 532–535.
For US analyses Farris, P.W. & Buzzell, R.W. (1979) Why advertising and promotional costs vary: some cross sectional analyses. *Journal of Marketing*, **43**(3), 112–122; and Farris, P. & Albion, M.S. (1981) Determinants of the advertising-to-sales ratio. *Journal of Advertising Research*, **21**(1), 19–26.
For other comparisons, Zif, J., Young, R.F. & Fenwik, I. (1984) A transnational study of advertising-to-sales ratios. *Journal of Advertising Research*, **24**(3), June–July 58–63.
(4) Kennedy, S.H. & Corkindale, D.R. (1976) *Managing the Advertising Process*. Saxon House, Lexington Books.
Here Chapter 6, The allocation of monetary resources: setting advertising budgets, distinguishes usefully between the viewpoints of marketers, economists and researchers. It also reviews the various models available in the mid-70s.
(5) Broadbent, S. (1979) What makes a top brand? *The Nielsen Researcher*, No. 3, September.
(6) Bersted, H. (1978) Problems involved in planning a useful advertising budget. *Telephony*, June, 46.
(7) Gromer, F.J. (1985) *How Much Advertising is Enough?* Association of National Advertisers Media Workshop. Hotel Plaza, New York City, 27 February.
(8) From an Ogilvy and Mather introduction to this subject, quoted for example in:

Sissors, J. & Surmanek, J. (1986) *Advertising Media Planning* (2nd Edn). NTC Business Books.

(9) See Chapter 2, Ref. (24).

(10) Field, P. & Morgan, A. (1985) Hofmeister: a study of advertising and brand imagery in the lager market. *Advertising Works 3* (Ed. C. Channon). Holt, Rinehart & Winston, pp. 70–83.

(11) Naples, M.J. (1979) *Effective Frequency: the Relationship between Frequency and Advertising Effectiveness.* Association of National Advertisers.

This is a thorough review of the applications to media planning of learning theory, laboratory experimentation and market place field studies. It has an important reference section.

(12) Achenbaum, A.A. (1977) *Facing the New Media Reality.* Association of National Advertisers Annual meeting.

(13) McDonald, C. (1971) *What is the Short Term Effect of Advertising?* Marketing Science Institute, Special Report No. 71–142, February.

(14) Elliott, J. (1985) How advertising frequency affects advertising effectiveness: indications of change. *Admap*, October, 512–515.

IPA Appraisal No. 248 had this to say:

'*Summary*: This reports a repeat of the 1966 study, *Short Term Effects of Advertising*, analysed by Colin McDonald. This update was done in Autumn 1984, using AGB's TCA panel in Southern TV, and was commissioned by TVS and JWT. It reports again McDonald's findings for both "retentive effect" and "attractive effect". These were measured by, respectively, the percentage of occasions where the same brand is bought at the next purchase and the percentage where there is a switch to the brand in question at the next purchase. The 1966 study showed positive incremental effects for cases with 1 and 2 OTS in the individual's inter-purchase interval but sharply diminished increments for 3+ OTS. For the attractive effect, the second OTS is twice as effective as the first, whereas both first and second OTS had about equal retentive effects.

'Two rules of thumb relevant to FMCG with inter-purchase intervals of about two weeks are based on this finding:

1. *"Maintenance"* strategy, i.e. reinforce imagery, retain existing purchasers, light competitive activity: 1 or 2 OTS per purchase interval is optimum.
2. *"Change"* strategy, i.e. modify attitudes, alter behaviour, gain market share, heavy competition: 2+ OTS per purchase interval is better.

'Data are cited showing that:
(a) the % of all OTS which are 1 only peaks at around 60 TVRs;
(b) the % of all OTS which are 2+ starts to plateau at around 150 TVRs.

'The conclusions are drawn that the number of TVRs to use *per purchase interval* should be:
(i) 60–80 TVRs when the target is 1 OTS;
(ii) 120–140 TVRs when the target is 2+ OTS.

'Tentative conclusions from the 1984 study were:

1. In 1966 all product fields showed similar types of response, while in 1984

there is evidence of differences between product fields.

2. Thresholds for the "attractive" effect have, in some product fields, moved up from 2 OTS to 3 OTS; possibly a sign of the effect of greater advertising "clutter".

'*Comment*: This is an interesting and thought-provoking way of using old data to help schedule a given budget with a given commercial length. In particular, the distinction between "maintenance" strategies and "change" strategies is valuable. So is the idea of planning on the basis of purchase intervals rather than conventional four-week periods.

'There are, however, a number of potentially important issues which are not addressed in this article, although the author is, we are sure, aware of them and we may hope that he will publish further work which throws light on them.

1. The analysis appears to be carried out in terms of individuals' inter-purchase intervals which will vary both between and within individuals. Reassurance is desirable that the translation to average intervals is justified.

2. In the analysis reported here, no account appears to be taken of competitive OTS. For some markets this must be relevant and might change the conclusions.

3. No consideration is apparently given to time length. No doubt, for this purpose, it, like the budget, is taken as given. However, it is noteworthy that a given budget in 10 seconds would yield something like 3.5 times the average frequency as the same budget in 60 seconds. It would also be interesting to know how different time lengths were treated in the analyses.'

(15) Broadbent, S. (1986) 'Two OTS in a purchase interval' — some questions. *Admap*, November, 12–16.
IPA Appraisal 273 said:

'*Summary*: Some 20 years ago a paper by Colin McDonald on the short-term effects of advertising demonstrated from consumer panel data that two exposures to a commercial between purchasing intervals produced a higher degree of brand switching than higher or lower frequencies. This conclusion has been supported by further papers and is still in regular use by media planners.

'This paper re-examines the topic, using the more detailed and accurate purchasing and exposure data produced by BehaviourScan panels in the USA, and multivariate analysis techniques. It confirms the basic "McDonald finding", but demonstrates that a higher proportion of brand-switching behaviour can be explained if other factors are taken into account besides number of TV exposures (for example the medium-term effects of advertising as determined by "Adstock", price, and sales promotion activity).

'*Comment*: It is reassuring to see that a long-lived principle of advertising holds good over a period of 20 years. But it is a good sign that the better data and more sophisticated analysis techniques now available shed further light on the highly complex process of consumer decision-taking.

'It highlights the importance of integrating advertising with marketing activity, and holds out the promise of improvements in the efficiency of marketing when scanner data becomes available for econometric analysis in Britain.

'This is an important paper, and all numerate marketing and advertising people should read it.'

(16) McGuinness, A. (1987) The repositioning of Mazola. *Advertising Works 4* (Ed. C. Channon). Cassell, pp. 191–212.

(17) The process I am describing is a series of commonsense decisions, based on observing the environment, measuring how the brand is doing, and knowing the Company climate. It can, of course, be more formal. A programme of experiment-decision-experiment can be set up.

'The prime decision variable is the level of spending to obtain advertising exposure. With perfect information, the expenditures may be set at the level which will maximize profits. As the quality of information diminishes, the optimal spending level becomes increasingly more uncertain. The decrease in expected profits as a result of this additional uncertainty measures the value of information. The adaptive optimization model compares the value of additional information with the cost of collecting it. In this way, the model may be used to establish the optimum operating values for those variables which specify the design, dimensions and frequency of experimentation.'

Rich, K.L. (1971) *An Adaptive Optimization Model for Setting Advertising Budgets.* Marketing Science Institute Working Paper.

(18) See Chapter 2, Ref. (2).

(19) Jones, J.P. (1988) Private communication. The survey from which these results are quoted was carried out for J. Walter Thompson, New York.

(20) Peckham, J.D. (1974) *Marketing Advertising Patterns.* ESOMAR Congress, Hamburg.

Reprinted in Broadbent, S. (1980) *Market Researchers Look at Advertising.* Sigmatext.

(21) Barnard, N. & Smith, G. (in preparation) *Market Modelling: Principles, Purpose and Practice.* IPA.

The four sections of the current draft of this introductory booklet are:

1. What a model is.
2. What a model can be used for.
3. Does the model make sense?
4. Practical modelling issues.

(22) Bogart, L. (1967) *Strategy in Advertising.* Harcourt, Brace & World.

(23) See Chapter 2, Ref. (6).

(24) A good review, if pessimistic, is found in
Donius, J. (1986) *Marketplace Measurement: Tracking and Testing Advertising and Other Marketing Effects.* Association of National Advertisers.

(25) 'To isolate advertising's effects, the respondent should not be allowed to determine whether he will be exposed to the advertising.'

'Self-selection bias lies behind more ambiguous results in advertising research than any other culprit.'

'Randomly assign at least three of a random sample of experimental units to each treatment under test.'

This and much other good advice may be found in

Ramond, C. (1976) *Advertising Research: the State of the Art.* Association of National Advertisers.

(26) Stewart, M. (1980) *Measuring Advertising Effects by Area Tests. Admap*, March, 110–114.

Bloom, D. & Twyman, W.A. (1978) The impact of economic change on the evaluation of advertising campaigns. *Journal of the Market Research Society*, **20**(2), April, 73–85.

(27) Dhalla, N.K. (1977) How to set advertising budgets. *Journal of Advertising Research*, **17**(5), October, 11–17.

(28) Zufryden, F.S. (1982) Predicting trial, repeat, and sales response from alternative media plans. *Journal of Advertising Research*, June–July, **22**(2), 45–52.

(29) Corkindale, D.R. & Kennedy, S.H. (1975) *Measuring the Effect of Advertising.* Saxon House/Lexington Books.

The reference is to Chapter 4: 'An appraisal of the experimental approach to determining advertising expenditure effectiveness', pp. 100–125.

(30) San Augustine, A.J. & Foley, W.F. (1975) How large advertisers set budgets. *Journal of Advertising Research*, **15**(5), October, 11–16.

The above report spurred on surveys in other fields, for example:

Permut, S.E. (1977) How European managers set advertising budgets. *Journal of Advertising Research*, **17**(5), October, 75–79.

Gilligan, C. (1977) How British advertisers set budgets. *Journal of Advertising Research*, **17**(1), February, 47–49.

Blasko, V.J. & Patti, C.H. (1984) The advertising budgeting practices of industrial advertisers. *Journal of Marketing*, **48**, 104–110.

Lynch, J.E. & Hooley, G.J. (1987) Advertising budgeting practices of industrial advertisers. *Industrial Marketing Management*, **16**, 63–69.

(31) Hooley, G.J. & Lynch J.E. (1985) How UK advertisers set budgets. *International Journal of Advertising*, **3**(3), 223–231.

This was commissioned by the Institute of Marketing, while the following work was funded by the Economic and Social Research Council as part of a national survey of marketing executive attitudes and practices: Lynch, J.E., Hooley, G.J. & Shepherd, J. (1988) *The Effectiveness of British Marketing.* Interim Report on ESRC project (F20250017). University of Bradford Management Centre.

Chapter 6

(1) Anon (1978) How to introduce a new product. *Media Decisions*, September, 64–65, 101–104.

(2) Schonfeld, E.P. (1981) More common sense rules in setting ad budgets. *Industrial Marketing* January, 70–75.

(3) Peckham, J.O. (1975) *The Wheel of Marketing.* Nielsen. Also in McNiven (1969); see Chapter 4, Ref. (1).

(4) Gold, L.A. (1987) *The Evolution of Television Advertising — Sales Measurement:*

Past, Present and Future. Advertising Research Foundation Workshop, 18 June.

(5) The following paper gives a long and useful list of technical references, including, for example, papers on the best-known new product models. It is not recommended reading for non-specialists, despite its title.

Wilson, R.D. & Machleit, K.A. (1985) Advertising decision models: a managerial review. In *Current Issues and Research in Advertising*, University of Michigan, pp. 99–187.

(6) McNiven, M.A. (1980) Reprinted by permission of the *Harvard Business Review*. Excerpt from 'Plan for more productive advertising' by Malcolm A. McNiven (March–April 1980). Copyright © 1980 by the President and Fellows of Harvard College; all rights reserved. pp. 130–136.

Geographical allocations are discussed very practically in Chapters 5 and 6 of: Sissors, J. & Surmanek, J. (1986) *Advertising Media Planning* (2nd Edn). NTC Business Books.

(7) Rao, V.R. (1981) New product sales forecasting using the Hendry System. In Wind, Y., Mahajan, V. & Cardoza, R.J. (Eds.) *New Product Forecasting*. Lexington Books, pp. 499–517.

(8) See Chapter 2, Ref. (2), pp. 86–87.

(9) Abramson, D. & Lynton, L. (1987) Fear of shopping. *DMNews/Catalog Business*, 1 October, 28–30.

(10) Rapp, S. & Collins, T.L. (1987) *MaxiMarketing*. McGraw-Hill.

See also the bi-weekly *Direct Marketing News* and publications from the Direct Marketing Association.

(11) Nolan, A. (1986) *How to Acquire Tight Leads to Ensure Bottom-line Profit*. 18th Montreux Direct Marketing Symposium, pp. 111–114.

(12) Brann, C. (1971) *Direct Mail and Direct Response Promotion*. Kogan Page.

(13) Waud, C.G. (1986) *How Head Office Can Provide Marketing Support for Their Life Assurance Sales Force*. 18th Montreux Direct Marketing Symposium, pp. 106–110.

(14) Nash, E. L. (1982) *Direct Marketing*. McGraw-Hill Book Company, p. 49.

(15) Thomson, A. (1988) Are they corporate ads with coupons . . . ? *Direct Response*, March, 120–121.

(16) Ray, M. (1980) *Recruitment Advertising*. Institute of Personnel Management.

(17) Brann, C. (1984) *Cost-effective Direct Marketing*. Collectors' Books Limited.

This book recommends agreeing a definition of a 'unit of achievement', which is, for example, a lead for a salesman or a physical unit sold. Then the marginal revenue per unit is required — the amount you are better off when a unit is achieved. Next, the whole of the costs to reach this goal are worked out — and also profit. In effect, a residual method is suggested: spend all you can after all other costs are allowed for.

The detail of applying this, of course, depends on your forecasts of sales turnover and the expected result of the media investment. At first these figures are estimates, carefully based on experience. No one stops there, as the records kept about a particular campaign, and the testing which should be continuous, guide you quickly on the next decision.

A useful chapter in this book is the short one on testing. A lot of the mystery is dispelled.

(18) Worcester, R. (1986) Why corporate advertising is the key to public goodwill. *Campaign*, 16 May, 33–34.

(19) Garbett, T.F. (1985) What happens when you cut corporate advertising? *Business*

Marketing, February, 52–56.

(20) Garbett, T.F. (1981) *Corporate Advertising*. McGraw-Hill Book Company.

(21) Worcester, R. (1983) Measuring the impact of corporate advertising. *Admap*, September, 441–445.

(22) Naples, M.J. & Wulfsberg, R.M. (1987) The ARF/ABP study of the relationship between business to business advertising and sales. *Journal of Advertising Research*, Special Issue, August–September.

(23) Lynch, J.E. & Hooley, G.J. (1987) Advertising budgeting practices of industrial advertisers. *Industrial Marketing Management*, **16**, 63–69.

(24) Wayte, D. (1988) Do advertisers overvalue the South-east? *Admap*, March, 35–36.

Chapter 7

(1) The OHerlihy models are more complex than those outlined here, and the services offered are wider than econometric analysis and the answers to what-if questions about the advertising budget alone. A brochure describing the consultancy is available from OHerlihy Associates. It covers pricing and promotions work as well as advertising. See also various articles in *Admap*, the most recent at the time of writing being OHerlihy, C. (1987) The desk top consultant. *Admap*, July–August, 66–71.

(2) Broadbent, S. (1983) Practical economics and computing at brand level. *International Journal of Advertising*, **2**, 3–15.

This gives examples of the application of the methods described here. Other details, including the collection of advertising and price elasticities, are in Broadbent, S. (1980) Price and advertising, volume and profit. *Admap*, November, 532–540.

An excellent and non-technical paper, which covers some of the points in Chapter 3 and in this chapter, is Roberts, A. (1986) *Setting Advertising Budgets*. Advertising Association Seminar, 10 March.

The IPA Appraisal No. 267 commented on this and an article which put forward views on cutting marketing budgets when times are hard: Collis, R. (1986) Selling your way out of trouble. *Director*, October, 25.

'*Summary:* Both these papers point out the dangers of regarding advertising and marketing expenditure as a "variable, discretionary expense" rather than as an essential ingredient in gaining sales revenue.

'As a result, in times of sluggish sales advertising is cut first, as a relatively easy source of short-term cost saving. Yet advertising spend should logically be higher when sales are difficult to achieve than when they are easy.

'The Collis article recommends zero-based budgeting for all cost-centres, so that expenditure is first cut where it is used inefficiently, rather than where it is on short-cancellation dates.

'Roberts goes into more detail about objective statistical methods of measuring the effects of different parts of the marketing mix on sales volume and value. He describes, with examples, how econometric techniques permit direct comparison of the effects on sales and profits between (say) cutting price and spending more in advertising.

'*Comment:* Under the inevitable pressures that most companies face in at least two years out of each five-year business-cycle, marketing tends to suffer the most, and by its very flexibility the advertising budget has tended to feel the sharpest edge of the axe.

'Yet to break out of the cycle of lost sales leading to cuts in selling expenditure leading to yet lower sales; marketing has to put forward quantified financial arguments, as cogent as those put forward by (say) production, distribution and accounting. This has never been easy, but the recent rapid increase in availability of operational research at economical costs has offered the chance to companies with good data-bases to quantify the short-term effects of marketing on sales.

'Those who are not yet fully aware of these techniques and what they can do will find these articles enlightening.'

(3) This condition is part of the Dorfman–Steiner theorem: Dorfman, R. & Steiner, P.O. (1954) Optimal advertising and optimal quality. *American Economic Review*, **64**(5), 826–836.

The equations in this section are not of course new: this ground has been well-trodden. See especially Kotler, P. (1974) *Marketing Decision-making: a Model-building Approach*. Holt, Rinehart & Winston, New York.

(4) See Chapter 5, Ref. (21).

(5) For an authoritative review, see Little, J.D.C. (1979) Aggregate advertising models: the state of the art. *Operations Research*, **27**(4), July–August, 629–667.

This includes salutary warnings: 'Econometric models . . . generally fail to represent advertising processes except possibly over a limited range . . . add the problems of collinearity, autocorrelation and simultaneity . . . '

The last three terms mean that two so-called independent factors may actually be related, sales this period may depend on sales in earlier periods, changes in advertising may happen at the same time, and even be caused by, changes in sales. I could add weaknesses in the price and in the advertising data, the restriction in most cases to short-term effects, and so on.

For a good British review of modelling problems: Corlett, T. (1985) Modelling the sales effects of advertising: today's questions. *Admap*, October, 486–500.

An academic view, more practical than most, but not up to date, of brand management and econometrics, is Watkins, T. (1986) *The Economics of the Brand*. McGraw-Hill Book Company (UK).

(6) From an advertisement for Henry Stewart Conference Studies, 1987.

(7) See Chapter 1, Ref. (5), for examples of econometric estimates of elasticities in real case histories. For example, 0.19 in the Dettol paper (1981), 0.31 in the Super Noodles paper (1983) and the range 0.1 to 0.4 for different campaigns for Bran Flakes (1985).

(8) Tolley, B.S. (1987) *It's Easy and It's Hard: Copy Testing Newspaper Ads*. Advertising Research Foundation Workshop, 18 June.

(9) Numbers, of course, often drive out judgement. An example follows of consultants analysing split panel data. The correct disclaimer is included about only short-term effects being studied, rather than long-term. It is even explicitly stated that brand image changes and trade effects are excluded. Nevertheless, the plans deduced from the test 'would result in essentially the same product sales volume as the current sales volume, but a higher profit return than the current spending level of advertising'. One plan called for a budget cut of more than 60%.

Sunoo, D.H. & Lin, L.Y.S. (1979) A search for optimal advertising spending level. *Journal of Advertising*, **8**(3), 25–28.

(10) 'Don't worry about overspending as much as underspending' is Rule 4 in: Schonfeld, E. (1979) Commonsense rules in setting ad budgets. *Industrial Marketing*, December, 53–58.

Tull, D.S. et al (1986) 'Leveraged' decision making in advertising: the flat maximum principle and its implications. *Journal of Marketing Research*, **23**, February, 25–32.

IPA Appraisal 263 summarizes the short-term sales and profit implications calculated by the authors. It also spells out the additional reasons for over- rather than underspending:

'*Summary:* The authors examine the sales and profit implications of departure of up to 25% from the optimum advertising budget. They do this for three forms of sales response function: (a) diminishing returns, (b) saturation and (c) quadratic.

'Their analysis concentrates on an advertising elasticity of 0.15, which they argue is representative. They report these results for the difference from the sales and profit at the optimum budget level.

Advertising Budget Is:

	25% below optimum		25% above optimum	
	sales loss (%)	profit loss (%)	sales gain (%)	profit loss (%)
Diminishing returns	4.2	0.6	3.4	0.4
Saturation [a]	5.6	2.2	2.6	1.4
Quadratic[a]	9.1	6.2	1.6	6.2

[a] Saturation response is like diminishing returns but approaches a ceiling level of sale by a constant percentage for every £1000 of extra advertising without ever actually getting to the ceiling. Quadratic response first rises with diminishing returns but after a point actually shows sales falling in response to additional advertising.

'For 'Diminishing returns' they also report results for over-advertising by 25% when the advertising elasticity is 0.05 and 0.50. Profit loss is 0.1% and 1.4%, respectively.

'The most important conclusion they draw is that, in a wide region around the optimum budget, profits tend to be very flat. They further argue that over-advertising may often, therefore, be an inexpensive way of buying market share.

'*Comment:* The article usefully spells out a feature of the advertising–profit relationship that others have mentioned. The authors might have stengthened their argument by widening the range of their analysis to encompass larger departures from the optimum, higher levels of advertising elasticity and perhaps different levels of contribution to overheads. This would tend to confirm the soundness of their conclusion.

'Justification for erring on the side of "over-advertising" does not, however, seem to lie in buying market share, since the sales gains also tend to be modest. Better justification surely lies in the fact that estimates of advertising elasticity made from econometric analysis or from market experiments are likely to ignore the really long-term contribution of advertising. To secure more of these long-term benefits a small sacrifice of short-term profit may be well worthwhile. Moreover, in some circumstances a larger than optimum budget may be warranted in order to deter actual or potential competitors.'

(11) The main problems in estimating long-term effects by modelling are that many different models and assumptions have been proposed. In addition, the time intervals used have serious effects: see Clarke, Chapter 2, Ref. (7).

Another difficulty is the way 'carry-over' is defined; it is probably affected by factors other than advertising (loyalty and product characteristics, for example). See Weiss, D.L. & Windal, P.M. (1980) Testing cumulative effects: a comment on methodology. *Journal of Marketing Research*, **XVII**, August, 371–378.

Aaker, D.A., Carman, J.M. & Jacobson, R. (1982) Modelling advertising–sales relationships involving feedback: a time series analysis of six cereal brands. *Journal of Marketing Research*, **XIX**, February, 116–125.

(12) A review and taxonomy of published models and of some traditional methods gives at least a reading list and quick summary: Riordan, E.A. & Morgan Jr, F.W. (1979) A taxonomic evaluation of advertising budgeting models. *Journal of Advertising* (US), Winter, 8(1), 33–38.

An unusually clear description of model-fitting and the use of the results is in Doyle, P. & Corstjens, M. (1982) Budget determination for highly advertised brands. *Journal of Advertising* (UK), **1**, 39–48. See also Chapter 6, Ref. (5).

(13) Butler, D. (1985) *How to Determine What Spending Levels to Test*. Advertising Research Foundation Advertising Heavy Spending Tests Workshop. The New York Hilton. 19 April. See also Chapter 6, Ref. (6), and Chapter 5, Ref. (6).

(14) Little, J.D.C. (1981) *Decision Support Systems for Advertising Allocation*. Association of National Advertisers annual meeting, 7–10 November, San Francisco. See also Little, J.D.C. (1970) Models and managers: the concept of a decision calculus, *Management Science*, **16**(8), 466–485. See also Chapter 5, Ref. (4).

Chapter 8

(1) Peckham, J.O. (1976) Why advertise established brands? *Nielsen Researcher*, No. 3, 1–12.

(2) Prentice, R.M. (1977) How to split your marketing fund between advertising and promotion. *Advertising Age*, 10 January, 41–44.
See also Strang, R.A., Prentice, R.M. & Clayton, A.G. (1975) *The Relationship between Advertising and Promotion in Brand Strategy*. Marketing Science Institute.
Prentice, R.M. (1986) *Why Most Promotions Cost Four Times as Much as Advertising (but Still Can't Build an Enduring Consumer Franchise)*. Association of National Advertisers Promotion Management Workshop, New York, 13 November.

(3) Cooper, A. & Cook, B. (1986) How advertising helped Mazda (UK) to sell a more profitable mix. *Advertising Works 4* (Ed. C. Channon). Cassell, pp. 129–147.

Index